Praise for *When Harry*

During this "transgender moment," a government-enforced tyranny of false presumptions about nature besieges the American family. *When Harry Became Sally* provides the empirical information needed to refute the transgender suppositions, and—in a most original way—makes historic sense of this social misdirection by noting how the "gender-fluid" pseudoscientific claims of today's transgender ideologues derive from dubious arguments previously passed around amongst second-wave feminists. Learn from Ryan Anderson how another craze about the workings of the mind has come to beset American households and put thousands of people at risk.

— PAUL McHUGH,
UNIVERSITY DISTINGUISHED SERVICE PROFESSOR OF PSYCHIATRY,
JOHNS HOPKINS UNIVERSITY SCHOOL OF MEDICINE

When Harry Became Sally is an eminently readable and insightful guide for all who find themselves perplexed by today's debates on gender identity. Ryan Anderson's analysis of the ideas that are fueling the transgender movement, their human costs, and their political implications will be a valuable resource for parents, educators, and policymakers.

— MARY ANN GLENDON,
LEARNED HAND PROFESSOR OF LAW, HARVARD UNIVERSITY,
AND AUTHOR OF *RIGHTS TALK* AND *A NATION UNDER LAWYERS*

For an informed and sensitive presentation of gender identity issues, *When Harry Became Sally* is a must-read book. It is especially a must for those in psychiatry, psychology, and counseling.

— PAUL VITZ,
PROFESSOR EMERITUS OF PSYCHOLOGY, NEW YORK UNIVERSITY,
AND SENIOR SCHOLAR, INSTITUTE FOR THE PSYCHOLOGICAL SCIENCES

I always read Ryan Anderson with great admiration. *When Harry Became Sally* is an always focused, informative, fair-minded, lucid, and fact-based guide to just and reasonable policies in place of government- and corporation-mandated falsification of science, medicine, public records, and history; suppression of free speech and family rights; and many-sided, often irreversible injustice to the vulnerable.

— JOHN FINNIS,
PROFESSOR OF LAW & LEGAL PHILOSOPHY EMERITUS,
UNIVERSITY OF OXFORD

"Do no harm" is a fundamental tenet of medical ethics. But sadly—as shown by Ryan Anderson's careful examination of the research—people with gender dysphoria are now commonly given treatments that involve grave health hazards and few (if any) lasting benefits. Regardless of political persuasion, all concerned citizens, especially parents, policymakers, and health-care professionals, should give serious consideration to the evidence presented in this thoughtful and balanced book.

— MELISSA MOSCHELLA,
ASSISTANT PROFESSOR OF MEDICAL ETHICS, DEPARTMENT OF MEDICINE,
COLUMBIA UNIVERSITY

Ryan Anderson forthrightly calls out the suspension of disbelief that has led us into ever more bizarre denials of reality, blindfolding our eyes and our heads in the name of political ideology and ensuring the suffering of the mentally ill. Everyone concerned with the welfare of children should read *When Harry Became Sally*.

— MARGARET A. HAGEN,
PROFESSOR OF PSYCHOLOGICAL AND BRAIN SCIENCES,
BOSTON UNIVERSITY

People who experience gender dysphoria deserve to be treated with compassion, kindness, and respect—just like everyone else. It is wrong to despise them, ridicule them, or disrespect them in other ways. As Ryan Anderson shows in his rigorously argued critique of transgender ideology, we can speak and stand up for the truth while loving those who identify as transgender as our neighbors. *When Harry Became Sally* confirms Anderson's standing as one of our nation's most gifted young intellectuals, and without doubt the most fearless.

— ROBERT P. GEORGE,
MCCORMICK PROFESSOR OF JURISPRUDENCE,
PRINCETON UNIVERSITY

Ryan Anderson takes up the challenging topic of the "transgender moment" in a clear and biologically well-informed manner. He writes in a thoughtful and accessible manner, and he succeeds in his goal of providing "a sober and honest survey of the human costs of getting human nature wrong." *When Harry Became Sally* raises important questions for anyone who is sincerely concerned about the well-being of those struggling with their gender identity.

— MAUREEN CONDIC,
ASSOCIATE PROFESSOR OF NEUROBIOLOGY AND ANATOMY,
UNIVERSITY OF UTAH

When Harry Became Sally

RYAN T. ANDERSON

When
Harry
Became
Sally

Responding to the
Transgender Moment

Encounter
BOOKS
New York • London

First American edition published in 2018 by Encounter Books,
an activity of Encounter for Culture and Education, Inc.,
a nonprofit, tax exempt corporation.
Encounter Books website address: www.encounterbooks.com

Manufactured in the United States and printed on
acid-free paper. The paper used in this publication meets
the minimum requirements of ANSI/NISO Z39.48–1992
(R 1997) (*Permanence of Paper*).

First paperback edition published in 2019.
Paperback edition ISBN: 978-1-64177-048-4

THE LIBRARY OF CONGRESS HAS CATALOGUED
THE HARDCOVER EDITION AS FOLLOWS:

Names: Anderson, Ryan T., 1981– author.
Title: When harry became sally : responding to the transgender moment /
Ryan T. Anderson.
Description: New York : Encounter Books, [2018] |
Includes bibliographical references and index.
Identifiers: LCCN 2017031504 (print) | LCCN 2017033229 (ebook) |
ISBN 9781594039621 (Ebook) | ISBN 9781594039614 (hardback : alk. paper)
Subjects: LCSH: Transgender people. | Identity (Psychology)
Classification: LCC HQ77.9 (ebook) | LCC HQ77.9 .A556 2018 (print) |
DDC 306.76/8—dc23
LC record available at https://lccn.loc.gov/2017031504

For Anna

Contents

Preface to the Paperback Edition   xi

Introduction   I

CHAPTER ONE   Our Transgender Moment   9

CHAPTER TWO   What the Activists Say   27

CHAPTER THREE   Detransitioners Tell Their Stories   49

CHAPTER FOUR   What Makes Us a Man or a Woman   77

CHAPTER FIVE   Transgender Identity and Sex "Reassignment"   93

CHAPTER SIX   Childhood Dysphoria and Desistance   117

CHAPTER SEVEN   Gender and Culture   145

CHAPTER EIGHT   Policy in the Common Interest   175

Conclusion   205

Postscript to the Paperback Edition   215

Acknowledgments   219

Notes   221

Index   251

Preface to the
Paperback Edition

The Sunday following Thanksgiving 2018, Andrea Long Chu published a heartfelt and heartbreaking op-ed in the *New York Times* on life with gender dysphoria. While the piece was clearly intended as a statement in favor of "sex reassignment," it communicates almost the exact opposite message, revealing painful truths about many transgender lives. Even the title conveys ambivalence: "My New Vagina Won't Make Me Happy."[1]

Chu was scheduled to undergo vaginoplasty surgery several days later. "Next Thursday, I will get a vagina," wrote Chu. "The procedure will last around six hours, and I will be in recovery for at least three months." Would this bring happiness? Probably not, Chu admitted, but that was beside the point: "This is what I want, but there is no guarantee it will make me happier. In fact, I don't expect it to. That shouldn't disqualify me from getting it."

Chu argues that the simple desire for sex reassignment surgery should be all that is required for a patient to receive it. No further consideration for authentic health and well-being should enter in. No concern about poor outcomes should prevent a doctor from performing the surgery if a patient wants it, and "no amount of pain, anticipated or continuing, justifies its withholding." According to Chu, "surgery's only prerequisite should be a simple demonstration of want."

This is a rather extreme stance with regard to the basis for a medical procedure, and we'll come back to it later on. But as the op-ed builds to this radical conclusion, Chu discloses many truths about transgender lives that are seldom acknowledged—truths that we should attend to.

1. Sex Isn't "Assigned," and Surgery Can't Change It

Chu acknowledges that the surgery won't actually "reassign" sex. On the contrary, "my body will regard the vagina as a wound; as a result, it will require regular, painful attention to maintain."

Indeed, sex reassignment is quite literally impossible. Surgery can't actually reassign sex, because sex isn't "assigned" in the first place. As I explain in this book, sex is a bodily reality: the reality of how an organism is organized with respect to sexual reproduction. That reality isn't "assigned" at birth or any time afterward. Sex—maleness or femaleness—is established at a child's conception; it can be ascertained by technological means even at the earliest stages of embryological development; it can be observed visually well before birth with ultrasound imaging. And the biological reality goes deeper than anything that can be changed by cosmetic surgery and cross-sex hormones.

People who undergo sex reassignment procedures do not become the opposite sex. They merely masculinize or feminize their outward appearance.

2. Gender Dysphoria Is Deeply Painful

Chu describes the deep pain of gender dysphoria, the sense of distress over one's bodily sex and alienation from one's own body:

> Dysphoria feels like being unable to get warm, no matter how many layers you put on. It feels like hunger without appetite. It feels like getting on an airplane to fly home, only to realize mid-flight that this is it: You're going to spend the rest of your life on an airplane. It feels like grieving. It feels like having nothing to grieve.

People with gender dysphoria don't choose it and aren't faking it. They really are suffering. And we should take their testimony seriously.

3. "Transitioning" May Not Bring Relief from the Pain

Chu acknowledges that "transitioning" may not make things better and could even make things worse. "I feel demonstrably worse since I started on hormones," Chu writes. And continues: "Like many of my trans friends, I've watched my dysphoria balloon since I began transition."

Would completing the process help? Not according to the best medical findings. The evidence suggests that sex reassignment does not adequately address the psychosocial difficulties faced by people who identify as transgender. Even when the procedures are successful technically and cosmetically, and even in cultures that are relatively "trans-friendly," transitioners still face poor outcomes.

Even the Obama administration admitted that the best studies do not report improvement after reassignment surgery.[2] In August 2016, the Centers for Medicare and Medicaid noted that "the four best designed and conducted studies that assessed quality of life before and after surgery using validated (albeit non-specific) psychometric studies did not demonstrate clinically significant changes or differences in psychometric test results after GRS [gender reassignment surgery]."[3]

What does that mean? A population of patients is suffering so much that they would submit to amputations and other radical surgeries, and the best research the Obama administration could find suggests that those drastic measures bring them no meaningful improvements in quality of life.

4. Suicide Is a Serious Risk

Chu acknowledges a struggle with suicidal ideation beginning *after* the transition treatment started: "I was not suicidal before hormones. Now I often am."

The Obama administration acknowledged that this is often a reality of life after such treatments. In a discussion of the largest and most robust study on outcomes of sex reassignment, the Centers for Medicare and Medicaid pointed out: "The study identified increased mortality and psychiatric hospitalization compared to the matched controls. The mortality was primarily due to completed suicides (19.1-fold greater than in control Swedes)."[4]

These results are tragic. And they directly contradict the most popular media narratives about "sex reassignment," as well as many of the snapshot studies that do not track people over time. Long-term studies are crucial because, as the Obama administration noted, "mortality from this patient population did not become apparent until after 10 years."[5] So when the media tout studies that track outcomes for only a few years, and claim on this basis that reassignment is a stunning success, there are good grounds for skepticism.

* * *

Given these acknowledged problems with gender reassignment as a treatment path, let's look again at Chu's argument that "surgery's only prerequisite should be a simple demonstration of want." What are the grounds for this assertion?

Why should a doctor perform surgery when it won't make the patient happy, it won't accomplish its intended goal, it won't improve the underlying condition, it might make the underlying condition worse, and it might increase the likelihood of suicide? Chu wants to turn the profession of medicine on its head, so that medical doctors would simply carry out instructions from their patients, rather than use their knowledge to lead patients to healing and wholeness.

Unfortunately, Chu isn't alone in holding this belief. Many health professionals themselves now view health care—including mental health care—primarily as a means of fulfilling patients' desires, whatever those are. In this view, as Leon Kass explains,

> The implicit (and sometimes explicit) model of the doctor-patient relationship is one of contract: the physician—a highly competent hired syringe, as it were—sells his services on demand, restrained only by the law (though he is free to refuse his services if the patient is unwilling or unable to meet his fee). Here's the deal: for the patient, autonomy and service; for the doctor, money, graced by the pleasure of giving the patient what he wants. If a patient wants to fix her nose or change his gender, determine the sex of unborn children, or take euphoriant drugs just for kicks, the physician can and will go to work—provided that the price is right and that the contract is explicit about what happens if the customer isn't satisfied. [6]

This vision of medicine and medical professionals gets it wrong. Professionals ought to profess their devotion to the purposes and ideals they serve. That's what makes them professionals, not just service providers. Teachers should be devoted to fostering knowledge, lawyers to ensuring justice under law, and physicians to "healing the sick, looking up to health and wholeness." Healing is "the central core of medicine," Kass writes; "to heal, to make whole, is the doctor's primary business."

Chu's vision of medicine instead turns the doctor into someone who merely satisfies desires, even if what is desired isn't good for the patient. Concerning the upcoming surgery, Chu writes:

I still want this, all of it. I want the tears; I want the pain. Transition doesn't have to make me happy for me to want it. Left to their own devices, people will rarely pursue what makes them feel good in the long term. Desire and happiness are independent agents.

Whatever might be said of this as a philosophy of life, it offers no compelling reason why physicians should be duty-bound to fulfill the patient's desires. Sound medicine isn't about desire, it's about healing.

Serving the patient's medical interests requires an understanding of human wholeness and well-being. Mental health care must be guided by a sound concept of human flourishing, so that our minds can serve our well-being. Our brains and senses are designed to bring us into contact with reality, connecting us with the outside world and with the reality of ourselves. Thoughts and feelings that disguise or distort reality are misguided, and they can cause harm. In this book, I argue that we need to do a better job of helping people who struggle with thoughts and feelings that undermine their own well-being.

Transgender activists have misrepresented my purposes and my disposition toward people who suffer from gender dysphoria. Chu, for example, writes:

> Many conservatives call this [gender dysphoria] crazy. A popular right-wing narrative holds that gender dysphoria is a clinical delusion; hence, feeding that delusion with hormones and surgeries constitutes a violation of medical ethics. Just ask the Heritage Foundation fellow Ryan T. Anderson, whose book "When Harry Became Sally" draws heavily on the work of Dr. Paul McHugh, the psychiatrist who shut down the gender identity clinic at Johns Hopkins in 1979 on the grounds that trans-affirmative care meant "cooperating with a mental illness." Mr. Anderson writes, "We must avoid adding to the pain experienced by people with gender dysphoria, while we present them with alternatives to transitioning."

Of course I never call people with gender dysphoria "crazy." And in this book I explicitly state that I take no position on the technical question of whether someone's thinking that he or she is the opposite sex is a clinical delusion. That's why Chu couldn't quote any portion of my book demonstrating that I have said it is.

Throughout the book, I stress that the feelings reported by people who identify as transgender are real—that these individuals really do feel a disconnect with their bodily sex—but I also highlight the fact that those feelings don't change bodily reality. I recognize the real distress that gender dysphoria can cause, but never do I call people experiencing it crazy.

I repeatedly acknowledge that gender dysphoria is a serious condition, that people who experience a gender identity conflict should be treated with respect and compassion, and that we need to find more humane and effective ways to help people who find themselves in that situation.

Chu dismisses all this as merely "compassion-mongering," and claims that it amounts to "peddling bigotry in the guise of sympathetic concern." For the record, Chu never contacted me regarding my research or my book.

Nor did the *Times* contact me to verify any of the claims made about me in the op-ed. Indeed, this was the *second* time that the *New York Times* published an op-ed with inaccurate criticisms of this book.[7]

Americans disagree about gender identity and about the best approaches to treating gender dysphoria. We need to respect the dignity of people who identify as transgender while also doing everything possible to help them find wholeness and happiness. This will require a better conversation about these issues, which is why I wrote this book. And presumably it's why Chu wrote the op-ed. Instead of personal attacks and name-calling, we need sober and respectful truth-telling, and a willingness to credit the good intentions of people who disagree with us.

Chu may regard me as a "bigot," but I regard Chu as a fellow human being made in the image and likeness of God who is struggling with a painful and dangerous condition. As such, Chu deserves care and support that will bring health and wholeness—not the on-demand delivery of "services" that even Chu acknowledges are unlikely to make life better and could make it very much worse.

All of us have a role to play in making this "transgender moment" as short as possible. Lives are at stake. My hope is that this book will equip you to do your part.

Introduction

In 1989, the classic film *When Harry Met Sally* dealt with one thorny issue: Can a man and a woman really be "just friends"? That question may still be up in the air, but Hollywood took on a more fundamental one with the 2015 film *The Danish Girl*: Can a man really become a woman? The answer from Hollywood was a resounding "yes."

The Danish Girl is based on the true story of Einar Wegener, a painter in Copenhagen who in 1930 became the first known subject of "sex reassignment" surgery. He had long thought of himself as having a female identity that he called "Lili Elbe," but whether those drastic medical procedures made him truly a woman is another matter. The idea that a person could have been born into a body of the wrong sex and might be transformed into the other sex by surgery and hormones would remain marginal for some time. Now it is rapidly becoming a mainstream view that social and medical "transition" is the appropriate treatment for people, including children, who feel at odds with their biological sex.

America is in the midst of what has been called a "transgender moment."[1] Not long ago, most Americans had never heard of transgender identity, but within the space of a year it became a cause claiming the mantle of civil rights. A discordant gender identity is said to represent who the person *really is*, by contrast with the sex "assigned at birth," and therefore any failure to accept and support a transgender identity amounts to bigotry. We are told that not treating people as the gender they claim to be is discriminatory. But is it true that a boy could be "trapped" in a girl's body? Is our sex merely "assigned" to us? Can modern medicine "reassign" sex? What is the most loving and helpful response to the condition of gender dysphoria, a profound and often debilitating sense of alienation from one's bodily sex? Should our laws accept and enforce a subjective notion of gender?

These shouldn't be difficult questions. In the late 1970s, Dr. Paul McHugh thought he had convinced the vast majority of medical professionals not to go along with bold claims about sex and gender that were being advanced by some of his colleagues. McHugh received a world-class education at Harvard College and Harvard Medical School. As chair of psychiatry at Johns Hopkins Medical School and psychiatrist-in-chief at Johns Hopkins Hospital, he put a stop to sex reassignment surgery at that facility in 1979. Many other medical centers across the country followed the elite institution's lead. But recent years have brought a resurgence of these procedures—not in light of new scientific evidence, mind you, but under the pressure of ideology.

The people increasingly in the spotlight of the transgender moment are children. In 2007, Boston Children's Hospital "became the first major program in the United States to focus on transgender children and adolescents," as its website brags.[2] A decade later, more than forty-five pediatric gender clinics had opened their doors to our nation's children.[3] Parents are told that puberty blockers and cross-sex hormones may be the only way to prevent their children from committing suicide. Never mind that the best studies of gender dysphoria (studies that even transgender activists cite) show that between 80 and 95 percent of children who express a discordant gender identity will come to identify with their bodily sex if natural development is allowed to proceed.[4] And never mind that "transitioning" treatment has not been shown to reduce the extraordinarily high rate of suicide attempts among people who identify as transgender (41 percent, compared with 4.6 percent of the general population).[5] In fact, people who have had transition surgery are nineteen times more likely than average to die by suicide.[6] These statistics should be enough to halt the headlong rush into "transitioning" and prompt us to find more effective ways to prevent these tragic outcomes. Most of all, we shouldn't be encouraging children to "transition," or making heroes and role models of those who have done so.

In this book, I argue that Dr. McHugh got it right. The best biology, psychology, and philosophy all support an understanding of sex as a bodily reality, and of gender as a social manifestation of bodily sex. Biology isn't bigotry. Every human society has been organized around a recognition that men and women are different, and modern science shows that the differences begin with our DNA and development in the womb. It is true that men and women differ among themselves, and that some people have difficulty identifying with their bodily sex. But this doesn't mean that sex is either fluid or subjective, as transgender ideology maintains. This book is an effort to provide a nuanced view of our sexed embodiment, a balanced approach to policy issues involving transgender identity and gender more broadly, and a sober and honest survey of the human costs of getting human nature wrong.

The first chapter focuses on our transgender moment in three different realms: culture, law, and medicine. It looks at recent developments in popular culture that have changed American opinion on gender identity, and legal developments during the Obama administration that redefined "sex" as "gender identity." Then it examines how medical practice has shifted, with particular attention to Johns Hopkins, Dr. McHugh's institution. In 2016, pressure by transgender activists resulted in a course reversal there, away from good medical practice and into what is becoming a transgender-affirmative mainstream. In a more disturbing story from Canada, a world-renowned expert on gender dysphoria had his clinic closed down by the government because he did not uncritically support transition therapies for children.

Chapter 2 shines a light on the thinking behind these trends by letting transgender activists speak for themselves. It's important to note that most people with a discordant gender identity are not activists of any sort. But there are activists pushing a transgender ideology on the nation, and their views have greatly influenced how our society responds to gender dysphoria. The chapter begins with transgender ontology—the assertion that a "trans boy" *is* a boy, plain and simple, not a girl who identifies as a boy. Second, it looks at transgender medicine—the recommended four-step treatment process of social transition, puberty blockers, cross-sex hormones, and surgery. Third is transgender policy, including access to sex-specific facilities and programs, the lessons that children are taught in school about gender, the criminalization of "misgendering" someone, and the provision of desired medical services. In all these areas, concerns about religious liberty, parental authority, and even privacy and public safety fall by the wayside.

Activists tend to be uncompromising in their demands, yet their worldview is fraught with contradictions. It holds that the real self is fundamentally separate from the material body, yet insists that transforming the body is crucial for personal wholeness. It attaches a notion of authentic gender identity to stereotypical activities and dispositions, yet it grows from a philosophy holding that gender is an artificial construct. It promotes a radical subjectivity in which individuals should be free to do whatever they wish and to define the truth as they choose, yet it calls for enforced conformity of belief in transgender dogma.

After listening to trans activists, we will hear from their victims: people who have transitioned and come to regret it. Chapter 3 presents the stories of several people who found that transitioning didn't bring the peace and wholeness they sought, but only new problems. The stories of detransitioners complicate the sunny picture frequently presented in the media. Many of these people recall a feeling of being pushed into transitioning, as if there were no other options, and they wish that medical professionals had made an effort to help them understand the deeper psychological issues that alienated them from their own bodies. Many regret the permanent damage done to their bodies, and some who transitioned as teenagers believe they were not mature enough to make such consequential decisions. Some feel that their dysphoria resulted from social hostility to people who don't conform to gender norms or who have same-sex attractions. In this light, social conservatives (including myself) should take care to be respectful and compassionate toward people we may disagree with. We should also call on transgender activists to stop trying to silence detransitioners. As this book went to press, the *Telegraph* (UK) ran a report with the headline: "Sex change regret: Gender reversal surgery is on the rise, so why aren't we talking about it?"[7] The answer to the question is political correctness. But it's better to be correct than politically correct where human lives are concerned.

Chapter 4 lays out a foundation for understanding why the "reassignment" approach is misguided. Looking at the biology and philosophy of sex, it answers questions about our nature as a sexually dimorphic species; about how our development as male or female begins at conception; about the many biological differences that result. Contrary to the claims of activists, sex isn't "assigned" at birth. It's a bodily fact that can be recognized well before birth with ultrasound imaging. The sex of an organism is defined by its organization for sexual reproduction. Secondary differences between the two sexes— attributes that may be visibly altered by hormone treatment—are not what make us male or female. It's impossible even to make sense of the *concept* of sex apart from the ways our bodies are organized for reproduction. That organization starts to develop well before birth. Chromosomal and hormonal pathologies may disrupt normal development, though in fact these abnormalities have essentially nothing to do with transgender ideology—except insofar as activists want to relabel such abnormalities as mere "differences," in an effort to normalize disorders.

Attempts to find biological explanations for discordant gender identities have come up short, as Chapter 5 explains. Notwithstanding the media hype over supposed differences in brain structure, there is no solid scientific evidence that transgender identities are innate or biologically determined, and there is some evidence that other factors are most likely involved. But in truth, very little is understood about the causes of discordant gender identities. Many psychologists and psychiatrists think of gender dysphoria as being much like other kinds of dysphoria, or serious discomfort with one's body, such as anorexia. These feelings can lead to mistaken and harmful beliefs. The most helpful therapies do not try to remake the body to conform with thoughts and feelings—which is impossible—but rather to help people find healthy ways to manage this tension and move toward accepting the reality of their bodily selves. This therapeutic approach rests on a sound understanding of physical and mental health, and of medicine as a practice aimed at restoring healthy functioning, not simply satisfying the desires of patients.

Children especially develop best when parents and professionals help them understand and accept their embodied selves as male or female. Chapter 6 focuses on gender dysphoria in children and the experimental therapies that have rapidly become commonplace. As recently as 2012, the *Washington Post* reported that "the very idea of labeling young children as transgender is shocking to many people."[8] Starting a young child on a process of "social transitioning" followed by puberty-blocking drugs was virtually unthinkable not long ago, and the treatment is still largely experimental. Unfortunately, many activists have given up on caution, let alone skepticism, about drastic treatments. They assert that puberty blockers are safe and reversible, but in fact these drugs carry long-term health risks, and development occurring at age sixteen that usually happens around age ten cannot be considered normal. There are potential psychological consequences, too, since blocking puberty may interfere with the developmental mechanisms that normally help children accept themselves as male or female.

A more cautious therapeutic approach begins by acknowledging that the vast majority of children with gender dysphoria will grow out of it naturally. An effective therapy looks into the reasons for the child's mistaken beliefs about gender, and addresses the problems that the child believes will be solved if the body is altered. Dr. McHugh finds that other psychosocial issues usually lie beneath the child's false assumptions, and his therapy focuses on remedies for those issues. Chapter 6 concludes with case studies of children who received effective therapy that offered strategies for accepting themselves.

An effective treatment plan for children will help them develop a more nuanced view of gender, so they understand that real boys and real girls don't all conform to narrow stereotypes. But this doesn't require adopting the view that gender norms are purely "social constructs," and hence artificial and oppressive. Chapter 7 traces our cultural gender confusion to its roots in gender theory and in certain strains of feminist thinking about our embodiment. First-wave feminism was a campaign to liberate women from an overly restrictive concept of gender, so they could be free to fulfill their nature, but it gave way to a movement seeking to make women identical to men. From the error of inflexible stereotypes, our culture swung to the opposite error of denying any important differences between male and female. The result is a culture of androgyny and confusion. An agenda of nullifying the distinction between men and women might seem opposed to the insistence on the absolute reality of transgender identity—i.e., an inner sense of being truly male or female—yet both start by severing gender from biological sex.

Between stereotypes on the one hand and androgyny on the other, the virtuous mean is a view of gender that reveals meaningful sex differences and communicates the difference they make; a view that takes sex differences seriously while upholding the fundamental equality of the sexes as complements to one another. It acknowledges what sex differences mean for marriage and family, for friendship and education. Our sexual embodiment is precisely what makes marriage possible, and a host of social practices, including how we nurture boys and girls, are shaped with the good of marriage in view. On average, boys and girls, men and women have different needs and inclinations, so our law and culture should not take the male way of being human as the norm. This means that women should not be forced to live, work, and compete as if they were men—which is what some people would prefer, with proposals to ban stay-at-home moms. Society should accept that men and women may, on the whole, have different preferences and freely make different choices.

From the realm of culture, we turn in Chapter 8 to law and public policy, covering issues like access to single-sex facilities, pronoun policing, and health-care mandates. There are five distinct areas of concern surrounding such policies: (1) privacy interests when men who identify as women can enter female-only spaces; (2) safety concerns when predators abuse gender-identity access policies; (3) equality concerns when biological males can compete against females in sports and other arenas where sex differences are relevant; (4) liberty interests when people are forced to speak or act in ways contrary to their best judgment and deeply held beliefs; and (5) ideology concerns about confusing messages that schoolchildren receive when they are taught that gender is fluid, falls along a spectrum, and is essentially detached from bodily sex. Children are especially vulnerable, so we must do everything possible to protect them and provide an environment that fosters healthy development. We need to respect the dignity of people who identify as transgender, but without encouraging children to undergo experimental transition treatments, and without trampling on the needs and interests of others. And we need to acknowledge that taking our sexual embodiment seriously in public policy is not discriminatory.

Transgender ideology may appear to be establishing a firm place in our culture, yet there are signs of defensiveness among its advocates, as if they realize that their claims are contrary to basic, self-evident truths. The transgender moment may turn out to be fleeting, but that doesn't mean we should expect it to fade away on its own. We need to insist on telling the truth, and on preventing lives from being irreparably damaged.

CHAPTER ONE
....

Our Transgender Moment

B efore the primetime interview of Bruce Jenner (as he was then called) by Diane Sawyer on ABC's *20/20* in 2015, many Americans had never had a conversation about transgender issues. It's a conversation we need to have, as radical doctrines of gender spread through the culture, into our schools and public policy. But political and cultural elites have tried to shut down the discussion before it starts by imposing a politically correct orthodoxy on the nation, an ideology in which "gender identity" is both a subjective matter and a category meriting civil rights protection.

The Jenner interview wasn't the first media effort to normalize transgender identity, but it had an especially big impact. For one thing, it involved the celebrity Kardashian family. More surprisingly, it was about a famous Olympian, a decathlon champion who had been an image of powerful masculinity to millions of Americans. There was also the timing of the interview, the weekend before oral arguments at the Supreme Court on same-sex marriage. This allowed LGBT activists to emphasize a unity of purpose between the T and the LGB parts of their constituency—to the consternation of many gay and lesbian Americans who feel that "gender identity" and "sexual orientation" have little in common. But the conjunction of events helped to represent the demands of transgender activists as another civil rights issue. Indeed, shortly after the Supreme Court redefined marriage, the Obama administration redefined "sex" to mean "gender identity" in our nation's civil rights laws, and then imposed these "gender identity" policies on schools and health-care providers. The transgender cause was officially mainstream.

Normalizing Transgender Identities in Popular Culture

Though the Jenner interview made a big splash, a series of earlier media events had been preparing the ground for our transgender moment. One was the premiere of *Becoming Chaz* at the Sundance Film Festival and on the Oprah Winfrey Network in 2011. The film tells the story of how Chastity Bono, the daughter of Sonny and Cher Bono, transitioned to identify as a man, called Chaz, at age forty. Media reports were punctilious in using the "correct" pronouns, encouraging viewers to "follow Chaz Bono through a significant part of the process that took place in 2010, including hormone treatments and the surgical removal of his breasts."[1] *His* breasts. (These edgy locutions are popular in the media, giving us headlines like "First Ever Pregnant Man..." and "What It's Like to Chestfeed.")[2] Chastity Bono had been only a second-hand celebrity, by contrast with Jenner, but many people saw Chaz on *Dancing with the Stars* in the autumn of 2011.

The gender identity theme made its way into TV dramedy in 2013 with the popular Netflix show *Orange Is the New Black*, featuring a transgender actor, Laverne Cox, in the role of a transgender prisoner. In 2014, Cox became the first person who openly identifies as transgender to appear on the cover of *Time* magazine,[3] and the first to be nominated for an Emmy Award.[4] Cox, a man who identifies as a woman, was named Woman of the Year for 2014 by *Glamour* magazine, whose editors declared that Cox "teaches us that gender identity lives, first and foremost, in our hearts and minds."[5] When the *Chicago Sun-Times* published a syndicated op-ed by Kevin Williamson pointing out that Cox was in fact not a woman, activists forced the newspaper to retract the column and apologize.[6] Dissent is not tolerated in the transgender moment.

Earlier in 2014, Amazon Studios released a Web TV comedy called *Transparent*, about a father transitioning to become a mother. The producer aimed to promote transgender identity behind the scenes as well as onscreen. Bathrooms were labeled as gender-neutral, and a "transfirmative action program" gave preference to transgender candidates for all positions working on the show. But the lead character, a transgender woman, was played by a "cisgender" man, which created some controversy.[7] That lead actor and the show's director both won Emmys in September 2016.[8] Around that time, the director, Jill Soloway, said in an interview, "The time has come where it's unacceptable for cis men to play trans women. It's pretty ironic coming from me, where I have a television show where a cis man plays a trans woman."[9]

Several other significant media events happened in the meantime, including the ABC special with Bruce Jenner in April 2015, and in July a cover story titled "Call Me Caitlyn" in *Vanity Fair*.[10] Also in July, Jenner won the Arthur Ashe Courage Award from ESPN.[11] Later that year came the Woman of the Year award from *Glamour*, which explained this choice by noting that Jenner "made the decision to transition publicly—so that in the future kids don't have to wait until they're 65 years old to discover who they are."[12] In the eyes of the mass media, a Woman of the Year award going to a biological man for the second consecutive year was less controversial than Jenner identifying as a Republican. Jenner also launched his own documentary series, *I Am Cait*, but it lasted only two seasons.[13]

A cable reality show called *I Am Jazz* entered its third season in 2017, profiling a teenage boy, Jazz Jennings, who identifies as a girl. Diagnosed with gender dysphoria at age four and socially transitioned at five, Jazz had been promoted as a model for transgender children for several years already. There was an interview by Barbara Walters in 2007, a documentary in 2011, a book titled *I Am Jazz* in 2014, and another book in 2016, *Being Jazz: My Life as a (Transgender) Teen*. The first book, *I Am Jazz*, is marketed to schools across the nation for preschool through the third grade. *Being Jazz* is marketed to teens. (We will see more in the next chapter about efforts to indoctrinate children in the schools.)

The summer of 2015 was "shaping up as the moment when transgender went mainstream—at least in the media," said *Fortune* magazine in reporting on a reality series that ran briefly on ABC Family.[14] *Becoming Us* was a show presented from the perspective of a teenage boy whose father and girlfriend's father were both in the process of transitioning. Later that year came *The Danish Girl*, the film based on the life of "Lili Elbe," one of the earliest sex reassignment patients. This film garnered the Academy Award for Best Supporting Actress as well as a Best Actor nomination.

National Geographic got in on the act in January 2017 with a "special issue" on what it called the "Gender Revolution." Two different covers were created for this issue, one that went to subscribers and another that appeared at newsstands.[15] The subscriber cover featured Avery Jackson, a nine-year-old boy who identifies as a girl, "the first transgender person to appear on the cover of *National Geographic*," the editors boasted. The cover text quotes Avery saying, "The best thing about being a girl is, now I don't have to pretend to be a boy."[16] The newsstand cover has a photo of seven young adults of various gender identities and expressions. Among the eight people on the two covers combined, there are three boys or men who identify as girls or women, a girl who identifies as a boy, individuals who identify as "bi-gender," "intersex nonbinary," and "androgynous," and even someone who is just "male," but not one girl who is comfortable being female.[17]

"Gender Identity" Policies, Public and Private

While Hollywood sought to mainstream transgender ideology, the federal government mandated it. The Obama administration pushed "gender identity" policies as a matter of civil rights in various domains—education, health care, housing, the military. In 2010, before the media parade began, the Office for Civil Rights at the Department of Education issued a "Dear Colleague" letter redefining the word "sex" in Title IX (an antidiscrimination law passed in 1972) to include "gender identity" for the purposes of antibullying programs. The department would apply this new interpretation to school bathrooms, locker rooms, showers, sports teams, and dorm rooms in a series of actions involving the Arcadia School District in California (2013), the Palatine School District 211 outside of Chicago (2015), and the Gloucester County Public Schools in Virginia (2015). Finally, in May 2016, the DOE and the Department of Justice jointly issued a "Dear Colleague" letter mandating that all public schools allow access to sex-specific facilities based on gender identity rather than biological sex.[18] So Title IX, a law designed to protect women and girls from discrimination at school, would be used to violate the privacy, safety, and equality of women and girls.

At the same time, in May 2016, the Office for Civil Rights at the Department of Health and Human Services announced that a ban on "sex" discrimination in Obamacare was now being interpreted to ban "gender identity" discrimination. This would require all health-care plans regulated under Obamacare to cover sex reassignment procedures, and all relevant physicians to perform them.[19] What was most remarkable about this new mandate was that it directly conflicted with the conclusions of the Obama administration's own medical experts. A month after HHS declared sex reassignment to be a civil right, the Centers for Medicare and Medicaid Services released a report explaining that they were *not* mandating insurance coverage of sex reassignment surgery because clinical evidence did not demonstrate it to be beneficial:

> Based on a thorough review of the clinical evidence available at this time, there is not enough evidence to determine whether gender reassignment surgery improves health outcomes for Medicare beneficiaries with gender dysphoria. There were conflicting (inconsistent) study results—of the best designed studies, some reported benefits while others reported harms. The quality and strength of evidence were low due to the mostly observational study designs with no comparison groups, potential confounding and small sample sizes. Many studies that reported positive outcomes were exploratory type studies (case-series and case-control) with no confirmatory follow-up.[20]

So while the Medicare plans run by the federal government weren't required to cover sex reassignment procedures, the federal government's civil rights office was requiring it of private insurance plans and physicians covered in those plans.

Both the education mandate and the health-care mandate were blocked by a federal judge before they went into effect. The Trump administration changed course from Obama-era policy at the federal level, but any policy made by executive decree can be reversed again by another administration.

Other agencies also advanced the transgender agenda during the Obama years. The administration had once been willing to admit that granting access to sex-specific emergency shelters based on biology was not bigotry. That changed in September 2016, when the Department of Housing and Urban Development required shelters for the homeless and for battered women, among others, to allow access based on gender identity. No exemption was granted for shelters run by religious organizations.[21]

The military too has been swept up in the moment, and it now pays for sex reassignment surgery—even for convicted spies. Bradley Manning, sentenced to thirty-five years in prison for leaking classified information, announced himself to be Chelsea Manning, and the taxpayers picked up the tab for his sex reassignment procedures. In January 2017, President Obama commuted Manning's sentence. As this book went to press, the Trump administration was reexamining the military policy concerning people who identify as transgender.

While the Obama administration was lenient on Manning, it had brought the full force of the Justice Department to bear on North Carolina, suing the state in May 2016 for allegedly violating the 1964 Civil Rights Act. At issue was the state's House Bill 2, a law under which access to bathrooms, locker rooms, and other sex-specific facilities in public schools and other government buildings is to be determined primarily by biological sex as indicated on a birth certificate, while private schools, restaurants, stores, and other businesses are free to establish access policies as they choose.[22]

North Carolina's HB2, like similar "bathroom bills," is simply common sense. It represents a reasonable compromise and makes accommodations for individuals who identify as transgender. For example, the North Carolina Department of Health and Human Services noted that "Anyone who has undergone a sex change can change their sex on their birth certificate."[23] HB2 allows local school authorities and managers of government offices to provide special arrangements for people who identify as transgender, such as single-occupancy bathrooms or letting students have controlled access to faculty locker rooms. Such measures would protect women and girls from finding biological males in places where they expect some privacy, while also granting people who identify as transgender a safe place. Compromise policies of this kind acknowledge the reason we have sex-specific facilities in the first place: it's because of biology, not an inner sense of gender identity. Separate facilities are designed to offer privacy with respect to our bodies.

Nevertheless, North Carolina's reasonable policy was attacked in the media and by the Obama administration. In announcing the lawsuit against the state, the attorney general, Loretta Lynch, suggested that basing bathroom and locker-room access on biological sex was as repulsive as basing it on skin color. "It was not so very long ago that states, including North Carolina, had signs above restrooms, water fountains and on public accommodations keeping people out based upon a distinction without a difference," she said.[24] The attorney general seemed to miss the fact that some distinctions do indeed make a difference. Whereas our skin color is irrelevant to which bathroom or locker room we use, our bodily differences as male or female are precisely why we have "men's rooms" and "women's rooms."

Liberal city and state governments also aimed to punish North Carolina for its "bathroom bill." The mayor of San Francisco issued an order "to bar any publicly-funded City employee travel to the State of North Carolina that is not absolutely essential to public health and safety."[25] Governor Andrew Cuomo did the same regarding state employees of New York. In response, Governor Pat McCrory of North Carolina asked how Cuomo's action with respect to HB2 was consistent with his trip to Cuba to promote trade with that country.[26] Is Cuba better on human rights than North Carolina? Or was Cuomo being a bit hypocritical?

Meanwhile, Big Business piled on too. IBM, PayPal, Apple, Facebook, Google, and Salesforce all came out against the North Carolina law.[27] The CEO of PayPal announced that the company was cancelling plans for a $3.6 million expansion in the state that would have created four hundred jobs because of "PayPal's deepest values and our strong belief that every person has the right to be treated equally, and with dignity and respect."[28] Really? PayPal never explained why its international headquarters are in Singapore, where people who engage in private, consensual homosexual acts can face two years in jail. PayPal never explained why it announced in 2012 that it would open offices in the United Arab Emirates, which reportedly jails people who identify as gay or transgender.[29]

Even Big Sports jumped into the action against North Carolina. The NBA moved the 2017 All-Star Game out of Charlotte, a decision that was particularly amusing given that the NBA and its sister organization, the WNBA, determine participation in their leagues according to biology. The NBA and WNBA are free to have gender-neutral basketball teams, and to have gender-neutral restrooms at their games. That they boycotted a state in an effort to force a policy they haven't voluntarily adopted for themselves was the height of hypocrisy.

Transgender Medicine at Johns Hopkins

The most striking aspect of the transgender moment may be the influence of ideology on medical practice. Johns Hopkins Hospital is a prime illustration on account of its prestige and its history involving the treatment of discordant gender identities. The institution was a forerunner in offering sex reassignment procedures, largely due to John Money, a professor of medical psychology at Johns Hopkins University who in the 1960s advanced a radical notion that gender is only a social construct without any real connection to biology.

Indeed, Money appears to have been the first person to use the term "gender" in this way in the academic literature.[30] He famously claimed to have helped a family successfully raise their twin sons as brother and *sister* after a botched circumcision destroyed one boy's penis. Money presented this case, along with findings from his work with "intersex" children, as proof that infants aren't born with a specific gender and that any child might be raised as either a boy or a girl (perhaps with medical assistance). In reality, the young boy raised as a girl always felt that something was wrong, despite all the hormones and surgery and social conditioning he was subjected to. When he was fourteen, his parents told him the truth. Both twins took their own lives in their mid-thirties.[31] Yet Money never backed away from his radical claims.

A transgender activist might say that the tragic end for the twins only means that the one boy didn't really have a female gender identity. But Money's broader theory of gender as something separate from bodily sex would be influential in transgender advocacy. Money promoted his notion of gender fluidity across the United States, and together with a plastic surgeon he founded the Johns Hopkins Gender Identity Clinic in 1965.

A young professor of psychiatry at Hopkins, Dr. Paul McHugh, tried to dissuade his colleagues from rushing into the fad of transgender-affirming treatment and "sex reassignment." Decades later he recounted his experience:

> When the practice of sex-change surgery first emerged back in the early 1970s, I would often remind its advocating psychiatrists that with other patients, alcoholics in particular, they would quote the Serenity Prayer, "God, give me the serenity to accept the things I cannot change, the courage to change the things I can, and the wisdom to know the difference." Where did they get the idea that our sexual identity ("gender" was the term they preferred) as men or women was in the category of things that could be changed?[32]

Hormones and surgery cannot actually transform a man into a woman or a woman into a man, McHugh argued. His colleagues responded by introducing him to patients they claimed had successfully transitioned. They thought that if he met enough sexually reassigned people, he would come to see the benefit. But as McHugh recalls, "none of these encounters were persuasive."[33]

For a while, he could simply avoid what his colleagues were doing in sex reassignment. Then he was promoted to head of the psychiatry department, so everything that went on there necessarily concerned him. "I realized that if I were passive I would be tacitly co-opted in encouraging sex-change surgery in the very department that had originally proposed and still defended it," he wrote. McHugh believed it was necessary to know more about the results of the drastic procedures being recommended under his authority. "I decided to challenge what I considered to be a misdirection of psychiatry and to demand more information both before and after their operations."[34]

McHugh encouraged Jon Meyer, a psychiatrist and psychoanalyst at Hopkins, to follow up with adults who had undergone sex change operations at the hospital and determine whether the surgery was beneficial in the long term. Meyer found that only a few of the patients he tracked down some years after their surgery actually regretted it, yet most did not appear to have benefitted psychologically. "They had much the same problems with relationships, work, and emotions as before. The hope that they would emerge now from their emotional difficulties to flourish psychologically had not been fulfilled." While the surgery may have provided some subjective satisfaction, it brought little real improvement in well-being. After studying the evidence, McHugh decided that sex change surgery was bad medicine and was "fundamentally cooperating with a mental illness." Psychiatrists, he thought, could better help patients with gender dysphoria by "trying to fix their minds and not their genitalia."[35]

Similar studies were conducted in Toronto and arrived at similar conclusions. With a better understanding of what was really being done through sex change operations, McHugh and his colleagues stopped prescribing those procedures for adults at Hopkins. Some of the hospital's plastic surgeons, he added, were relieved at no longer being "commandeered to carry out the procedures."[36]

Dr. McHugh regards his profession as too inclined to chase fads and bend to political pressure instead of adhering to objective science. When patients claim to have discovered a "true" sexual identity at odds with their body, psychiatrists focus on "preparing them for surgery and for a life in the other sex," which he considers a distraction from trying to understand the causes of their mental confusion. "We have wasted scientific and technical resources and damaged our professional credibility by collaborating with madness rather than trying to study, cure, and ultimately prevent it."[37]

Medical professionals can be committed to an ideology just like anyone else. McHugh says that in his profession it is difficult "to gain agreement to seek empirical evidence for opinions about sex," and that "there is a deep prejudice in favor of the idea that nature is totally malleable."[38] A postmodern worldview is changing medicine from a profession that restores health and wholeness, into a set of techniques to provide customers with what they desire. It is eroding the very foundations of objectively sound medical practice, as McHugh observes:

> Without any fixed position on what is given in human nature, any manipulation of it can be defended as legitimate. A practice that appears to give people what they want—and what some of them are prepared to clamor for—turns out to be difficult to combat with ordinary professional experience and wisdom. Even controlled trials or careful follow-up studies to ensure that the practice itself is not damaging are often resisted and the results rejected.[39]

The politicizing of medical problems is not good for anyone, says McHugh. Because actual "sex change" is biologically impossible (as will be explained in more detail later), no one truly benefits from the insistence that surgical intervention for that purpose is a civil right. Today, "policy makers and the media are doing no favors either to the public or the transgendered by treating their confusions as a right in need of defending rather than as a mental disorder that deserves understanding, treatment and prevention."[40]

McHugh suggests that our cultural confusion on the topic of gender identity is much like the famous Hans Christian Andersen tale, *The Emperor's New Clothes*, in which the spectators all pretend not to notice that the emperor in fact is not regally garbed but is strutting through the streets without a stitch on. They all worry that speaking an obvious truth would endanger their own social standing. Likewise, "onlookers to the contemporary transgender parade" know well that "a disfavored opinion is worse than bad taste," so they shrink from stating clear facts. McHugh says, "I am ever trying to be the boy among the bystanders who points to what's real. I do so not only because truth matters, but also because overlooked amid the hoopla...stand many victims." Too many parents are finding no one, "not doctors, schools, nor even churches," who will actually help them spare their children from the lifelong problems of transitioning.[41]

Truth tellers and healers are being punished by government and by society. In several states, McHugh points out, "a doctor who would look into the psychological history of a transgendered boy or girl in search of a resolvable conflict could lose his or her license to practice medicine," but there is no penalty for putting such a patient on drugs to block puberty, which may cause a host of problems.[42]

Dr. McHugh's evidence-based approach to gender dysphoria prevailed at Johns Hopkins for a few decades, but in 2016 the hospital announced that it would start performing sex reassignment procedures again. This was not a consequence of new scientific evidence. *LGBTQ Nation* reported that the policy reversal came about "thanks to mounting criticism against the respected medical center—and faculty member and psychiatrist Paul McHugh in particular."[43] According to *ThinkProgress*, the institution was trying to "reclaim a reputation it once had as the leading academic medical institution when it comes to providing affirming care for transgender people, but it has nearly four decades of damage to repair."[44]

In short, political pressure and a shift in cultural attitudes explain the policy reversal at Hopkins. But changes in the culture don't all happen spontaneously by a kind of natural evolution, as is often implied by the very people who have agitated for those changes. The cultural shift that led to our transgender moment has largely been the result of a targeted campaign by transgender activist organizations.

The Human Rights Campaign (HRC), a large and lavishly funded LGBT activist group, publishes a "Foundation Overview" documenting the work it has done to advance transgender "rights" on campuses, at workplaces, in medical institutions, even in houses of worship, aiming to force cultural and legal change. For example, HRC created a "Corporate Equality Index" to push businesses to implement transgender-friendly policies, and it appears to be having an effect. In 2002, only 3 percent of Fortune 500 companies included "gender identity" in their nondiscrimination policies, but 75 percent did so by 2016.[45] In 2002, not a single Fortune 500 company offered "transgender-inclusive healthcare coverage," but 511 did so by 2016.[46]

Another HRC publication, *Transgender Americans: A Handbook for Understanding* (2005), asserts that it is discriminatory to exclude from insurance coverage a certain kind of medical therapy for purposes of gender "transition" if that therapy is covered when used "for some other medical reason" by "non-transgender" individuals. "For example, testosterone therapy will be paid for by insurance policies if a non-transgender man has a low level of the hormone, but a transsexual man who uses the same hormone as part of his medically supervised gender transition would not be covered." It seems lost on HRC that using a certain medicinal agent or technique for different purposes is not medically the same thing. In the view of HRC, it is unacceptable that "transgender people must often pay out-of-pocket—for lifelong needs, such as hormone therapy, or for expensive one-time costs, such as sex-reassignment surgery—even when medical experts deem them necessary."[47]

Of course, the costs of the surgeries and lifelong hormone treatment are exorbitant no matter who pays for them, and meanwhile many Americans have unmet needs for essential health care. The question of what "medical experts deem necessary" in cases of discordant gender identity is a matter of controversy. But as HRC boasted, those "discriminatory exclusions" in insurance coverage were gradually disappearing. Indeed, businesses across the country have been falling in line: whereas only 13 companies had a perfect score on the HRC Equality Index in 2002, the count was 407 companies in 2016.[48]

HRC also created a "Healthcare Equality Index" as a means of pressuring medical facilities to offer sex reassignment therapies. Making the grade became a bragging point for Johns Hopkins. In the summer of 2016, the dean of the medical faculty and the president of the Johns Hopkins Health System sent out a "Dear Colleagues" letter to mark "Pride Month," noting that "All six Johns Hopkins member hospitals achieved recognition from the Human Rights Campaign Foundation's 2016 Healthcare Equality Index." The letter also touted the decision to begin, once again, offering "gender-affirming therapies for transgender patients."[49]

But that wasn't enough. After being awarded a perfect score on the Healthcare Equality Index, Hopkins scored considerably lower in 2017. The reason was that the institution did not publicly condemn Dr. McHugh and another researcher, Dr. Lawrence Mayer, over a report they published in August 2016, a 143-page literature review on what science showed, and didn't show, about sexual orientation and gender identity. HRC blasted their findings as "transphobic." NBC reported that the conclusions of McHugh and Mayer had "triggered an unprecedented review by HRC," along with warnings that the medical school would be removed from an "elite classification" in the Healthcare Equality Index unless Johns Hopkins officially disassociated itself from the literature review. A warning that HRC sent to the institution said: "Failure to take significant steps to distance Johns Hopkins Medicine from this line of Dr. McHugh's personal beliefs and opinions will be considered an activity that undermines LGBTQ equality and patient care for the purposes of the Healthcare Equality Index score for Johns Hopkins Hospital."[50] Note that HRC characterized McHugh's survey of scientific research as his "personal beliefs and opinions."

In the spring of 2017, HRC made good on its threat. As Jonathan Last pointed out, since no change of policy at Hopkins could account for a lower score, this action by HRC "would reveal that the essence of the Healthcare Equality Index was mau-mauing, not Science." HRC found a way around the problem: it changed the scoring methodology, particularly by adding a new criterion called "responsible citizenship." Medical institutions "could not *earn* any points for being responsible citizens. But they could be docked 25 points if the Human Rights Campaign decided that they had *not* been responsible citizens," Last explains. "Of the 590 institutions in the 2017 index, you'll never guess which was the *only one* to be deemed an 'irresponsible citizen.'"[51] Actually, you probably will guess. The scoring criterion of "responsible citizenship" was a patently ideological one.

While activists have attacked the Mayer-McHugh review (which will be discussed in some detail later on), they haven't been able to specify any errors or flaws. As Last observes,

> It's an extremely cautious document that relies entirely on published research and presents both sides of all arguments. If you had to boil Mayer and McHugh's conclusions down to a single sentence, it would go something like this: *Human sexuality and gender are incredibly complicated, a lot of what's presented as "fact" has no sturdy basis in scientific research, and we really ought to study the entire subject more rigorously.*

But even this modest, empirically based view is regarded as blasphemy against LGBTQ orthodoxy.[52]

Mayer and McHugh found numerous claims in that orthodoxy to be scientifically weak. They have insisted on a careful consideration of the evidence, free from political agendas. That's how science is supposed to work. Unfortunately, people who arrive at "incorrect" conclusions on hot-button issues can expect to be attacked and made to pay a price.

Taking Down an Enemy

At least McHugh and Mayer got to keep their jobs. That wasn't the case for Dr. Kenneth Zucker when activists trained their sights on him. Zucker is a psychologist who ran the Centre for Addiction and Mental Health (CAMH) in Toronto for three decades and directed its Gender Identity Clinic (GIC).

He is perhaps the most frequently cited name in research on gender identity and the editor of the journal *Archives of Sexual Behavior*. Zucker has been at the forefront of developing treatments for people with gender dysphoria, and he headed the group that wrote the entry on gender dysphoria for the *Diagnostic and Statistical Manual of Mental Disorders*, the official handbook of the American Psychiatric Association. Yet he was abruptly fired from the Toronto clinic one morning in December 2015, becoming a casualty of a campaign by activists who viewed him as insufficiently pro-trans. Never mind that he had recommended transition therapies for scores of patients over the years and had never tried to "detransition" a patient. He was targeted for his belief that *children* represent a special kind of gender dysphoria, and that their long-term well-being may not be served by automatically encouraging them to transition. For that sin, he was subjected to a show trial by the hospital (CAMH).

The World Professional Association for Transgender Health (WPATH) is partly responsible for Zucker's ousting. The organization objected to something published in the journal he edited: a Swedish study that found substantially elevated rates of suicide and other mental health problems among adults who identify as transgender even after hormonal and surgical transitioning treatments. WPATH pressured the study's authors to retract their conclusions, but Zucker refused to permit a retraction. He was attacked by activists, and then the Canadian government shut down his clinic.[53]

Transgender activists celebrated their "spectacular victory" in taking down one of their biggest enemies, as Jesse Singal reported in *New York* magazine. That's hardly a conservative outlet, and Singal is a trans-friendly journalist, but his account of what happened to Zucker is fair and detailed. In his telling,

> The activists had won what seemed like a satisfying end to a simple, sad story. "Infamous Reparative Therapy Clinic For Transgender Youth Set To Close," trumpeted ThinkProgress. "Hooray! A Big, Bad Conversion Therapy Clinic For Trans Youth In Canada Is Shutting Down," went the MTV headline. Good prevailed over evil, in other words. Those innocent children would never suffer again....
>
> [But] if you look closely at what really happened—if you read the review (which CAMH has now pulled off of its website), speak with the activists who effectively wrote large swaths of it, examine the scientific evidence, and talk to former GIC clinicians and the parents of patients

they worked with, it's hard not to come to an uncomfortable, politically incorrect conclusion: Zucker's defenders are right. This was a show trial.[54]

In reality, Zucker was not doing "reparative therapy" or "conversion therapy," but his clinic took a cautious approach to treating children. The clinicians "viewed it as preferable for a child to become comfortable with his or her natal gender" instead of beginning a process of social transition, a process that tends to become self-reinforcing because "children naturally respond to the messages they get from parents and peers and society," Singal explains. A large majority of those children would eventually desist from their gender dysphoria, so "why nudge them prematurely toward accepting a cross-gender identity?" At the same time, the clinic often helped patients, especially the older ones, transition to their felt gender, "providing a wide range of services that included hormone referrals."[55]

But activists demanded total capitulation. And the hospital capitulated, first by commissioning an external review, which Singal describes as "a markedly unprofessional document that takes many of the worst claims about the GIC at face value—without bothering to check them." The most explosive claim against Zucker—that he had mocked one of his patients, calling him a "hairy little vermin"—was shown to be entirely false, which led the hospital to remove the external report from its website and substitute a toned-down summary. This possibly libelous charge was "the most serious single problem with the External Review, but it's just one of many," Singal remarks. "It simply does not read, at any point, like a serious attempt to evaluate the Gender Identity Clinic, and it is riddled with sloppiness."[56]

Judging from the evidence, it's pretty clear that the review was initiated to achieve a preordained result: firing Zucker and shuttering his clinic. This is all because the question of how best to treat gender dysphoria in children has become a focus of political warfare—between those who understand it as similar to other dysphorias, and those who insist that it should be accepted at face value as evidence of a fixed transgender identity, as who the child really is. One strange result of this politicization, as Singal comments, is that the professional psychiatrists who conducted the external review were "concerned that it's harmful or improper to help patients in a mental-health clinic understand why they are the way they are."[57] If this concern were to be generalized across the field, it would render *any* mental health work harmful or improper.

In the activists' view, Zucker's offense was to approach gender dysphoria in the same way as other psychological symptoms, such as anxiety or depression, trying first to understand the causes and then to resolve the underlying problems. Parents interviewed for *New York* magazine were thankful to Zucker and his clinic for their services, Singal reports:

> I spoke with five mothers of GIC patients or former patients who went into CAMH to defend Zucker (out of the seven parents who did, total), and they told me all about their experiences with him and his clinic. None was happy about the closing, and none could point to any examples of Zucker or the other clinicians acting unprofessionally or disrespectfully. Their children, all but one in their teens or younger, are in very different places, reflecting the wide range of clients who were seen at the GIC, but all of them, their parents insisted, had been helped by the GIC and what they said was a nurturing, exploration-focused environment.

With one exception, the parents that Singal spoke with didn't exhibit "a whiff of discernible transphobia." One had a child who was continuing to identify as transgender, and another child was still ambivalent.[58]

Parents appreciated Zucker's methods and his care in looking deeper into their children's distress. But too many parents today are pressured "to embrace the [trans]gender-affirmative approach," Singal says:

> According to an influential strain of trans politics, Zucker's more nuanced, "Why?"-focused method is offensive. This sounds like a caricature, but right there in the External Review that helped get him fired and his clinic shuttered, two professional psychiatrists state that asking "why" is improper. What needs to be done is to accept the child for who they are, and anything less than that is ignorant, if not bigoted.[59]

Simply accepting the self-declaration of a gender-dysphoric child and encouraging persistence in a transgender identity does not constitute sound, science-based medicine. But politics now rules the debate. If one of the world's leading experts on gender dysphoria can be railroaded in this way, it means that medical practice is seriously compromised by an ideological agenda. Far from being a stable and coherent set of beliefs, it is an ideology that changes with political expediency, but what is lacking in logical coherence is more than compensated by the uncompromising zeal of its advocates. It's to this ideology and its promoters that we turn in the next chapter.

....

CHAPTER TWO

What the Activists Say

In March 2017, I debated a board member for Equality Texas on the subject of school policies on gender identity. The debate was sponsored by the Federalist Society chapter at the University of Texas at Austin School of Law. UT Austin isn't exactly a bastion of conservatism, but I had spoken there before and always without incident. The room was packed, and it was colorful—lots of pink and rainbows. But what I remember most about the debate was that several protesters interrupted and started chanting over a megaphone: "Trans lives are not a debate. F**k this guy and f**k this state."

The protesters were right about one thing: trans lives are not a debate. The topic at issue that day was not whether people who identify as transgender have a right to their lives; it was what sort of public policies best respect the lives of students who identify as transgender *and the lives of all other students.* Activists have a rather radical idea of what is required in terms of public policy to respect trans lives, and Texas wasn't going along with that agenda. A bill had recently been introduced in the state house of representatives to allow reasonable accommodations for people who identify as transgender, but not give unfettered access to the bathrooms, locker rooms, and showers of their choice. Activists found that outrageous.

While the colorful language of the protesters left the most vivid memory, something else about that debate has stuck with me. My opponent, a lawyer and LGBT activist, opened his remarks with a simple statement of what guided his thinking on these policy questions: a transgender boy *is* a boy, and thus should be treated like all other boys; a transgender girl *is* a girl, and thus should be treated like all other girls. This statement conveys a radical idea, and it reflects a shift of thinking among activists in recent years. No longer do they admit that a transgender boy is a biological girl who *identifies as* a boy, or that a transgender girl is a biological boy who *identifies as* a girl. Now they assert that people actually *are* the sex they claim to be.

This change in thinking is illustrated in the language favored by the Human Rights Campaign. When the organization published *Transgender Americans: A Handbook for Understanding* in 2005, it defined gender dysphoria as a person's "discomfort from the strong internal sense that their true gender identity does not match their physical sex." The handbook noted, without quibble, that gender dysphoria "remains listed as a mental disorder in the *Diagnostic and Statistical Manual of Mental Disorders*."[1] That was then. Now the HRC website gives this advice (with bolding and italics) to journalists for reporting about transgender people: "Refrain from contrasting trans men and women with **'real' or 'biological' men and women.** *Contrasting transgender people* with 'real' or 'biological' men and women is a false comparison. They are real men and women, and doing so contributes to the inaccurate perception that transgender people are being deceptive when, in fact, they are being authentic and courageous."[2]

This is a dramatic shift: from an emphasis on transgender identity being at odds with physical sex, to the idea of gender identity being essentially the *determinant* of sex; from acknowledging gender dysphoria as a mental disorder, to regarding transgender identities as just a variety of normal human development. These radical beliefs give rise to some equally radical demands.

This chapter presents the claims and demands of transgender activists in their own words: what they assert to be the truth about gender identity, and what they seek in terms of medical treatment and public policy. Special attention is focused on what they say about children, the demands made on our nation's schools, and the efforts to bypass parental authority. For the most part, this chapter simply reports what activists say, avoiding extended engagement with their arguments but noting some of the more outrageous and inaccurate statements along the way. In subsequent chapters we will assess these claims in more detail. It is easy to get things wrong; getting them right takes hard work.

Three realities about transgender activists will become clear. First, they are always changing their creed and expanding their demands: yesterday's mandatory vocabulary will become tomorrow's epithets; yesterday's enlightenment will be tomorrow's benighted bigotry; yesterday's requirements of Science and Medicine and Justice are tomorrow's suicide-inducing oppression. Second, even as their own position shifts, the activists are absolutely closed off to contrary evidence: they call for the censure of honest researchers; they refuse to give any consideration to competing interests of privacy or safety; they reject alternative therapies that may be favored by parents or doctors. Third, because the transgender movement is so close-minded, it inclines toward coercion. All of this suggests a posture of defensiveness—that activists know their claims can't stand up to scrutiny.

Transgender Ontology

People say that we live in a postmodern age that has rejected metaphysics. That's not quite true. We live in a postmodern age that promotes an alternative metaphysics. At the heart of the transgender moment are radical ideas about the human person—in particular, that people *are* what they claim to be, regardless of contrary evidence. A transgender boy *is* a boy, not merely a girl who *identifies as* a boy. It's understandable why activists make these claims. An argument about transgender identities will be much more persuasive if it concerns who someone *is*, not merely how someone *identifies*. And so the rhetoric of the transgender moment drips with ontological assertions: people *are* the gender they prefer to be. That's the claim.

Transgender activists don't admit that this is a metaphysical claim. They don't want to have the debate on the level of philosophy, so they dress it up as a scientific and medical claim. And they've co-opted many professional associations for their cause. Thus the American Psychological Association, in a pamphlet titled "Answers to Your Questions about Transgender People, Gender Identity, and Gender Expression," tells us, "*Transgender* is an umbrella term for persons whose *gender identity*, *gender expression*, or behavior does not conform to that typically associated with the sex to which they were assigned at birth."[3] Notice the politicized language: a person's sex is "assigned at birth." Back in 2005, even the Human Rights Campaign referred instead to "birth sex" and "physical sex."[4]

The phrase "sex assigned at birth," i.e., imposed from outside, is now favored because it makes room for "gender identity" as the real basis of a person's sex. In an expert declaration to a federal district court in North

Carolina concerning House Bill 2, Dr. Deanna Adkins stated, "From a medical perspective, the appropriate determinant of sex is gender identity."[5] Dr. Adkins is a professor at Duke University School of Medicine and the director of the Duke Center for Child and Adolescent Gender Care (which opened in 2015). When there is not a "complete alignment among sex-related characteristics," she says—and she includes "gender identity" among these characteristics—then "a more careful consideration of sex assignment is needed." And in these cases, "medicine and science require" that the carefully considered basis of sex assignment be "gender identity rather than other sex characteristics."[6] This is a remarkable claim, not least because the argument recently was that gender is only a social construct, while sex is a biological reality. Now, activists claim that gender identity is destiny, while biological sex is the social construct.

Adkins argues that gender identity is not only the preferred basis for determining sex, but "the only medically supported determinant of sex."[7] Every other method is bad science, she claims: "It is counter to medical science to use chromosomes, hormones, internal reproductive organs, external genitalia, or secondary sex characteristics to override gender identity for purposes of classifying someone as male or female."[8] Adkins doesn't say if she would apply this rule to all mammalian species. But why should sex be determined differently in humans than in other mammals? And if medical science holds that gender identity determines sex in humans, what does this mean for the use of medicinal agents that have different effects on males and females? Does the proper dosage of medicine depend on the patient's sex or gender identity? We'll look at that topic in Chapter 4; the crucial point here is the way "medical science" appears to be reconceived on a subjective foundation.

But what exactly is this "gender identity" that is supposed to be the true medical determinant of sex? Adkins defines it as "a person's inner sense of belonging to a particular gender, such as male or female."[9] Note that little phrase "such as," implying that the options are not necessarily limited to male or female. Other activists are more forthcoming in admitting that gender identity need not be restricted to the binary choice of male or female, but can include both or neither. The American Psychological Association, for example, defines "gender identity" as "a person's internal sense of being male, female, or something else."[10]

Adkins asserts that being transgender is not a mental disorder, but simply "a normal developmental variation." And she claims, further, that medical and mental health professionals who specialize in the treatment of gender dysphoria are in agreement with this view.[11]

These notions about sex and gender are now being taught to young children. Activists have created child-friendly graphics for this purpose, such as the "Genderbread Person," one of the first among them.[12] The Genderbread Person (shown on the following page) teaches that when it comes to sexuality and gender, people have five different characteristics, each of them falling along a spectrum. There's "gender identity," which is "how you, in your head, define your gender, based on how much you align (or don't align) with what you understand to be the options for gender." The graphic lists "4 (of infinite)" possibilities for gender identity: "woman-ness," "man-ness," "two-spirit," or "genderqueer." The second characteristic is "gender expression," which is "the way you present gender, through your actions, dress, and demeanor." In addition to "feminine" or "masculine," the options are "butch," "femme," "androgynous," or "gender neutral." Third is "biological sex," defined as "the physical sex characteristics you're born with and develop, including genitalia, body shape, voice pitch, body hair, hormones, chromosomes, etc." The final two characteristics concern sexual orientation: "sexually attracted to" and "romantically attracted to." The options include "Women/Females/Femininity" and "Men/Males/Masculinity." Which seems rather binary. The Genderbread Person tries to localize these five characteristics on the body: gender identity in the brain, sexual and romantic attraction both in the heart, biological sex in the pelvis, and gender expression everywhere.

The Genderbread Person presented here is version 3.3, incorporating adjustments made in response to criticism of earlier versions. But even this one violates current dogma. Some activists have complained that the Genderbread Person looks overly male. A more serious fault in the eyes of many activists is the use of the term "biological sex." *Time* magazine drew criticism for the same transgression in 2014 after publishing its profile of Laverne Cox, the "first out trans person" to be featured on the cover. At least the folks at *Time* got credit for trying to be "good allies, explaining what many see as a complicated issue," wrote Mey Rude in an article titled "It's Time for People to Stop Using the Social Construct of 'Biological Sex' to Defend Their Transmisogyny."(It's hard to keep up with the transgender moment.) But *Time* was judged guilty of using "a simplistic and outdated understanding of biology to perpetuate some very dangerous ideas about trans women," and failing to acknowledge that biological sex "isn't something we're actually born with, it's something that doctors or our parents assign us at birth."[13]

Today, transgender "allies" in good standing don't use the Genderbread Person in their classrooms, but opt for the "Gender Unicorn," which was

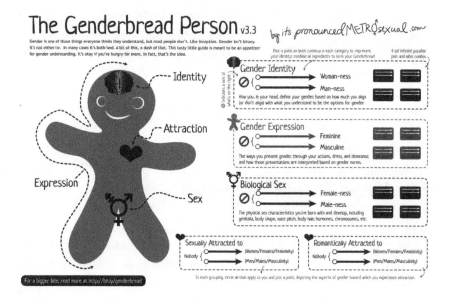

created by Trans Students Educational Resources (TSER).[14] It has a body shape that doesn't appear either male or female, and instead of a "biological sex" it has a "sex assigned at birth." Those are significant changes to the Genderbread Person, and they were made so that the new graphic would "more accurately portray the distinction between gender, sex assigned at birth, and sexuality." According to TSER, "Biological sex is an ambiguous word that has no scale and no meaning besides that it is related to some sex characteristics. It is also harmful to trans people. Instead, we prefer 'sex assigned at birth' which provides a more accurate description of what biological sex may be trying to communicate."[15] The Gender Unicorn is the graphic that children are likely to encounter in school. These are the dogmas they are likely to be catechized to profess.

While activists claim that the possibilities for gender identity are rather expansive—man, woman, both, neither—they also insist that gender identity is innate, or established at a very young age, and thereafter immutable. Dr. George Brown, a professor of psychiatry and a three-time board member of the World Professional Association for Transgender Health (WPATH), stated in his declaration to the federal court in North Carolina that gender identity "is usually established early in life, by the age of two to three years old."[16] Addressing the same court, Dr. Adkins asserted that "evidence strongly sug-

The Gender Unicorn

Graphic by: **TSER**
Trans Student Educational Resources

Gender Identity
- Female/Woman/Girl
- Male/Man/Boy
- Other Gender(s)

Gender Expression
- Feminine
- Masculine
- Other

Sex Assigned at Birth
Female   Male   Other/Intersex

Physically Attracted to
- Women
- Men
- Other Gender(s)

Emotionally Attracted to
- Women
- Men
- Other Gender(s)

To learn more, go to:
www.transstudent.org/gender

Design by Landyn Pan and Anna Moore

gests that gender identity is innate or fixed at a young age and that gender identity has a strong biological basis."[17] (At no point in her expert declaration did she cite any sources for any of her claims.)

In seeking evidence of a biological basis for transgender identities, activists point to the brain. "Much of the evidence in support of a biological basis for gender identity is based on comparison studies of the brains of transgender persons," says Dr. Brown.[18] People with gender dysphoria, claims Dr. Adkins, "have brain structure, connectivity, and function that do not match their birth-assigned sex."[19] Even if these claims were supported by evidence—and later we'll see good reasons for doubt—it wouldn't tell us whether the brain differences are the *cause* of transgender identity or a *result* of identifying and acting as transgender, through what is known as "neuroplasticity." And regardless of how transgender identities and aspects of the brain might correlate, none of this speaks to the question of biological sex. Even if there is a biological basis for people to think they're the opposite sex, that wouldn't actually make them so. Dr. Brown seems to acknowledge as much when he concludes that "Individuals experiencing gender dysphoria are, in essence, psychologically in the 'wrong body' and suffer significant emotional distress as a result."[20] In other words, what they are experiencing is a *psychological* condition.

Transgender Medicine

Given the transgender ontology—the belief that an internal sense of gender determines a person's sex—it isn't surprising that transgender activists promote medical remedies designed to affirm "gender identity." In the view of Dr. Adkins, the "appropriate treatment for individuals who are transgender must focus on alleviating distress through supporting outward expressions of the person's gender identity and bringing the body into alignment with that identity."[21] This treatment begins with supporting social transition, helping the person live as if already the opposite sex, and eventually it involves transforming the body to make it look like the opposite sex, in an attempt to conform it to the mind.

Dr. Randi Ettner, the chief psychologist at the Chicago Gender Center, describes the standard of care promoted by transgender activists:

- Changes in gender expression and role, consistent with one's gender identity (also referred to as social role transition).
- Psychotherapy for purposes such as addressing the negative impact of stigma, alleviating internalized transphobia, enhancing social and peer support, improving body image, promoting resiliency, etc.
- Hormone therapy to feminize or masculinize the body.
- Surgery to alter primary and/or secondary sex characteristics.[22]

Dr. Adkins asserts in her court declaration that these treatments "have been very successful," but cites no sources.[23] In Chapter 5, we'll see that the evidence falls short in two ways. First, these treatments do not actually bring the body "into alignment" with gender identity, and second, they do not effectively alleviate distress.

While the treatment plan summarized above is often called "transitioning," some transgender activists regard that term as stigmatizing and inaccurate. That's the view of PFLAG, a group that started out as Parents, Families and Friends of Lesbians and Gays, but since that leaves out Trans, it now goes by the acronym alone. PFLAG says that the language of transition is "inaccurate to describe the process a transgender person is going through from that person's perspective." From the outside it looks like a change, but people who identify as transgender experience it is a process of "settling in to themselves" or "coming home" to what they always were inside.[24] For the same reason, activists now prefer to speak of gender-affirming therapies instead of sex reassignment therapies.

Activists believe that even small children have a *real* gender identity that may not align with the body, so they call for "affirming" transgender identities in young children through social transition, followed by puberty blockers and eventually cross-sex hormones. This is the standard of care that WPATH and other transgender organizations promote. A guide for schools prepared by several prominent activist groups including the ACLU and HRC says that children develop a gender identity "between the ages of two and four," and that very young "transgender" children "are often insistent and persistent about their gender, differentiating their behavior from a 'phase' or imaginative play." Parents and teachers are instructed to support these children by "allowing them to live in a manner consistent with their gender identity, which helps them develop self-esteem and grow into happy, healthy members of society."[25]

A three-year-old child is just beginning to learn the difference between boys and girls, so how could that child have any sense of being really a boy when everyone says she's a girl? Yet some "experts" insist that a preschooler can have a "valid" sense of gender identity, independent of bodily sex. In his declaration to a federal court, Dr. Scott Leibowitz stated: "Peer-reviewed research demonstrates that pre-pubertal children asserting a different gender identity from the one they were assigned at birth are cognitively capable enough to be aware of the gender they are asserting. The meaning of a child's gender identity assertion at a younger age is no less valid than the meaning of a gender identity assertion of an older child."[26] On what other subject is the assertion of a two-year-old "no less valid" than that of an older child or an adult? PFLAG claims that "children know a lot about themselves and their gender from a very early age. And whether they reveal themselves to be gender expansive, transgender, or eventually neither, the most important thing we can do is listen to what our children are telling us, and really hear them."[27] On what other issue is it "most important" that parents take "what our children are telling us" at face value? PFLAG says parents can know that a child is truly transgender because "the 'consistent, persistent, and insistent' declaration of being a different gender is unique to kids who are transgender."[28]

Diane Ehrensaft, the director of mental health at the Child and Adolescent Gender Center at Benioff Children's Hospital, University of California San

Francisco, also believes that adults should be learning from children. Young transgender people, she says,

> are our best teachers in alerting us to the reality that gender exists primarily between our ears—in our brains and minds—and not necessarily by what is between our legs, our genitalia, or in our accompanying XX or XY chromosomes, as many are mistakenly prone to believe. We demonstrate how much we have yet to learn when we say, "But, honey, you can't be a girl, you're a boy because you have a penis. Boys have penises and girls have vaginas."[29]

On what other subject do we consider children to be "our best teachers"? Ehrensaft goes on to describe how young children can teach adults by "rearranging" their gender identity and expression:

> They refuse to pin themselves down as either male or female—maybe they are a boy/girl, or a gender hybrid, or gender ambidextrous, moving freely between genders, living somewhere in-between, or creating their own mosaic of gender identity and expression. As they grow older, they might identify themselves as agender, or gender neutral, or gender queer. Each one of these children is exercising their gender creativity, and we can think of them as our gender-creative children.[30]

In the activist view, these "gender-creative" children are more gender-wise than the adults, so parents and teachers are obliged to support them in living out their gender identity.

Consequently, all other medical approaches are to be discredited. Speaking of therapies that try "to bring the individual's gender identity into alignment with [biological] sex," Adkins asserts that they have been "unsuccessful and incredibly harmful. Deep depression, psychosis, and suicide frequently resulted."[31] She acknowledges that the rate of attempted suicide among people who identify as transgender—over 40 percent—is far higher than for most other medical conditions, but claims that the only way to prevent those suicide attempts is "to recognize the gender identity of patients with gender dysphoria."[32] But depression, psychosis, and suicide occur frequently both before and after sex reassignment therapies. And there are effective therapies to help children with gender dysphoria feel comfortable in their bodies; indeed, 80 to

95 percent of such children do not persist in a transgender identity. Yet Adkins told the court that a transgender identity "is fixed, cannot be changed by others, and is not undermined or altered by the existence of other sex-related characteristics that do not align with it."[33]

Activists use such claims to support the contention that *any* therapy other than promoting transition is unethical. Dr. George Brown claims that any effort to align transgender people's thoughts and feelings with their bodies— an approach that he labels "reparative therapy" or "conversion therapy"—is "widely considered to be unethical by professional organizations."[34] In the same vein, a "guide for parents" produced by the Children's National Medical Center suggests that social attitudes are the real problem, and therefore "a red flag should be raised when the therapist seems to focus on the child's behaviors as the problem rather than on helping the child cope with intolerance and social prejudice."[35] In other words, we should be alarmed (say the activists) if a professional tries to help a boy who thinks he's a girl come to understand that he is actually a boy, seeking to understand the reasons for his false belief and to help him identify with his body.

Transgender Policy

Because they believe that social attitudes may be the biggest problem for people who identify as transgender, activists demand sweeping changes in public policy. One proposal, the so-called "Equality Act," would add the phrase "gender identity" as a protected class to practically every federal civil rights law that protects individuals from racial discrimination. Besides expanding those laws beyond their current reach, the Equality Act would explicitly reduce protections of religious liberty. It would cover "Public Accommodations, Education, Federal Financial Assistance, Employment, Housing, Credit, and Federal Jury Service," thus going well beyond the proposed (but never enacted) Employment Non-Discrimination Act (ENDA), which applied only to employment.[36]

Transgender activists push for similar policies at the local, state, and federal levels. They see unlawful "discrimination" in actions that do not treat people in accordance with their self-professed gender identity when it comes to the sex-specific facilities they wish to use, the medical procedures they desire—such as removing a healthy uterus from a woman who wants to be a man—or the pronouns they want others to use in referring to them, which might be "ze" or "hir." In New York City, you can now be fined up to a quarter million dollars for intentionally "misgendering" someone by using pronouns other than those the person prefers.[37] And in October 2017, the governor of California signed a new law that could send health-care workers *to jail* for failing to use a person's chosen pronouns.[38]

Activists are particularly intent on promoting their policy agenda in schools, with serious consequences not only for students' privacy and safety, but also for their development: for what is taught about biological sex and gender identity, and for whether children with gender dysphoria will be helped or harmed. We can see what this agenda looks like in a document titled *Schools in Transition: A Guide for Supporting Transgender Students in K–12 Schools*, which was jointly produced by the ACLU, the Human Rights Campaign, Gender Spectrum, the National Center for Lesbian Rights, and the National Education Association. That's right: the nation's largest teachers' union partnered with LGBT organizations to formulate the guidelines for schools. They start out by articulating their "guiding principles," including this:

> The expression of transgender identity, or any other form of gender-expansive behavior, is a healthy, appropriate and typical aspect of human development. A gender-expansive student should never be asked, encouraged or required to affirm a gender identity or to express their gender in a manner that is not consistent with their self-identification or expression. Any such attempts or requests are unethical and will likely cause significant emotional harm. It is irrelevant whether a person's objection to a student's identity or expression is based on sincerely held religious beliefs or the belief that the student lacks capacity or ability to assert their gender identity or expression (e.g., due to age, developmental disability or intellectual disability).[39]

The National Education Association endorses the activists' view that transgender identities are a healthy and normal aspect of human development, that children should always be encouraged to act in ways consistent with their self-identification (whatever it is), that any attempt to help a child feel more comfortable in his or her body is unethical and likely to be harmful, that all this applies even to very young and mentally disabled children, and that the religious beliefs and religious liberty rights of parents and teachers don't matter. This is coming to a school near you, if it isn't already there.

An entire chapter of the guidelines is devoted to "the use of chosen names and pronouns, student confidentiality and student records, restroom and locker room access, sports and other sex-separated activities and harassment or bullying."[40] The gist of these guidelines is pretty straightforward: "Ultimately, the school environment must be set up so that transgender girls are treated like all other girls and transgender boys like all other boys."[41] Again, transgender policies follow from transgender ontology. But the guidelines don't stop with a gender binary of boys and girls; they tell schools to recognize that "a growing number of gender-expansive youth are identifying themselves outside the gender binary, and many use gender-neutral pronouns." Adapting to such usage may be difficult, but "it is still important to do so in support of the student."[42]

There is guidance on nonbinary pronouns, but nothing on how "gender-expansive youth" should be treated when it comes to uniforms, bathrooms, locker rooms, or sports teams. On those practical questions, the guidelines simply accept the normal gender binary and instruct schools to treat students in accordance with their self-asserted gender identity as male or female. As for concerns that boys will claim to identify as girls just to get into the girls' locker room, the guidelines assert that any such tomfoolery would be "easily discernable." A school administrator who has "credible doubts" can ask for "some documentation that the student has asserted a transgender identity in other settings."[43] But requesting evidence of a consistent gender identification goes against transgender activists' own claims about gender fluidity. A CNN report on the subject in 2016 said that gender identity and expression "can change every day or even every few hours," and this fluidity "can be displayed in how we dress, express and describe ourselves." Moreover, it added, "Everyone's gender exists on a spectrum."[44]

While activists don't provide much practical guidance to schools concerning nonbinary or highly fluid gender identities, they make it clear that young children should be considered the authorities on their own gender: "A student's age and maturity—or that of their peers—should never be a basis for denying a transgender student an opportunity to transition in a safe and supportive environment." The guidelines claim that "experience from schools across the country" shows children to be capable of discussing transgender issues in elementary school, and to be generally "much more flexible in their thinking and capacity for understanding a peer's assertion of their authentic gender."[45] That's a crucial point: Part of the program is to "educate" students to be "flexible" in their understanding of "authentic gender."

This agenda becomes abundantly clear in the section on bullying. The guidelines counsel against relying on suspension or expulsion of bullies, as it doesn't change the behavior. Instead, they recommend "restorative justice programs and positive behavior interventions" in order to "create a school-wide culture of inclusion and respect for difference."[46] Once implemented, this "culture of inclusion" will look an awful lot like politically correct indoctrination.

The guidelines show concern for the privacy of *some* students, emphasizing that a student's "transgender status, legal name or sex assigned at birth is confidential."[47] For all others, privacy doesn't matter so much. Other students may not be told that they will be sharing a bathroom or locker room or shower, or a dorm room or hotel room during field trips, with a student who identifies as transgender. Concerning overnight field trips, a "school has an obligation to maintain the [transgender] student's privacy and cannot disclose or require disclosure of the student's transgender status to the other students or their parents."[48] This means that girls will have no advance notice that a boy who identifies as a girl but has all of the standard male body parts will be undressing in their locker room or shower, or spending the night in their hotel room. The privacy concerns of non-transgender students are never discussed, except to be dismissed as merely a matter of being "uncomfortable." The guidelines say that "respect for the transgender student should be the starting point." They concede that "school officials have a responsibility to ensure the safety of all students," but only after saying that "being uncomfortable is not the same as being unsafe."[49]

If a female student feels that her privacy is violated upon discovering a biological male in a women's facility, the guidelines suggest first trying to indoctrinate her in transgender ontology. She should be taught to discard "the false idea that a transgender boy is not a 'real' boy, a transgender girl is not a 'real' girl."[50] If this effort fails and a student still feels that her privacy is not being respected, the guidelines suggest an accommodation, but one that gives priority to the feelings of the transgender student: "Any student who feels uncomfortable sharing facilities with a transgender student should be allowed to use another more private facility like the bathroom in the nurse's office, but a transgender student should never be forced to use alternative facilities to make other students comfortable."[51] The guidelines reiterate this instruction in nearly the same words, driving home the principle that the "comfort" of non-transgender students or personnel is of scant importance.[52]

Because the feelings of students who identify as transgender are paramount, even the creation of single-occupancy facilities to accommodate those students is deemed unacceptable. "Transgender students should never be forced to use a separate single-stall facility," the guidelines stress.[53] Instead, everyone else most conform to transgender ontology and policy.

When it comes to sports teams too, students should be treated in accordance with their self-professed gender identity. The guidelines pointedly dismiss the obvious concerns about the advantages that biological males would have in competition with girls, saying that such worries reflect an "erroneous" belief: "Concerns regarding competitive advantage are unfounded and often grounded in sex stereotypes about the differences and abilities of males versus females." After all, a transgender girl was simply "assigned male at birth," and the guidelines assure us that "she [*sic*] still falls within the wide range of athletic abilities of her [*sic*] female peers."[54] There is no guidance on athletic policies for students who are gender-fluid or who in other ways reject the gender binary. Recall the CNN report saying that "how one identifies can change every day or even every few hours." Suppose a student identifies as a boy on Mondays, Wednesdays, and Fridays, but as a girl on Tuesdays, Thursdays, and Saturdays, and as both on Sundays. Which team should this student play on for a weekend tournament? The guidelines don't say.

Transgender activists make these policy demands not only as a requirement of justice or equality, but also in the name of science and medicine. Dr. Brown, for example, stated to a federal court that "Access to sex-segregated bathrooms and changing facilities consistent with gender identity is an essential part of the social role transition." Moreover, he added, "Excluding transgender men from men's facilities and transgender women from women's facilities can result in depression, anxiety, trauma, and isolation that exacerbates the mental health issues associated with Gender Dysphoria."[55] In concluding his declaration to the court, Brown maintained that any laws or policies requiring that people who identify as transgender be treated in accordance with their biological sex are "psychologically harmful to those individuals, and are inconsistent with evidence-based best practices to promote the health and well-being of transgender people."[56]

Dr. Randi Ettner of the Chicago Gender Clinic declared to the court that "Use of facilities that correspond to one's lived experience and appearance is integral to social recognition of identity."[57] (Here, "appearance" seems to mean the person's self-presentation.) Therefore, failing to treat a gender-dysphoric person as the self-declared gender in all situations "is inconsistent with evidence-based medical practice and detrimental to the health and well-being of the individual, regardless of age."[58]

Even if these policy prescriptions were founded on good science (which they are not), the expert declarations nowhere even consider other concerns of public policy with respect to sex-specific facilities. They evince no awareness that there are competing considerations in this discussion. And they are frequently wrong in their characterization of the policies they criticize—policies that in fact do not force people who identify as transgender to use facilities that correspond with their biological sex, but only prevent them from using the opposite sex's facilities unless they have legally transitioned, and otherwise allow them to be reasonably accommodated, for example, with a single-occupancy facility.

Many activists—as we see in the school guidelines—object to any requirement that people who identify as transgender use a single-occupancy facility. In Ettner's view, "to insist that a transgender individual use a separate restroom, communicates that such a person is not a 'real' man or woman; or that the person is some undifferentiated 'other.'" This "othering," no matter the policy justification in terms of other people's privacy or safety, is unacceptable because it "interferes with the person's ability to consolidate identity and undermines the social-transition process."[59] Dr. Scott Leibowitz agrees, asserting that policies disallowing people who identify as transgender to have unfettered access to the sex-specific facility of their choice send a message that "their identity is invalid, wrong, or problematic," with harmful consequences for "their self-esteem, self-worth, ability to trust in others, and willingness to go out into the world."[60] Unsurprisingly, neither Ettner nor Leibowitz cites any studies to support these claims. No such research exists.[61]

Parental Authority

Privacy concerns for the school setting are entirely one-sided: carefully guarding the privacy of a student who identifies as transgender, while ignoring everyone else's concerns, and that includes the concerns of parents. Neither the other students nor their parents can be informed that they or their child will be sharing a hotel room or dorm room with a student of the opposite biological sex who identifies as transgender. Nor can the parents of *a student who identi-*

fies as transgender be given that information. These parents are likely to have the deepest concern for the well-being of their child, but the experts believe in going behind the backs of parents who might question transgender dogma.

The school guidelines devote a chapter to "approaches for working with unsupportive parents or parents who disagree about the appropriate response to their child's expressed gender identity."[62] The starting point is the conviction that "Privacy and confidentiality are critically important for transgender students who do not have supportive families. In those situations, even inadvertent disclosures could put the student in a potentially dangerous situation at home, so it is important to have a plan in place to help avoid any mistakes or slip-ups."[63] There's an eight-page worksheet on how to handle a gender transition in school while protecting a child's privacy—that is, keeping parents in the dark. The same strategy is promoted in the "Model District Policy on Transgender and Gender Nonconforming Students" produced by the National Center for Transgender Equality and GLSEN (another organization that left Transgender out of its original name, "Gay, Lesbian, and Straight Education Network," so it now goes only by the acronym). In the model policy, "School staff shall not disclose any information that may reveal a student's transgender status to others, including parents or guardians," unless absolutely required to do so by law.[64]

Transgender activists believe that schools should conceal from parents who do not embrace transgender ideology the fact that their child is identifying as transgender. The guidelines give advice on how to use a student's preferred name and pronouns in class, but the legal name and normal sex-specific pronouns in communications with parents, to hide their child's social transition. So parents whose ten-year-old son is identifying as a girl in school and being treated as a girl by his classmates and teachers could be intentionally kept clueless. If parents do find out and are "unsupportive," schools are instructed to "support the student's family in accepting their child's gender identity and seek opportunities to foster a better relationship between the student and their family."[65] Rather than respect parental authority in the education and health of their children, schools first deceive the parents and then try to change their beliefs. Indeed, the Transgender Equality and GLSEN model district policy states that "it is critical that parental/guardian approval is never a prerequisite for respecting a student's chosen name, appropriate gender, and pronouns," even if this goes against the medical and psychological care that the parents are pursuing for that child.[66]

If the parents disagree between themselves—one parent supporting transition and one favoring efforts to help the child identify with his or her body—then school officials may serve as impartial witnesses in a legal dispute, the guidelines say. Of course, their unbiased testimony can be expected to favor the parent who supports transition:

> School officials interact with the student on a daily basis and focus on supporting the student's growth and development, which gives school personnel unique insight into the student's needs without the biases parents can or are perceived to have. Sharing the school's experiences with the student before and after the student began identifying as transgender can help highlight to the judge the importance of affirming the student's gender identity. Describing the academic, social or emotional changes that school personnel observed will strengthen the testimony and give the judge a fuller understanding of the child's needs and what would be in that child's best interests.[67]

Puberty blockers and cross-sex hormones may be in "that child's best interests," according to the activists. These medications, they claim, "act as a pause button and give the youth an opportunity to explore their gender identity without the distress of developing the permanent, unwanted physical characteristics of their assigned sex at birth." Then a treatment plan can be worked out, which may include "cross-sex hormones to induce a puberty that is consistent with their gender identity."[68]

What if the family doesn't want to go along with puberty blockers and cross-sex hormones? Activists suggest that Child Protective Services might then intervene, on the grounds that the home is a "toxic environment" for the child. At a 2017 meeting of USPATH, the U.S. chapter of the World Professional Association for Transgender Health, a social worker speaking in a session called "Addressing Suicidality in Transgender Youth" set out a strategy for dealing with "family non-acceptance":

> This is where you have a family who is saying, no, no, no...and then you realize that actually the family is contributing to some of that negativity at home. So the family is creating a toxic environment. And that's where we have let the young person know the potential ramifications of calling DHS and saying that this is an unsafe environment.

And that we've given the family every chance. To learn, to grow. And they're continuing to be part of the problem. So thankfully this was an important time when I realized it was worthwhile in starting the clinic at children's hospital to have lots of meetings with the lawyers in risk management. To be able to say, "alright. I have the ethicist, I have the lawyer, I have the guru from risk management, I'm gonna sit down and say, I need to describe a case to you and make sure this is actually parents being negligent in the healthcare needs of their child.["]

Thankfully we've had a lot of support in that realm. Because of the trainings we've done with DHS workers in Delaware, Pennsylvania, and New Jersey. DHS workers will go and say you're creating an unsafe environment for your child. And we need to have that stop...unfortunately staying in that home environment is going to result in a child's suicide.[69]

So it isn't just information that may be withheld from parents who aren't adequately pro-trans. Their child may be taken away from them too, and the parents will be told it's the only way to prevent the child from committing suicide.

Transgender Contradictions

If the claims presented in this chapter strike you as confusing, you're not alone. The claims of transgender activists are inherently confused and filled with internal contradictions. Activists never acknowledge those contradictions, but opportunistically rely on whichever claim is useful at any given moment.

Here I'm talking about transgender *activists*. Again, most people who suffer from gender dysphoria are not activists, and many of them reject the activists' claims. Many of them may be regarded as victims of the activists, as we'll see in the next chapter. Many of those who feel distress over their bodily sex know that they aren't really the opposite sex, and do not wish to "transition." They wish to receive help in coming to identify with and accept their bodily self. They don't think their feelings of gender dysphoria define reality.

But transgender activists do. Regardless of whether they identify as "cisgender" or "transgender," the activists promote a highly subjective and incoherent worldview. On the one hand, they claim that the real self is something other than the physical body, in a new form of Gnostic dualism, yet at the same time they embrace a materialist philosophy in which only the material world exists. They say that gender is purely a social construct, while asserting that a person can be "trapped" in the wrong body. They say there are no meaningful differences between man and woman, yet they rely on rigid sex stereotypes to argue that "gender identity" is real while human embodiment is not. They claim that truth is whatever a person says it is, yet they believe there's a *real* self to be discovered inside that person. They promote a radical expressive individualism in which people are free to do whatever they want and define the truth however they wish, yet they try to enforce acceptance of transgender ideology in a paternalistic way.

It's hard to see how these contradictory positions can be combined. If you pull too hard on any one thread of transgender ideology, the whole tapestry comes unraveled. But here are some questions we can pose:

If gender is a social construct, how can gender identity be innate and immutable? How can one's identity with respect to a social construct be determined by biology in the womb? How can one's identity be unchangeable (be immutable) with respect to an ever-changing social construct? And if gender identity is innate, how can it be "fluid"? The challenge for activists is to offer a plausible definition of gender and gender identity that is independent of bodily sex.

Is there a gender binary or not? Somehow, it both does and does not exist, according to transgender activists. If the categories of "man" and "woman" are objective enough that people can identify as, and *be,* men and women, how can gender also be a spectrum, where people can identify as, and *be,* both or neither or somewhere in between?

What does it even mean to have an internal sense of gender? What does gender feel like? What meaning can we give to the concept of sex or gender, and thus what internal "sense" can we have of gender, apart from having a body of a particular sex? Apart from having a male body, what does it "feel like" to be a man? Apart from having a female body, what does it "feel like" to be a woman? What does it feel like to be *both* a man and a woman, or to be *neither*? The challenge for the transgender activist is to explain what these feelings are like, and how someone could know if he or she "feels like" the opposite sex, or neither, or both.

Even if trans activists could answer these questions about feelings, that still wouldn't address the matter of reality. Why should feeling like a man—

whatever that means—*make* someone a man? Why do our feelings determine reality on the question of sex, but on little else? Our feelings don't determine our age or our height. And few people buy into Rachel Dolezal's claim to identify as a black woman, since she is clearly not. If those who identify as transgender *are* the sex with which they identify, why doesn't that apply to other attributes or categories of being? What about people who identify as animals, or able-bodied people who identify as disabled? Do all of these self-professed identities determine reality? If not, why not? And should these people receive medical treatment to transform their bodies to accord with their minds? Why accept transgender "reality," but not trans-racial, trans-species, and trans-abled reality? The challenge for activists is to explain why a person's "real" sex is determined by an inner "gender identity," but age and height and race and species are not determined by an inner sense of identity.

Of course, a transgender activist could reply that an "identity" is, by definition, just an inner sense of self. But if that's the case, gender identity is merely a disclosure of how one feels. Saying that someone is transgender, then, says only that the person has feelings that he or she is the opposite sex. Gender identity, so understood, has no bearing at all on the meaning of "sex" or anything else. But transgender activists claim that a person's self-professed "gender identity" *is* that person's "sex." The challenge for activists is to explain why the mere feeling of being male or female (or both or neither) *makes* someone male or female (or both or neither).

Gender identity can sound a lot like religious identity, which is determined by beliefs. But those beliefs don't determine reality. Someone who identifies as a Christian believes that Jesus is the Christ. Someone who identifies as a Muslim believes that Muhammad is the Final Prophet. But Jesus either is or is not the Christ, and Muhammad either is or is not the Final Prophet, regardless of what anyone happens to believe. So, too, a person either is or is not a man, regardless of what anyone—including that person—happens to believe. The challenge for transgender activists is to present an argument for why transgender beliefs determine reality.

Determining reality is the heart of the matter, and here too we find contradictions. On the one hand, transgender activists want the authority of science as they make metaphysical claims, saying that science reveals gender identity to be innate and unchanging. On the other hand, they deny that biology is destiny, insisting that people are free to be who they want to be. Which is it? Is our gender identity biologically determined and immutable, or self-created and changeable? If the former, how do we account for people whose gender identity changes over time? Do these people have the wrong sense of gender at some time or other? And if gender identity is self-created, why must other people accept it as reality? If we should be free to choose our own gender reality, why can some people impose their idea of reality on others just because they identify as transgender? The challenge for the transgender activist is to articulate some conception of truth as the basis for how we understand the common good and how society should be ordered.

The claims of transgender activists are confusing because they are philosophically incoherent. Activists rely on contradictory claims as needed to advance their position, but their ideology keeps evolving, so that even allies and LGBT organizations can get left behind as "progress" marches on. At the core of the ideology is the radical claim that feelings determine reality. From this idea come extreme demands for society to play along with subjective reality claims. Trans ideologues ignore contrary evidence and competing interests; they disparage alternative practices; and they aim to muffle skeptical voices and shut down any disagreement. The movement has to keep patching and shoring up its beliefs, policing the faithful, coercing the heretics and punishing apostates, because as soon as its furious efforts flag for a moment or someone successfully stands up to it, the whole charade is exposed. That's what happens when your dogmas are so contrary to obvious, basic, everyday truths. A transgender future is not the "right side of history," yet activists have convinced the most powerful sectors of our society to acquiesce to their demands. While the claims they make are manifestly false, it will take real work to prevent the spread of these harmful ideas.

Activists claim to represent the best interests of all those with discordant gender identities, insisting that their policies and treatment protocols are the only ethical ones, and that other approaches lead to depression and suicide. Popular media outlets are happy to report on people who seem to find contentment with sex reassignment procedures. We seldom hear the voices of people who discovered that hormones and surgery were not the answer but often the source of new problems. We will allow them to tell their stories in the next chapter.

CHAPTER THREE

....

Detransitioners Tell
Their Stories

In 2012, the UK's *Daily Mail* ran a story with this headline: "'I was born a boy, became a girl, and now I want to be a boy again': Britain's youngest sex swap patient to reverse her sex change treatment." Here's how that report began:

> Ria Cooper made headlines last year when she became Britain's youngest sex change patient aged 17, after years of begging her family and the NHS to turn her in to a girl.
>
> But now, having lived as a woman for less than a year the 18-year-old has decided to change back in to a man after suffering huge mental anguish as a woman.
>
> She has cancelled the full sex change operation that was scheduled for January and ceased the female hormone therapy that has seen her develop breasts saying that she has found the changes overwhelming and that they have made her deeply unhappy.[1]

At the time, seventeen years was considered young to be transitioning. The *Daily Mail* reported that Cooper had been given "a thorough psychological assessment and counseling" before the sex change therapy, but nevertheless "suffered such torment living as a woman that she has tried to commit suicide twice."[2]

Cooper described this suffering in an interview with the *Mirror*: "The hormones have made me feel up and down. One minute I feel moody and the next minute I feel really happy.... A couple of months ago I'd had enough and took a lot of paracetamol but my friend found me.... Just before that, I'd tried to slash my wrists and ended up in hospital. I get these dark moods when nothing seems right."[3] As Cooper tells the story, family rejection appears to have been a factor contributing to the depression—highlighting the importance of family love and support even amid disagreement.

More recently, in 2017, the UK *Guardian* ran an op-ed by someone who had started transitioning as a teenager and came to regret it as an adult. This time it was a girl who spent her childhood as a tomboy, and then as a teen started to live as a boy and began hormonal and surgical treatment:

> It wasn't until I was 15 that I found out about transitioning. Everything fell into place: this was who I was. I realised I could have the body I wanted. When I went to my GP, aged 17, I was told I was too old to refer to children's services and too young to be seen as an adult; I didn't get my first appointment until three months after my 18th birthday.
>
> After months of waiting and appointments, none of which included counselling, I finally started on testosterone gel, later switching to injections. It was a huge thing when, at university, my voice broke, and my figure started changing: my hips narrowed, my shoulders broadened. It felt right. Passing as a man, I felt safer in public places, I was taken more seriously when I spoke, and I felt more confident.
>
> Then I had chest surgery. It was botched and I was left with terrible scarring; I was traumatised. For the first time, I asked myself, "What am I doing?" I delayed the next steps of hysterectomy and lower surgery, after looking into phalloplasty and realising that I was going to need an operation every 10 years to replace the erectile device.[4]

For many people, surgery goes well as a cosmetic matter, but a botched surgery led this anonymous author to question what she was doing in the first place. And as she notes in her narrative, the medical professionals never provided any counseling to help her understand why she had felt so strongly that she wanted to be a man. "I had assumed the problem was in my body. Now I saw that it wasn't being female that was stopping me from being myself; it was society's perpetual oppression of women. Once I realised this,

I gradually came to the conclusion that I had to detransition." Here's how that process went:

> I have come off testosterone and, as my body has resumed production of its own hormones, I have become someone female who looks like a man. I will always have a broken voice and will never regrow breasts, but my hips and thighs are getting bigger. Being male was more comfortable for me, but remaining on hormones means I would have continued to focus on my body as the problem—when I don't believe it belongs there. What feels easiest isn't always what's right.
>
> I made the best possible decision in poisoned circumstances, and if I hadn't had treatment when I did, I might not be alive. But I do feel very sad when I think of my fertility: I want to be a parent one day, but it's likely that being on testosterone has made that more difficult. I'm now in my late 20s and won't know until I try to have children.
>
> I feel happy for those people transition has helped, but I think there should be more emphasis on counselling, and that [transitioning] should be seen as the last resort. Had that been the case for me, I might not have transitioned. I was so focused on trying to change my gender, I never stopped to think about what gender meant.[5]

The themes expressed in these newspaper accounts are echoed over and over in YouTube videos and blog posts by people who have transitioned only to discover that changing the body did not help the psyche. It may have seemed like the easiest solution to their distress, but "what feels easiest isn't always right," as the *Guardian* op-ed pointed out. Many of these people end up detransitioning and learning to embrace their bodily sex. No two people are the same—whether they've transitioned or not, whether they've detransitioned or not.

This chapter introduces several people who have spoken and written in depth about their experiences of transitioning and detransitioning. I have tried to get out of the way and let these individuals speak for themselves. Some are still hurting, for while they may have found better ways to deal with their issues, they have lasting pain from their ordeal and from continuing dysphoria. To make things worse, they are often attacked and silenced by trans activists. Some of these detransitioners will no doubt disagree with large portions of this book. Some will disagree with my previous books on marriage. Some continue to support transition as a helpful option for other people who identify as transgender, even if they found it unsatisfactory for themselves. Where we agree is that their voices deserve to be heard.

Some common themes emerge from the various stories related here: Many people report feeling pressured into transitioning, as if it were their only real option. They regret that medical professionals never explored the underlying psychological issues. They detransitioned because they didn't find the peace and wholeness they desired by changing their bodies, but did find it when they were able to address past trauma in their lives and come to a better understanding of gender. Many of these people regret the damage done to their bodies and their lost fertility. They feel they were too young to be making such life-altering decisions. They blame a society that was hostile to people like them—particularly to people with same-sex attractions and other gender-nonconforming people—as they believe this hostility contributed to their thinking that transition was the only option. This charge should prompt social conservatives (like myself) to be careful not to attack or marginalize people as we advocate for the truth. By the same token, we should insist that trans activists cease attacking and marginalizing detransitioners.

The media play up the "success" stories of people like Bruce Jenner becoming Caitlyn Jenner, but largely ignore the stories like those told in this chapter. While some common themes run through them, it is important to hear each person's story at length. I encourage readers to follow the links in the endnotes to learn more.

Cari

Cari Stella posted a YouTube video telling her story in 2016.[6] "I'm Cari and I'm a 22-year-old detransitioned woman," she says at the beginning of the video. "I transitioned socially at 15, I started hormones at 17, and I detransitioned just after my 22nd birthday." Cari stresses that the reason for her choice to detransition was not that people didn't accept her as trans, or because of "social pressure" or "nebulous unhappy feelings." It wasn't because of a botched surgery or a hostile family. Cari tells viewers that her family was "accepting" and the transition was going well; her insurance paid for her mastectomy and would have covered everything including a hysterectomy and "bottom surgery." She lives in "one of the most trans-friendly areas" of the

United States and her workplace "has trans people in its leadership." Indeed, "from all outer appearances, my transition was a success," she says. But her inner life was another story.

As Cari tells it, she realized that the social and medical transition was a way of running away from herself. "I detransitioned because I knew I could not continue running from myself, dissociating from myself, because acknowledging my reality as a woman is vital to my mental health."[7] She places a fair bit of blame on gender therapists for not helping her accept herself as she was, as a woman:

> The truth is that a lot of women don't feel like they have options. There isn't a whole lot of place in society for women who look like this, women who don't fit, women who don't comply. When you go to a therapist and tell them you have those kinds of feelings, they don't tell you that it's okay to be butch, to be gender nonconforming, to not like men, to not like the way men treat you. They don't tell you there are other women who feel like they don't belong, that they don't feel like they know how to be women. They don't tell you any of that. They tell you about testosterone.[8]

Cari was put on testosterone after only three or four visits with a therapist at the TransActive Gender Center in Portland, Oregon. She emphasizes the lack of effort to get to the root of her discomfort with herself, and the absence of any suggestion of alternative therapies:

> I was put on hormones after 3 months of therapy at the age of 17. In fact, because I was only seeing a therapist once per month, it was after 3 or 4 visits that I was prescribed testosterone, with no meaningful attempt made to process the issues that I brought up that led in part to my wish to transition.... When I was transitioning, no one in the medical or psychological field ever tried to dissuade me, to offer other options, to do really anything to stop me besides tell me I should wait till I was 18.... I want to ask you, how many other medical conditions are there where you can walk into the doctor's office, tell them you have a certain condition, which has no objective test, which can be caused by trauma or mental health issues or societal factors, and receive life-altering medications on your say-so?[9]

That question should be posed to all transgender activists and to physicians and staff at "gender clinics."

Cari made a video for USPATH (the American chapter of the World Professional Association for Transgender Health) in which she explains how she needed to do "a lot of unlearning of what I understood about myself," in order to recognize and deal with the root causes of her dysphoria:

> When I was transitioning I felt a lot of intense, very intense body dysphoria, that felt very innate, very integral, at the time, to the way I perceived myself and the world. And what I came to realize eventually was that this was not the case, that there were all these factors that played into my dysphoria: dissociation, and feelings of inferiority for being female, and depression, body dysmorphia, you know, all these things contributing to this kind of general sense of alienation, sense of otherness from the people around me, and specifically from other women.[10]

Cari concludes that "detransition for me was about firstly discovering and acknowledging that my dysphoria had these causes, and it wasn't just, you know, some innate identity. Basically that it was a maladaptive coping mechanism for me." Her way of "coping" was to keep changing herself more and more: "when I was on testosterone I wanted to change my name, once I changed my name I wanted a mastectomy, once I had a mastectomy I wanted a hysterectomy, bottom surgery, and so on and so forth." And this process may have lacked any clear goal, says Cari: "I could keep going and changing my body in search of this finishing point but I don't think I would have ever arrived. Transition didn't really make my dysphoria better, it just kind of kept moving the goalposts, so I felt like I was making progress, but I never got any closer to where I wanted to be or where I thought I wanted to be."[11]

A misguided coping strategy that entails radically transforming themselves can be particularly attractive to young people at an age when anxieties about fitting in are acute, Cari suggests:

> I think the prospect of completely changing your body, your life, your identity, is very compelling to a teenager who is just learning to cope with mental health issues, with trauma, with gender nonconformance, with being a lesbian, and that's especially true when the current rhetoric around transition really discourages any kind of questioning; it really

frames transitioning or trans identity as the solution to any kind of gender issues or gender confusion. And I think it's really important for therapists not to frame transition as the only solution, to really present options, and to encourage people not to take their feelings and urges entirely at face value, to be critical, to really think about where those thoughts are coming from.[12]

Cari argues that our culture as a whole, and gender therapists in particular, help create a climate in which people uncomfortable with their own bodies—and with the gender expectations attached to them—see transition as the only cure. "My decision to transition was not made in a vacuum," she says. "I decided to transition based on societal factors, based on my own understanding of my mental health issues, and the constant reassurance from therapists that yes, I was really trans, and that the treatment for that was transition."[13] But Cari sees no reason to think that the trans activists who promote transition are right:

I will say, from my own experience and from my conversations with other detransitioned and reidentified women: transition is not the only way, or even necessarily the best way, to treat gender dysphoria. I felt a strong desire, what I would have called a "need" at the time, to transition.... And it wasn't weeks, or months, that I stayed on hormones, before I realized that I needed to stop. I was on them for over three years, cumulatively. I know women who were on testosterone three, four, five, even ten years before they were able to recognize that it was f**king them over. It can be damn hard to figure out that the treatment you're being told is to help you is actually making your mental health worse. Testosterone made me even more dissociated than I already was.[14]

Social and medical transition can do harm, according to Cari. She urges people to be more cautious, especially with children, and to acknowledge that the vast majority of children with gender dysphoria will end up accepting and identifying with their bodies. She wants trans activists to take this "desistance" rate much more seriously:

When you say "why does this desistance rate even matter," you demonstrate your utter callousness towards the trauma we experienced going through transition. Obviously... statistics can be skewed, statistics can lie. But where are your statistics? Where are the statistics that say children do persist in trans identities when they grow up?[15]

Cari also wants activists to stop turning a deaf ear to the growing numbers of people who have detransitioned, "especially those individuals who transitioned underage," as she herself did. "You may not agree with us, but the fact is that we exist, we're going to continue to exist, and our numbers are growing. Sooner or later, we're going to have to start making changes. Sooner or later, you won't be able to ignore us any longer." In fact, Cari opened her video by explaining that she had wanted to document her experiences for a while, but feared being attacked for it:

> I wanted to make a video previously... so that folks can see that I'm a real live person, but didn't out of fear of showing my face. But I think it's important when we talk about these issues to really understand that women like us aren't just statistics, not just some dry data some gatekeeping doctor might throw at you, we're real people. This is a real outcome of transition. I'm a real live 22 year old woman with a scarred chest and a broken voice and 5 o'clock shadow because I couldn't face the idea of growing up to be a woman. That's my reality.[16]

Max

Another young woman who transitioned as a teenager likewise came to believe that she had been presented with a false choice—or with no real choice at all. Max began to transition socially at age sixteen, presenting herself as a boy. Hormone therapy and a mastectomy followed shortly thereafter. Transitioning seemed to be the only alternative to suicide, says Max, because no other option was suggested to her:

> I felt I had no choice but transition for a long time, and the reason I felt that way was because other choices were not offered to me. I didn't know anyone who had survived feelings like mine without transition, and I didn't have any ideas about how someone might do that. That's a problem! How can someone give informed consent to transition when

they believe the only alternative is a miserable life eventually cut short by suicide? People who transition believing it's absolutely the only way they can ever experience any relief are people whose community and healthcare professionals have failed them.

Max criticizes trans activists who "see advice for coping with distress that doesn't involve medication or surgery as inherently invalidating."[17] These activists take the view that any therapy other than affirming and supporting a person's inner gender identity amounts to devaluing the person. Indeed, Max herself once believed that the only valid response to feelings of gender dysphoria was to initiate a transition, and she used the standards of care recommended by WPATH to promote her own transition: "I used them to self-advocate in medical offices as a teenager who met the diagnostic criteria for GID [gender identity disorder], believing I'd kill myself if they didn't give me what I needed. I didn't know there were ways to get relief from those feelings that didn't come from a therapist, endocrinologist, or surgeon."[18]

Max expected that having a male body would be the cure for all the ways she felt inadequate as a woman:

On some level, when I was transitioning at 16, I had thought of "being a woman" as everything I wasn't—pretty, compliant, content with the way I was treated as a woman and with my female body. I thought that women didn't ever hate their bodies the way I did or believe they'd be better off as a man. This isn't true. I learned many women, especially lesbians, have experienced periods of wanting to be men in intense and visceral ways, ways that met the diagnostic criteria for GID or gender dysphoria, but were eventually really glad that they had instead made peace with themselves as one type or another of unconventional women. I learned, from connecting with other women, that womanhood could hold women like me.[19]

As Max tells it, sex stereotypes were at the heart of her thinking that she needed to transition, and she found only short-term relief by doing so: "Having a set of steps to focus on completing in order to acquire some peace of mind gave me hope and a sense of direction for a while, until I had completed all the steps I had wanted to accomplish and was extremely disappointed to find myself still facing pretty much the same issues I had as a teenager."[20]

There was another step she had not yet taken before she reassessed her situation and decided to change course. Max says, "I count myself as extremely lucky that I had misgivings about the hysterectomy I was about to schedule a while before I stopped transitioning. I am extremely grateful that, at this point in my life, I can usually stay far away from the [medical] fields that I feel did me an awful lot of harm."[21]

Max bristles when people assert that she could not really have had gender dysphoria to begin with and claim that her experience and that of other detransitioners is irrelevant to their cause. "I didn't stop transition because I 'was never trans,'" she says. "I stopped because I found other ways of coping that worked better, did less damage, and in my case, allowed me a higher degree of autonomy in that I no longer relied on anything from endocrinologists—a luxury not afforded to those who received hysterectomies as a part of their transition."[22] That last line refers to the twice-yearly visits to hormone specialists that people who remove their sex glands typically must make, since their bodies can no longer produce these hormones.

Detransitioning was not forced on her "by anyone, or by any circumstances," Max emphasizes. But coming to see it as a possibility was not easy:

> Realizing I could stop transition was extremely challenging at first—I had years of unexpressed emotions to work through when those walls started coming down. Ultimately, though, reconciling with my femaleness has been profoundly healing for me. A lot of detransition, for me, has been about listening to myself, and learning to take the pain I experienced as a result of transition seriously. Paying Dr. Curtis Crane to cut away healthy tissue from my body, being seen as a man when I'm not one, side effects from testosterone...I can name the ways they hurt me now. I am grateful for the perspective transition has given me on how the medical-industrial complex fails women and girls in pain.[23]

Max doesn't seek to discount the stories of people who have had different experiences. Each person is unique. But she does want people to stop discounting the experiences of detransitoners like herself: "I know others who feel their transitions were lifesaving. That's their story and they're free to tell it, just like I was free to tell the same story when I believed it to be true. Now, *this* is my story. I understand why someone would feel transition saved their life. Do others understand that transition can also do profound harm?"[24]

Crash

For another example of how transitioning can do harm, consider the story told by Crash, a young woman who began "living as a man" when she was eighteen and started on testosterone at twenty. Crash reports that she did "experience some relief" by taking these steps.[25] But it didn't provide what she really needed, and so she detransitioned at twenty-seven.

> Taking testosterone didn't get to the root of my suffering, it only relieved it temporarily. I came out of my transition with many of the same problems I had before and then some. Being supported in my trans identity didn't help me, letting go of it and accepting myself as a woman did. Changing my body didn't help me find lasting peace. I helped myself by tracing back my trans identity and dysphoria to trauma and working through how I'd been hurt.[26]

Crash rejects the idea that she was a boy trapped in a girl's body. Instead, she says she wanted to identify as a boy because of personal trauma and a misogynistic culture. When she began to understand her distress in this light, she decided that she needed to detransition: "I realized that my dysphoria and trans identity were rooted in trauma and internalized misogyny. I was severely bullied and harassed starting when I was a young girl and continuing throughout my teenage years." The bullying and harassment weren't the only causes of her discomfort with herself, says Crash: "I also see a connection between my decision to transition and my mom's suicide. She killed herself when I was 20 and I started hormones about three months after she killed herself. We greatly physically resembled each other and I think one of my motivations for changing my body is I wanted to differentiate myself from her."[27]

Dealing with the effects of those traumatic events brought more lasting peace. "Since I've started to accept myself as a woman and work through my trauma I've gotten a whole lot more satisfaction and I feel much happier and much more functional overall," Crash reports. She now understands her transition and her transgender identity as "coping mechanisms for dealing with traumatic events" in her life, and explains her dysphoria as "a kind of dissociation that was a result of trauma." Now, instead of trying to figure out "how to express an internal gender identity," she has been trying to "heal and recover from traumatic events that I lived through." The result: "I've achieved way more relief overall."[28]

But her experience with mental health professionals and gender specialists has left her wounded, regardless of how sympathetic and well-meaning they were. Crash describes one doctor in particular:

> She was the one everyone wanted to see because she was so chill and respectful. I really liked seeing her, my trans and genderqueer friends liked seeing her too.... I really enjoyed how she treated me when I went to appointments with her and she helped me take a drug that gave me problems that I'm still dealing with. It's hard for me to wrap my head around those conflicting pieces of information. I know she was trying to help me and other suffering people.... The way she treated us with understanding and respect meant a lot to me and other trans people....
>
> And she hurt me, helped me hurt myself. That definitely wasn't her intention but that's still what happened. This contradiction is difficult to face and understand. She treated me like I wanted to be treated at the time. She was supporting me and helping me do what I was convinced was best for me and I appreciated that a lot. I appreciated all the support I got when I was transitioning. I thought taking t [testosterone] was what I needed to do and it seemed to be helping me. I liked how easy it was to get on testosterone and I liked how I was treated when I went to my appointments. I liked how my friends all supported me and thought it was cool that I was transitioning, that they saw it as a positive thing. I also thought of it as a positive thing.
>
> And now when I look back I'm horrified and creeped out. There's something disturbing about doing something you think is good for yourself but that turns out to be really self-destructive and it's even worse when so many other people were helping you and making it easier for you to do it. It's hard enough taking in how I managed to hurt myself when I was trying to find happiness and express my true self. How am I supposed to deal with how all these people in my life were trying to be helpful but were actually enabling? How am I supposed to make sense of that?[29]

Crash writes movingly about how her transition treatments have left her reluctant to trust medical professionals—the people she hoped would heal her:

When someone tries to do good and ends up hurting you it makes it hard to trust them. I did trust my providers (as much as I can trust any medical professional) and they helped me destroy myself. Can they accept whatever responsibility they had in that or will they deny it? If I open myself up and tell them how the drugs they gave me affected my life in the long run will they be able to face that? Are they going to say it was all my fault and I should've known better? Will they actually be able to do anything that will help me now? Are they going to treat me like I'm crazy? Are they going to get defensive? What should I expect if I tell my old providers that I transitioned because I was severely harassed for being a lesbian and traumatized by my mom's suicide?

I ask myself what reaction I'd most want if I did tell my old providers about how transitioning hurt me. I'd want them to apologize to me. I'd want them to recognize the harm they were a part of. Not take it all on themselves but accept their role in it. Just hearing something simple like "I didn't mean to hurt you and I'm sorry I did" would be enough.[30]

In concluding her post, Crash tells us what she would like to say to her old doctors—acknowledging their good intentions, but suggesting that they misunderstood her needs and ended up hurting her:

You thought you were doing good but you were giving me tools to hurt myself. I thought I needed to come to you to get what I needed to be happy but I was wrong. We both had no idea what we were doing, what was really going on. Your good will didn't end my suffering, it increased it. You supported the splits in myself. Your kindness led to more scars, not less. I know you want to do good, so show me what your compassion looks like when someone comes back to tell you that your efforts almost ruined them. I can forgive you if you can face what you've done to me as I've had to face what I've done to myself. I'll feel more at peace if I can see doubts rise across your face, if you have the strength to consider that I may not be an isolated case. Listen, you did not help me except to move me further away from myself. You did not help me, I helped myself come back from the damage we both took part in. I found what I needed on my own, found the strength to put my knowledge into practice with the help of other women. I don't need your acceptance or your chemical offerings, I don't need to come back to you anymore. This is the last you'll hear from me. I never needed your help and now I'm working hard to let other women know they don't need your help either.[31]

TWT

Many of the people who have gone public about their detransition are women. An anonymous man who goes by the initials TWT online created a website called *Third Way Trans* after reading some of their testimonials, in the hope that his own story might be helpful to men like himself: "This is inspired by several of the detransitioned women that have been recently making videos and so I decided that there should be videos from the detransitioned men as well."[32] TWT started his blog "to help people deal with their dysphoria," adding:

> One of the things that I discovered in this journey is that there were other ways to deal with my dysphoria that would work better and also would have been less harmful. I had to go through this whole transition first in order to figure all that out and I had to spend 20 years being transitioned. I transitioned when I was 19 and detransitioned when I was 39. I'm 42 now. I spent all this time transitioned and modified my body in many ways which is still causing problems to this day and I want to help people be able to deal with these issues without having to go through that.[33]

He takes a nuanced position, acknowledging that others may have different experiences and voicing sympathy with those who choose transitioning. "I don't oppose transition," he says, "and I really understand how debilitating gender dysphoria can be." But he also wants people to understand that transitioning brings a new set of problems: "I don't think these treatments should be eliminated but at the same time we should help as many people as possible to work through these issues without having to go through that because it's a horrible thing to go through, and it's imperfect and leads to social problems and potential medical problems including sterility." He highlights that last concern as one of particular importance, although it may not seem so to minors who are considering transition, because "having children is very important to many people and may not seem so important when you are young."[34]

TWT sees the recent spike in transitioning partly as the result of a more accepting culture, but partly too as a product of "social contagion," which encourages people to transition when they might be better off not doing so: "People who would have not transitioned in other times but in this time consider it, are probably the ones who maybe have better ways to deal with their issues and so I think there's definitely a problem going on. I think it's a problem with therapists that rubber-stamp people's transitions."[35] TWT has some professional expertise to back up this conclusion, since he is pursuing a Ph.D. in clinical psychology and has worked in several clinics, where some of his clients identify as transgender. "One of the things I learned in my clinical training," he writes, "is just in general how little you know about someone when you see them once or twice or three times. There's so much we don't know."[36]

He was given hormones after only two sessions with a therapist, who didn't know the whole story behind his feeling that he would be happier as a woman:

> When I was a child I experienced trauma issues with bullying. When I was young I was physically the slowest boy but also very intellectually advanced like a child prodigy. By fourth grade I was going to the high school to take high school math, and on the other hand I was the weakest. So I was singled out for being a kind of super nerd. This didn't make me popular at all. It made me popular with the adults actually but not my peers. So I suffered a lot of bullying and violence. It peaked in middle school where every day I would have some sort of violence directed at me.
>
> When I was a child I started to have this fantasy of being a girl, because it meant I could be safe and not suffer from this violence due to being at the bottom of the male hierarchy. I could also be more soft. I used to cry a lot and that was also something that was not seen as good for a boy. I could be free of all of that and also still be intellectual because everyone was saying that girls can be smart too. Of course I didn't understand the complexity of society then and all the prior sexism behind that message because I was six. It became a fantasy that kept me comfortable, not something that could really happen, more like a fantasy I had.
>
> Then when I got to adolescence it continued and became tied to sexuality. I was also attracted to women so it was confusing, and my dating life didn't go well when I was a young teenager. I was a late bloomer but

eventually once I got to be a junior in high school I did have some success in dating and had several different girlfriends. After that my gender dysphoria declined.

When I got to college, in the first few months I didn't meet any women and it felt like a real step back and my gender feelings resurfaced again. Now I understand that one of the reasons I was successful in dating as a high school senior was because I was at the top of the heap and then when I became a freshman in college I was at the bottom of the heap.[37]

TWT writes that his gender dysphoria "reappeared with a vengeance" when he discovered a new online forum called "alt.transgendered," which made him hopeful for a remedy. "I couldn't believe there were people in the real world that felt like me! Also I was dealing with the stress of newly being in college and being away from home for the first time. I felt so euphoric when I discovered people with similar feelings, and begun to believe that it was possible for me to transition."[38] It was "like a revelation" to learn that others were struggling the same way, and they seemed to have an answer. "Other people had these feelings too and I could relate to them. It meant you could really do this. It could really happen!"[39]

This was when he decided to visit the campus health office and was referred to a gender clinic: "I went to the clinic and told the psychologist my story and that I wanted to be female. I didn't talk about bullying and I was unaware that it was related in any way. This is something I sorted out later when I was in real therapy." After just two sessions, he was prescribed estrogen, and it seemed easy: "I was just like this is who I am and this is who I want to be and they were like that's great."[40]

At first, he thought the treatment was working: "I came to believe that I had an essential transgender identity and it was important to express it. Both the community and the therapist I saw twice before being prescribed hormones confirmed it. I was on a high dose of estrogen and it created a kind of euphoria and emotional intensity I hadn't experienced before. This was considered to be confirmation that I found my true self." And he succeeded in passing as a woman: "I got quite a bit of attention from men, many of them the same sort of men that used to bully me as a teenager. This attention validated my then fragile sense of self-worth and validated I was on the right path."[41]

For twenty years, TWT attempted to live as a woman, but it didn't cure his dysphoria. "It just made me uncomfortable with different parts of my body that weren't feminine," he recalls. "I had really big hands and a big jaw and so I still had the same problem of hating parts of my body."[42] He also found there were new social problems, both with people who knew he was trans and with people who did not:

> If they weren't aware there was a sense of I can't tell them about it, and that really closes off intimacy because you can't share this really important part of your life. If they did know about it there would be lots of different reactions. Some people were fine. A lot of people were fine on the surface, but they would really act differently towards me. It almost felt like having no gender at all and being outside of humanity. It was a really awful feeling.[43]

Eventually, he started seeing a normal therapist—not a gender therapist—and began dealing with the deeper reasons for his disconnection from his body:

> I wasn't working on my gender, but on why I couldn't have relationships and why my body was so tense. I started to do therapy and all of these embodied practices. I got involved in meditation. I got involved in doing dance practice. I got involved in doing a practice called Biodanza which is a sort of practice where you learn to connect to yourself and other people. I eventually became aware I was really disconnected to my body.... I came gradually to the realization that this was actually a problem. That this whole transition was actually a problem. It was still difficult because I still had this feeling like maybe I should be a man, but it was totally unsafe emotionally and I couldn't do it. I did a lot more therapy and eventually came to understand the roots of this with the bullying and feeling unsafe about being myself and a man in the world. I didn't see things this way in an intellectual sense, but in a visceral. So, it was a long process and eventually I worked through. It was also a big revelation because I thought my gender identity of being female was fundamental. It seemed like an absolute truth and an absolute axiom, and then it turned out not to be that at all. It turned out to be something that could be changed.[44]

This discovery that a transgender identity is not innate and immutable was "very surprising" to TWT because of all the talk about gender identity as something permanent and unchangeable. He points out the confusion of trans activists on the subject of gender identity, which they describe as "permanent but it also can be fluid and it can also change but it doesn't change and there is no real kind of consistency in the whole ideology behind it." TWT wishes that he had known about this inconsistency back when he was nineteen. He wishes that he had been aware of the possibility that his gender dysphoria could be treated with therapy before he went about altering his body, which is "really something I would not have wanted to go through because it'd be much better to have dealt with my issues without changing my body so that I wouldn't have the difficulties I have now."[45]

There are remaining difficulties because some procedures cannot be reversed, particularly the removal of the sex organs that create and regulate the sex hormones: "I can't really get my hormones right. I take testosterone but it doesn't work right, it's always a problem because I can't find the right balance of it and never get it right. I know I can't recover my body all the way." He continues: "Things are not perfect, as it is impossible to replicate the natural cycle of a complex endocrine system using external hormones but they are still much better than they were."[46]

For all of these reasons, he urges caution: Don't rush into transitioning. Consider alternatives. He notes that being put on hormones after just two visits to a therapist fell short of the medical standards of care back then—but not today: "At that time they said you had to have at least 12 sessions of therapy for hormones. That's not true anymore. Lots of people are doing it after just one, two or three sessions. This thing that was harmful in my life has now become standard practice in the clinical community."[47]

So as he pursues a Ph.D. in psychology, he wants to urge clinicians to consider ways of helping people with gender dysphoria that don't rely on hormones and surgery: "We should be working on this a lot more even if we support transition. I do support it for some people. We should still simultaneously be working on how we can help people deal with these issues without doing that because it would save people a lot of trouble and a lot of expensive imperfect medical interventions."[48] Most of all, TWT wants to spare children the pain that he has suffered. He concludes a letter to youths considering transition with this: "I do know I see some of the same patterns that led me to transition, and it concerns me. Looking back it would have been nice to avoid all of that unnecessary suffering. I also see your doubts being brushed aside by rampant cheerleading, and that is dangerous."[49]

Carey Callahan

So far, we've heard from individuals who started to transition as teenagers, but others begin the process well into adulthood. Carey Callahan is a woman who transitioned at age thirty because she felt a deep alienation from her body, regarding it as a kind of "enemy." Now she looks back in consternation at the doctors who didn't seem to respect her body either, but treated it as something to experiment on:

> I had the idea that my body was wrong, that it was disgusting, that it was incorrect and that it kept people from seeing the real me.... I just felt like kind of a hostility towards my body and so I didn't really care. I didn't care...to know what the rates of ovarian cancer were, I didn't care to know what the rates of stroke were. I think on some level I felt like my body was my enemy. But once I saw that disrespect reflected in medical professionals for the bodies of people who experience gender dysphoria then I got pissed. If you look at the relationship between people with gender dysphoria and doctors what you'll see through the history is that doctors are very willing to do experiments on us.[50]

Transitioning didn't help, but only made the dissociation from her body worse. As Carey recalls it, "every step of the process for me, every step I took toward affirming that trans identity—life got worse."[51] Indeed, she says, "The longer I chased that disassociation—the more I asked people to call me special pronouns, the more I tried to change my body, the more I ensconced myself in a community that would affirm a trans identity—the worse I felt."[52]

Today, Carey is dismayed that medical professionals would have subjected her to such drastic procedures, in view of her mental confusion and unaddressed trauma:

> I do not believe I was in a clear state of mind, and I absolutely think that I was operating under some delusional ideas about what it would take for me to pass as a dude. I think that the feelings that I had interpreted as gender dysphoria were actually long-term trauma symptoms that I had never addressed. So I had a chronic and disruptive fantasy of what

my life would be like if I was a dude—I thought about it all the time. Any time I had an upsetting interaction, I thought, "This wouldn't be happening if they didn't view me as a woman. I'm not a woman, that's the problem here." And this was especially prominent when I would talk to other women about my experiences. They would be like, "Oh, that doesn't sound like that big of a deal," and I would be like "Oh my gosh, I'm so upset by it; it must be that I'm in the wrong gender." ... This kind of obsessive identification with men rather than women, because a lot of the way that women seemed to react to the world and interact with the world seemed really foreign to me.[53]

Because of her difficult experience with transitioning as a young adult, and her belief that she was plunged into it without a clear understanding of her own problems, Carey finds it especially concerning that teenagers and young children would be considered capable of making a decision to go down the same path:

I so strongly feel that people under 18 should not be empowered to make these medical decisions. Now at the base level, I don't think they should be empowered because I got that shit wrong at 30, so if I could be 30 and think that my best life was a trans guy ... and then come to understand that on so many levels that life didn't work for me and on so many levels that life caused its own problems for me and just worsened my anxiety and put me in social situations that were not ok ... if I could get it wrong at 30, a 9-year-old for sure can get it wrong. A 13-year-old for sure can get it wrong. Absolutely I think an 18-year-old can get it wrong.[54]

And yet trans activists argue that children should start social transition in kindergarten, puberty blockers at nine, cross-sex hormones at sixteen, and surgery at eighteen. While Carey thinks eighteen-year-olds can get this wrong, she also thinks they'll have to be free to make their own decisions—and live with the consequences. After all, "that's the age that we let you go off to war. So I guess that's the age that we accept that that's when you get to start making real decisions about the unsafe circumstances you want to put your body through."[55]

Walt Heyer

After undergoing sex reassignment surgery in his forties, Walt Heyer detransitioned in his fifties. Now, in his seventies, Walt says it all started when he was a young boy and his grandmother would dress him up as a girl:

> My grandmother withheld affirmations of me as a boy, but she lavished delighted praise upon me when I was dressed as a girl. Feelings of euphoria swept over me with her praise, followed later by depression and insecurity about being a boy. Her actions planted the idea in me that I was born in the wrong body. She nourished and encouraged the idea, and over time it took on a life of its own.[56]

As a consequence, his uncle began mocking him and then sexually abusing him, and his parents didn't believe it when he told them.

Walt eventually married and had children, but he still couldn't shake the persistent feeling that he was actually a woman inside, thirty-six years after it all began. "The seeds sown by Grandma developed deep roots," he explains. "Unbeknownst to my wife, I began to act on my desire to be a woman. I was cross-dressing in public and enjoying it. I even started taking female hormones to feminize my appearance."[57]

Next, Walt sought professional help from a renowned gender specialist, Dr. Paul Walker, the lead author of the first edition of what's now known as the WPATH *Standards of Care for the Health of Transsexual, Transgender, and Gender Nonconforming People*. Walt reports that Dr. Walker said he had "a clear-cut case of gender dysphoria" and told him that "the only way to get relief was to surgically change genders." So at age forty-two, after decades of cross-dressing, Walt had sex reassignment surgery and began living as a transgender female.[58] "My new identity as Laura Jensen, female, was legally affirmed on my birth record, Social Security card, and driver's license. I was now a woman in everyone's eyes."[59]

The transition went well as a cosmetic and legal matter, but it didn't resolve Walt's underlying psychological issues: "Hidden deep underneath the make-up and female clothing was the little boy carrying the hurts from traumatic childhood events, and he was making himself known. Being a female turned out to be only a cover-up, not healing."[60] The relief that Walt found was only transient:

> To a person undergoing gender transition, in the beginning it feels like the right thing to do, even exciting, for the first few months or years. I felt at peace for the first four or five years after I transitioned. Then I realized the high cost of that tenuous peace. Being transgender required destroying the identity of Walt so my female persona, Laura, would feel unshackled from Walt's past, with all of its hurt, shame, and abuse. It's a marvelous distraction for a while, but it isn't a permanent solution when the underlying issues remain unaddressed.[61]

Living as a woman brought him "no lasting peace." Instead, says Walt, "My gender confusion only seemed to worsen."[62]

After eight years of living as "Laura," Walt found his way toward detransitioning through college courses he was taking as an adult: "While studying psychology in a university program, I discovered that trans kids most often are suffering from a variety of disorders, starting with depression—the result of personal loss, broken families, sexual abuse, and unstable homes. Deep depression leads kids to want to be someone other than who they are."[63] This was when he finally received an accurate diagnosis:

> During an internship in a psychiatric hospital, I worked alongside a medical doctor on a lock-down unit. After some observation, he took me aside and told me I showed signs of having a dissociative disorder. Was he right? Had he found the key that would unlock a childhood lost? Rather than going to gender-change activist psychologists like the one who had approved me for surgery, I sought the opinions of several "regular" psychologists and psychiatrists who did not see all gender disorders as transgender. They agreed: I fit the criteria for dissociative disorder.
>
> It was maddening. Now it was apparent that I had developed a dissociative disorder in childhood to escape the trauma of the repeated cross-dressing by my grandmother and the sexual abuse by my uncle. That should have been diagnosed and treated with psychotherapy. Instead, the gender specialist never considered my difficult childhood or even my alcoholism and saw only transgender identity. It was a quick jump to prescribe hormones and irreversible surgery. Years later, when

I confronted that psychologist, he admitted that he should not have approved me for surgery.[64]

Walt regrets that he didn't know anything about dissociative disorder or its link to gender dysphoria before he underwent sex reassignment surgery. He wishes that Dr. Walker had been required first to inform him about a Johns Hopkins study showing that surgery did not alleviate severe psychological problems, and another that found continuing unhappiness and a high rate of suicide in the transgender population even after hormone treatment and reassignment surgery. "This information might not have stopped me from making that disastrous decision," Walt acknowledges, "but at least I would have known the dangers and pain that lay ahead."[65]

Now he has started a mutual-support network of detransitioners. "Every single one of them," says Walt, "had unwanted pain caused by sexual abuse, deep trauma, mental disorders, horrible loss, or terrible family circumstances in early life."[66] One of the people who wrote to Walt told his own story of disappointment with transitioning and regret over the permanent consequences:

I transitioned to female beginning in my late teens and changed my name in my early 20s, over ten years ago. But it wasn't right for me; I feel only discontent now in the female role. I was told that my transgender feelings were permanent, immutable, physically deep-seated in my brain and could NEVER change, and that the only way I would ever find peace was to become female. The problem is, I don't have those feelings anymore. When I began seeing a psychologist a few years ago to help overcome some childhood trauma issues, my depression and anxiety began to wane but so did my transgender feelings. So two years ago I began contemplating going back to my birth gender, and it feels right to do so. I have no doubts—I want to be male!

I did have orchiectomy [the removal of one or both testicles], and that happened before my male puberty had completed, so I have a bit of facial hair which I never bothered to get electrolysis or laser for, and so the one blessing about all this is that with male hormone treatment I can still resume my male puberty where it was interrupted and grow a full beard and deep voice like I would have had if transgender feelings hadn't intruded upon my childhood. My breasts are difficult to hide though, so I'll need surgery to get rid of them. And saddest of all,

I can never have children, which I pray God will give me the strength to withstand that sadness.[67]

From his own experience and his communications with others, Walt concludes: "Treating psychological pain with sex change surgery doesn't work."[68] He wants people to understand that "transgender feelings are not permanent, immutable, or deep-seated in the brain. Feelings, no matter how powerful, do not justify taking hormones and undergoing surgery."[69]

Reconnecting with One's Body

The stories recounted in this chapter tell us, at a minimum, that transitioning is not the "only solution" to gender dysphoria. They tell us, furthermore, that trying to align the body with a transgender identity does not resolve the deep issues that led to alienation from one's own body. Walt Heyer says, "The world of regretters that I see and support is vastly different from the world of the transition advocates, those in a relentless pursuit to convince the world that being transgender is the ultimate of all genders." The sad reality is that many people who detransition "live in secret and hide the shame and disappointment of falling for the fraud of gender change."[70]

Their predicament is partly the fault of journalists and medical professionals who consistently tout the success of sex reassignment procedures and overstate the evidence in their favor. Perhaps that's because they are looking only at *surgical* results, as Heyer explains:

> The advocates say that regret is rare, and that 98 percent of surgeries are successful. While that figure might be true for surgical complications, before we accept a narrative of surgical success we should consider the evidence. To evaluate success or failure, we need to go beyond the mechanical skill of the surgeon to examine the emotional and psychological wholeness of the patient afterwards—and not just in the first few months, but in the years to come.[71]

Few studies have been done to track long-term emotional and psychological outcomes for people who transition. Among those that do exist, very few are rigorous. A review of studies on gender reassignment done by the aggressive research intelligence facility (Arif) at Birmingham University in 2004 found that the researchers in many of the studies had "lost track of more than half of the participants." The director of the review suggested that this dropout rate "could reflect high levels of dissatisfaction or even suicide among post-operative transsexuals," and concluded that while "some people do well with gender reassignment surgery, the available research does little to reassure about how many patients do badly and, if so, how badly."[72] A decade later, another research firm assessed the scientific literature and found that the evidence on long-term results was still limited, but some rigorous studies have shown poor outcomes. One study from 2011, for example, found suicide rates for people who have transitioned that are nineteen times higher than those of the general population.[73] (We'll look at these findings in more detail in Chapter 5.)

In this light, it's dismaying that people who found more problems after transitioning would be ignored or even attacked by transgender activists. Women who transition and then detransition can be special targets for hate. After a prominent activist criticized people who had detransitioned, Crash penned an open letter in which she explained the reasons why people like her chose to transition in the first place, and why many of them have found it more harmful than helpful. I am closing this chapter with a large portion of the letter:

> We transitioned for a lot of different reasons. Many of us transitioned due to trauma. We lived through event(s) terrible enough that it damaged our sense of self and so we created a new self to cope and survive. That self was our trans or male or genderqueer identity. We transitioned because we got raped, because we're incest survivors, because we faced violence for being lesbians, because we were locked up in psych wards, because one of our parents killed themselves. We also live in a patriarchy that hates women and attacks female bodies constantly. Whatever trauma we lived through typically had something to do with being a woman. Sometimes bad things happened to us just for being female in a culture where women are violated every day and sometimes bad things happened because we're the wrong kind of woman, maybe too butch or "masculine" or loud or unemotional. One way or another, we didn't fit in with what other people and our culture expected women to be. Sometimes our bodies themselves were deemed not female enough and

treated as if they were freakish. That happened to me because I had traits like an adam's apple, body hair, an angular face and so on, leading many to speculate on what sex I was. Eventually, other people's judgments got inside my head and infected how I saw myself until I started questioning whether I was really female too.

Trauma and misogyny led us to dissociate from being female and then to transition. Transitioning was itself further trauma. First others attacked and wounded our bodies and distorted our self-perceptions and then we hurt ourselves in response. Transitioning was an act of self-destruction, enabled by medical professionals who were supposedly "helping" us to be our "true selves." It is truly horrifying to come out of that dissociated state and realize that not only were you suppressing and trying to destroy yourself but that other people were there encouraging and assisting you in doing so. Many of us came to see the "care" we received as unethical or a form of medical abuse. Many of us believe that the present "trans affirmative care" and "informed consent" models are misleading, irresponsible and do not truly ensure that people make realistic, fully informed choices.

Crash describes how testosterone treatment quickly begins changing a female body down to the cellular level, including "mitochondrial damage and damage to the leukocytes." Some of these changes are irreversible, so they act as a constant reminder of self-rejection and self-betrayal.

Many of the effects of testosterone are permanent and some of these irreversible effects, such as a deeper voice and in some cases facial hair, can manifest after only a few months of taking it. In many cases, the changes we made to our bodies felt right at the time but as we began to work through why we transitioned we came to feel very differently about them. The ways transitioning changed our bodies came to symbolize extreme self-denial rather than the self-affirmation we felt earlier.

We have to learn to live in a modified body and this usually involves grieving. All of us who took t [testosterone], whether for a few months or for years, all of us have altered voices. There is a very deep, painful symbolism behind losing your original voice and having no way of getting it back. For many of us it is not the physical changes themselves that are troubling but what they represent. I am not disturbed by changes like my facial hair or my deeper voice in and of themselves but they remind me constantly of what I did to myself, how I rejected and betrayed myself, how deeply I took other people's hatred into my own body. My body is now marked forever by that hatred and that can be a lot to carry. Many of us have struggled with feeling like we have ruined ourselves.

Crash rejects the idea that transitioning is the only solution, even for severe dysphoria, since it doesn't fix the "root problems," and it may actually deepen the alienation from one's body. The process of detransition requires learning how to deal with the underlying issues that transitioning did not resolve. It's a long process, she says, but worth the effort.

Detransitioning is as much about facing trauma as it is about figuring out how to live in an altered body. Transitioning was all about trying to get away from what hurt us and detransitioning is finally facing that and overcoming it. It's about making connections between how other people have treated us and how we've seen ourselves and our bodies. It's about remembering terrible, scary, upsetting memories and integrating them. It's about making sense of what happened, giving up old explanations that no longer work and coming up with new ones that fit our experience better. In the process we often reject much of what we believed when we were trans because it no longer suits us or seems true. It's about understanding how the society around us has influenced us and shaped how we thought, felt and came to view ourselves. It's not just figuring out how specific people hurt us but how our culture has restricted and attacked us and all women. It's about connecting both with other women who transitioned and then stopped and to women in general. Feeling like we couldn't be women, being cut off from other women is one of our deepest wounds and healing it means finally finding common ground and community with other women.

Detransitioning is learning to accept and be fully present in your body. It is about finding different ways to cope with and heal from dysphoria. Transitioning is not the only viable treatment for dysphoria, however severely it may manifest. We have learned this through experience and often with great difficulty and sacrifice. And many of us found that transitioning made our dysphoria worse instead of improving it. Many of us found some relief through changing our bodies but found even greater peace and happiness coming to accept our bodies as female. I was very satisfied with the physical changes caused by testosterone. They never felt wrong. But changing my body did not get at my root problems, it only obscured them further. My actual problems were trauma and hating myself for being a woman and a lesbian. Since I started dealing with my trauma and finding ways to be more present in my body, I have felt a lot more joy, strength and power than I ever felt taking t [testosterone]. Learning to accept the body and fully inhabit it is an effective way to treat many people's dysphoria. Many detransitioned and dysphoric women have found ways to re-connect with our bodies, such as meditating, yoga, working out, exercising or doing physical labor, and we combine these practices with working through the trauma that caused dissociation from the body in the first place. It is often a long and difficult process that takes years but the rewards are well worth it.[74]

CHAPTER FOUR

What Makes Us
a Man or a Woman

The case for "transitioning" as the answer to gender dysphoria rests on the notion that transgender identity is innate—that a person can simply be born as "a man trapped in a woman's body," or vice versa. Therefore, adjusting that person's hormone balance and restructuring the anatomy, to align the body with the inner sense of identity, should make things right. But is there any biological basis to believe that a man could be born in the bodily form of a female, invisible to those who "assign" a sex at birth? Is there reason to be confident that hormones and surgery can "reassign" sex? To answer these questions, we need to start by examining what science tells us about the biological genesis of sex.

In a way, understanding biological sex isn't all that difficult. When all goes right in the developmental process, it's relatively easy to discern a baby boy from a baby girl, even on an ultrasound. We don't have to wait until birth for sex to be "assigned," as is obvious to anyone who has ever joyfully sent an ultrasound photo to a loved one announcing "It's a girl!" or "It's a boy!"

What can be discerned on a grainy ultrasound is also abundantly manifest in real life: when all goes well, a person's sex is readily identifiable—not "assigned," but recognized. We all recognize it on a daily basis. Later we'll discuss those unfortunate cases when it doesn't all go well—when genetic or hormonal defects cause what doctors refer to as "disorders of sexual development" (DSD). First we'll look at what normally happens in human development.

While doing research for this book one day, I pulled three embryology textbooks off my bookshelf. About a decade ago I had been doing work on bioethics, focusing particularly on cloning and embryo-destructive stem cell research and all of the debates that swirled in that area. So I had purchased three of the standard embryology texts used in prominent medical schools. I wanted to cite the standard texts on when the life of a human being begins, and I found that the scientific community is rather clear on the matter when political debates aren't involved: the life of a new human organism—a human being—begins at conception, when sperm and egg fuse to form a single-cell embryo, a zygote.

The scientists who wrote these textbooks also had no difficulty pronouncing on when and how sex is determined. *Langman's Medical Embryology*, for example, concisely explains how the sex of a new organism is determined at fertilization: "An X-carrying sperm produces a female (XX) embryo, and a Y-carrying sperm produces a male (XY) embryo. Hence, the chromosomal sex of the embryo is determined at fertilization."[1] A new human organism of a particular sex is created at that moment.

William J. Larsen's *Human Embryology* is equally straightforward in its definition of "sex determination" in the glossary: "The male sex is determined by presence of a Y sex chromosome (XY), and female sex is determined by absence of a Y chromosome (XX)."[2] *The Developing Human: Clinically Oriented Embryology* gives more detail here: "The embryo's chromosomal sex is determined at fertilization by the kind of sperm (X or Y) that fertilizes the oocyte; hence, it is the father rather than the mother whose gamete determines the sex of the embryo. Fertilization by an X-bearing sperm produces a 46, XX zygote, which normally develops into a female, whereas fertilization by a Y-bearing sperm produces a 46, XY zygote, which normally develops into a male."[3]

Note the word "normally," which adds an important nuance: An XX embryo *normally* develops into a female and an XY embryo *normally* develops into a male. Chromosomal and hormonal pathologies can disrupt and prevent normal development, as we will see. In biological terms, these abnormalities have essentially nothing to do with transgender identities, except to the extent that some activists want to recast all such abnormalities as only "differences," in effect normalizing disorders.

So we know how X and Y chromosomes ordinarily determine whether an individual is one sex or the other. We will look at the unfolding process of sexual differentiation after fertilization, and then at bodily differences between males and females, behavioral differences in newborn babies, and medical and health differences between the sexes. But first, we need to consider what exactly it means for an organism to be male or female—that is, what biological sex really is.

What Is Sex in the First Place?

The basics of sex determination are relatively clear. Our genetic code determines our sexed body. But what do we even mean by a "sexed" body? Here's how the *Encyclopedia Britannica* defines sexual dimorphism: "the differences in appearance between males and females of the same species, such as in colour, shape, size, and structure, that are caused by the inheritance of one or the other sexual pattern in the genetic material."[4] In other words, there are physical differences between males and females that result from the sexual pattern in the genetic material. But what do we mean by "sexual pattern"? What do we mean by "males" and "females"?

To answer these questions, we have to understand how organisms are identified and classified by their organization. The neuroscientist Maureen Condic and her philosopher brother Samuel Condic explain: "The defining feature of an organism is organization: the various parts of an entity are organized to cooperatively interact for the welfare of the entity as a whole. Organisms can exist at various levels, from microscopic single cells to sperm whales weighing many tons, yet they are all characterized by the integrated function of parts for the sake of the whole."[5] Male and female organisms have different parts that are functionally integrated for the sake of their whole, and for the sake of a larger whole—their sexual union and reproduction.

Sex, in terms of male or female, is identified by the organization of the organism for sexually reproductive acts. Sex as a status—male or female—is a recognition of the organization of a body that has the ability to engage in sex as an act. More than simply being *identified* on the basis of such organization, sex is a *coherent concept* only on the basis of that organization. The fundamental conceptual distinction between a male and a female is the organism's organization for sexual reproduction. My frequent co-author Sherif Girgis explained this point in a discussion of the first U.S. Supreme Court case redefining marriage:

> After all, male and female are not just any two sexes, as black and white are just two races. Maleness and femaleness, and a certain social purpose, are necessarily inter-defined: one cannot fully explain either maleness or femaleness without reference to the other and to a certain social good. The reason is that what differentiates them are not just different anatomical or genetic features, but—at a deeper level of explanation—their joint (basic) physical potential for a biological task: reproduction. And this task, its social value, and its link to sexual composition are certainly not mere social inventions.[6]

The conceptual distinction between male and female based on reproductive organization provides the only coherent way to classify the two sexes.

Lawrence Mayer and Paul McHugh highlighted the same truth in a recent review of the scientific literature on sexuality and gender identity:

> The underlying basis of maleness and femaleness is the distinction between the reproductive roles of the sexes; in mammals such as humans, the female gestates offspring and the male impregnates the female. More universally, the male of the species fertilizes the egg cells provided by the female of the species. This conceptual basis for sex roles is binary and stable, and allows us to distinguish males from females on the grounds of their reproductive systems, even when these individuals exhibit behaviors that are not typical of males or females.[7]

Mayer is a scholar-in-residence in the Department of Psychiatry at Johns Hopkins University and a professor of statistics and biostatistics at Arizona State University. McHugh is a professor of psychiatry and behavioral sciences at the Johns Hopkins University School of Medicine, and for twenty-five years was the psychiatrist-in-chief at the Johns Hopkins Hospital. The editor of the *New Atlantis*, in the introductory note to their report, called McHugh "arguably the most important American psychiatrist of the last half-century."

After explaining the "binary and stable" conceptual basis for maleness and femaleness, Mayer and McHugh note that a structural difference for the purposes of reproduction is the only "widely accepted" way of classifying the two sexes:

In biology, an organism is male or female if it is structured to perform one of the respective roles in reproduction. This definition does not require any arbitrary measurable or quantifiable physical characteristics or behaviors; it requires understanding the reproductive system and the reproduction process. Different animals have different reproductive systems, but sexual reproduction occurs when the sex cells from the male and female of the species come together to form newly fertilized embryos. It is these reproductive roles that provide the conceptual basis for the differentiation of animals into the biological categories of male and female. There is no other widely accepted biological classification for the sexes.[8]

Males are organized to engage in sexual acts that donate genetic material, while females are organized to engage in sexual acts that receive genetic material and then gestate the resulting offspring. This fundamental difference in organization is what allows scientists to distinguish male from female. When Dr. Deanna Adkins called this "an extremely outdated view of biological sex" in her declaration to a federal court in North Carolina, Dr. Mayer responded in his rebuttal declaration: "This statement is stunning. I have searched dozens of references in biology, medicine and genetics—even Wiki!—and can find no alternative scientific definition. In fact the only references to a more fluid definition of biological sex are in the social policy literature."[9] Just so.

And this really isn't that controversial. Sex is understood this way across species. No one finds it particularly difficult—let alone controversial—to identify male and female members of the bovine species or the canine species. Farmers and breeders rely on this easy distinction for their livelihoods. It's only recently, and only in the human species, that the very concept of sex has become convoluted, and controversial.

How the Sex Distinction Begins

For much of history, people thought sex in humans was determined environmentally, in the womb. While sex is environmentally determined in some species—the sex of some reptiles is determined by the temperature in which the egg is incubated—we now know that for humans the starting point is the presence of an XX or XY chromosomal composition. In fact, we've known it since 1921. But it was only in 1959 that scientists were able to explain *why* these chromosomes make a difference and *how* they do it. Prior to this time, they were uncertain "whether femaleness was determined by the *presence* of two X chromosomes or by the *absence* of the tiny Y chromosome and, conversely, whether maleness was determined by the presence of a Y chromosome or by the presence of a *single* X chromosome."[10]

Scientists now know that "the *presence* of a Y chromosome determines maleness and its *absence* determines femaleness."[11] This is because the Y chromosome ordinarily carries the SRY ("sex-determining region on Y") gene. The SRY gene contains a transcription factor known as the testis-determining factor (TDF), which directs the formation of the male gonads.

For the first six weeks of human embryological development, males and females develop in more or less the same way. One textbook explains that "the early genital systems in the two sexes are similar; therefore the initial period of genital development is referred to as the *indifferent state of sexual development*."[12] As the gonads start to develop, they are referred to as "indifferent gonads" because under some circumstances they can develop as either male or female, independent of the genetic sex. The presence of a Y chromosome with the SRY testis-determining factor initiates the formation of testicular differentiation in week 7. The absence of SRY allows the indifferent gonads to continue development into the ovaries.

The formation of the gonads—testicles and ovaries—then directs subsequent sexual differentiation. As *The Developing Human* explains it, "the type of sex chromosome complex established at fertilization determines the type of gonad that differentiates from the indifferent gonad. The type of gonads present then determines the type of sexual differentiation that occurs in the genital ducts and external genitalia."[13] Once the ovaries and testes are formed, we read in the *Journal of Cellular Physiology*, they become "the primary regulators of mammalian sexual differentiation by secreting sex-specific hormones that regulate downstream developmental processes. Thus, these reproductive tissues impose body-wide and long-lasting phenotypic effects."[14] Genotype, you may recall, refers to our genetic composition, while phenotype refers to its physical manifestation, so an ordinary male has an XY genotype, which expresses itself in a male phenotype through the development of testes. The Y chromosome carrying the SRY gene initiates the formation of the testes, which in turn produce testosterone, which then masculinizes the body and contributes to the development of a male.[15] Otherwise, without a Y carrying SRY, the human will normally form ovaries and develop as a female.[16]

Continuing Sexual Differentiation

The primary development of our sexed bodies takes place in the womb with the formation of the gonads, either ovaries or testes. The secondary development of our sexed bodies takes place in two stages. It begins in the womb, with the development of our reproductive organs, external genitalia, and sex hormones. Then, it continues at puberty, when our bodies reach sexual maturity.

Apart from reproductive organs, boys and girls have remarkably similar bodies at birth, though newborn boys have longer bodies with more lean mass.[17] During puberty, however, bodily differences become more pronounced, as "the two sexes take increasingly divergent pathways, with girls passing through puberty earlier and ceasing to grow at a younger age."[18] Here is how one scholar put it in *Best Practice and Research: Clinical Endocrinology and Metabolism*:

> Females enter puberty earlier and undergo a more rapid pubertal transition, whereas boys have a substantially longer growth period. After adjusting for dimorphism in size (height), adult males have greater total lean mass and mineral mass, and a lower fat mass than females. These whole-body differences are complemented by major differences in tissue distribution. Adult males have greater arm muscle mass, larger and stronger bones, and reduced limb fat, but a similar degree of central abdominal fat. Females have a more peripheral distribution of fat in early adulthood; however, greater parity and the menopause both induce a more android fat distribution with increasing age. Sex differences in body composition are primarily attributable to the action of sex steroid hormones, which drive the dimorphisms during pubertal development. Oestrogen is important not only in body fat distribution but also in the female pattern of bone development that predisposes to a greater female risk of osteoporosis in old age.[19]

The result is that male and female bodies differ not only in their sex chromosomes (XX and XY) and in their organization for reproduction, but also, on average, in size, shape, bone length and density, fat distribution, musculature, and various organs including the brain. These secondary sex differences are not what define us as male or female; organization for reproduction does that. But this organization leads to other bodily differences. There are organizational differences and organism-wide differences in organs and tissues, as well as differences at the cellular and molecular levels. These differences affect not just our physiology, but also our minds.

Indeed, after the reproductive organs, the brain is possibly the most "sexed" organ in a human being. This is not to say that there are male brains and female brains, but that on average there are differences in the brains of males and females that tend to make a difference in how men and women experience emotion and pain, how they see and hear, and how they remember and navigate.

Larry Cahill, a neurobiologist at the University of California, Irvine, reviewed the literature for *Scientific American* in 2012 and reported "a surge of findings that highlight the influence of sex on many areas of cognition and behavior, including memory, emotion, vision, hearing, the processing of faces and the brain's response to stress hormones."[20] There are differences in the size of various regions and structures in the brain, as well as differences at the cellular level.[21] In the journal *Endocrinology*, Cahill cites "abundant evidence" showing that "sex influences on brain function are ubiquitous, found at every level of neuroscience."[22]

While male and female brains are similar in many ways, researchers have found "an astonishing array of structural, chemical and functional variations" between them. This is not to suggest that either men or women are smarter, and "no one has uncovered any evidence that anatomical disparities might render women incapable of achieving academic distinction in math, physics or engineering," Cahill stresses.[23] The documented differences between male and female brains, on average, cannot legitimately be used to justify stereotypes or discriminatory treatment, or to nullify the considerable variation among males and among females. We should appreciate each person's individuality, and we should honor the complementarity in the male and female ways of being equally human.

We know that differences between the sexes begin in the womb, and they are manifested in our behavior from infancy. Many researchers have found that young children show a distinct pattern in choosing toys: "Boys tend to gravitate toward balls or toy cars, whereas girls more typically reach for a doll," Cahill notes. Whether this difference comes from nature or nurture was long a subject of debate, until some researchers did an experiment to observe the play habits of vervet monkeys. Given a selection of toys, "male monkeys spent more time playing with the 'masculine' toys than their female counterparts did, and female monkeys spent more time interacting with the playthings typically preferred by girls."[24] These results cannot be explained away by reference to cultural stereotypes or the social pressures that operate among humans.

It's also difficult to blame socialization for the differences in how newborn human babies respond to objects and to people. Girls tend to show more interest in their mothers than boys do. Girls typically prefer movies showing faces, while boys prefer movies showing cars. Cahill cites a study that found these preferences in one-day-old infants, long before nurture could have any effect: the baby girls looked more at a face, while the baby boys looked more at a mechanical object. This pattern of behavior in the first day of life indicates that "we come out of the womb with some cognitive sex differences built in."[25] A recent study using MRIs suggested that, on the whole, "male brains are structured to facilitate connectivity between perception and coordinated action, whereas female brains are designed to facilitate communication between analytical and intuitive processing modes."[26]

Sex Differences Affect Our Health

When we step back from contentious political debates, we can see scientists acknowledging what might otherwise be an unpopular truth: that there are biological differences between men and women, and they are consequential for our health. Recognizing differences between the sexes is increasingly regarded as vitally important for good medical practice, because scientists have found that male and female bodies tend to be susceptible to certain diseases in different ways, to differing degrees, and they respond to treatments differently. For this reason, the best research protocols now require that both males and females be included in samples, and that the sex of participants be tracked so that any sex-specific results can be recorded.

The Institute of Medicine at the National Academy of Sciences published a report in 2001 titled *Exploring the Biological Contributions to Human Health: Does Sex Matter?* The executive summary answered the question in the affirmative, saying that the explosive growth of biological information "has made it increasingly apparent that many normal physiological functions—and, in many cases, pathological functions—are influenced either directly or indirectly by sex-based differences in biology."[27] Because genetics and physiology are among the influences on an individual's health, the "incidence and severity of diseases vary between the sexes." The difference between male and female is thus "an important basic human variable that should be considered when designing and analyzing studies in all areas and at all levels of biomedical and health-related research."[28]

The chapter titles of the report sum up basic truths about our bodily nature: "Every Cell Has a Sex." "Sex Begins in the Womb." "Sex Affects Behavior and Perception." "Sex Affects Health." Some of the biological differences between the sexes that bear on health derive from hormone exposure, but others come more directly from our genetic material. There are "multiple, ubiquitous differences in the basic cellular biochemistries of males and females that can affect an individual's health. Many of these differences do not necessarily arise as a result of differences in the hormonal regime to which males and females are exposed but are a direct result of the genetic differences between the two sexes."[29] Written into our genetic code are differences that manifest themselves at the cellular level, in ways that can affect our health.[30] Sexual differentiation begins at conception, progresses in the womb, and continues throughout life, notably at puberty but also significantly at menopause in females. "Hormonal events occurring in puberty lay a framework for biological differences that persist through life and contribute to the variable onset and progression of disease in males and females."[31]

Some people may overplay the differences between men and women, as in the popular phrase "men are from Mars, women are from Venus." But men and women do, on average, have biologically rooted differences in perception and behavior. These differences are undoubtedly influenced by culture and society, but culture and society themselves begin on a biological foundation. "Basic genetic and physiological differences, in combination with environmental factors, result in behavioral and cognitive differences between males and females," says the Institute of Medicine.[32] Females tend to display more verbal ability in general and to recover verbal skills better after suffering a stroke. Men tend to be more conceptual and more focused on action—as the studies with newborn babies show.

These biological differences seem to have consequences for mental health. An article in the *Neuroscience and Biobehavioral Review* points to well-known differences between men and women in susceptibility to mental disorders:

"Examples of male-biased conditions include autism, attention deficit/hyperactivity disorder, conduct disorder, specific language impairment, Tourette syndrome, and dyslexia, and examples of female-biased conditions include depression, anxiety disorder, and anorexia nervosa."[33] This is not to say that these are exclusively male or female conditions, but that one sex or another experiences them with greater frequency.

A literature review in the *Journal of Cellular Physiology* tells us that "men are able to synthesize serotonin, the neurotransmitter commonly associated with pleasant moods, at a greater rate than women," and therefore men have a lower incidence of major depression, anxiety, and multiple sclerosis, but a higher incidence of attention deficit hyperactive disorder and coronary artery disease.[34] There are also differences in susceptibility to Alzheimer's disease and dementia.[35] While scientists don't know how much of these differences are due to environment and how much to biology, they do know that "innate physiological differences between males and females may play a large role in sex differences in disease onset, susceptibility, prevalence, and treatment responses."[36]

Men and women also tend to respond differently to pain, which has important implications for the use of painkillers and other medicines. Men and women have "variable responses to pharmacological agents and the initiation and manifestation of diseases such as obesity, autoimmune disorders, and coronary heart disease, to name a few."[37] Differences in the chemistry and structure of the brain influence our response to stressful events and how we remember them.[38] The differences between men and women in memory formation surrounding "emotionally arousing incidents" have implications for the treatment for post-traumatic stress disorder.[39]

Acknowledging sex-based differences is vital for women's health, as Jill Goldstein and colleagues emphasize in a paper for *Frontiers in Neuroscience*. "We now know there are significant sex differences in many chronic diseases, including brain disorders," they write, so understanding the causes of these differences "is critical to understanding women's mental health and healthcare needs." They cite studies demonstrating, for example, that "the vulnerability for sex-dependent risk for MDD [major depressive disorder] begins in *fetal* development" (their italics). Neuroscience must therefore "adopt a 'sex-dependent' and/or 'sex-specific' lens on investigations of the brain."[40]

Of course, male and female bodies are alike in many ways, but there are notable differences in average male and average female bodies beyond our different organizations for reproduction. In other words, there is a fundamental, essential difference, and there are subsidiary, average differences. There is also wide variation among males and among females, and considerable overlap between them, even in the areas just discussed. While environmental factors are likely to influence many of these differences, there's no denying the role of biology.

Disorders of Sexual Development

We have seen what happens when human development follows the normal pattern. We've focused on the focal case, as Aristotle teaches. But what if something goes awry? Then the story is more complicated. We'll look at some abnormal situations now.

Disorders of sexual development (DSDs) occur in roughly one out of every 5,000 births.[41] They can result in ambiguous external genitalia, a mismatch between internal and external reproductive organs, the incomplete development of reproductive organs, and the formation of two sets of sex organs. These disorders in development are frequently caused by chromosomal or hormonal defects. People with DSDs do not constitute a third sex. Rather, DSDs are a pathology in the development and formation of the male or female body. This is the consensus view of medical experts who study and treat DSDs. As the pediatric endocrinologist Quentin L. Van Meter writes, "The exceedingly rare DSDs are all medically identifiable deviations from the sexual binary norm. The 2006 consensus statement of the Intersex Society of North America and the 2015 revision of the statement does not endorse DSD as a third sex."[42] After all, biological sex is grounded in the organism's organization for reproduction. There is no third gonad. With DSDs, what can develop are dysfunctional ovaries and testes.

Disorders of sexual development can have a variety of causes. They can arise from genetic mutations, hormonal influences, the formation of a chimera or mosaic as an early embryo, or chromosomal abnormalities at fertilization. To take this last example first, sometimes a chromosomal disorder at conception results in more than 46 chromosomes or fewer, leading to a disorder in sexual development. People with Klinefelter syndrome have 47 chromosomes and are XXY. They develop as males, but tend to have abnormal body proportions, with enlarged breasts, and they frequently suffer from sexual and reproductive problems including infertility. People with Turner syndrome have only 45 chromosomes, with a single X chromosome rather than XX or XY. They develop as women but are infertile, because two X chromosomes are necessary for normal development of the ovaries.[43]

People with disorders of sexual development are grouped into three general categories: those with an XY set of chromosomes who develop female characteristics, referred to as XY DSD; those with an XX set of chromosomes who develop male characteristics, referred to as XX DSD; and those with more than one set of chromosomes who develop both ovarian and testicular cell lines and genitals—what used to be called true hermaphroditism, now referred to as ovo-testicular DSD. There are dozens of specific types of DSDs that fall into these three categories. We will look at a few of them to illustrate the phenomena.

Consider two examples of XY DSD. As *The Developing Human* reminds us, "If a *normal* Y chromosome is present, the embryo develops as a male. If no Y chromosome is present, or the testis-determining region of the Y chromosome is absent, female development occurs."[44] Recall our earlier discussion about SRY, the gene that commences the formation of male gonads. The testes then produce testosterone, which influences the subsequent development of male reproductive organs and external genitalia. This is when development follows the typical pattern.

But some XY people lack the SRY gene or have a severe mutation in it. As a result, the testes never form and the body never masculinizes; these individuals develop as females who are infertile (because they lack a second X chromosome).[45] Other XY people have a functional SRY gene but develop as females because they suffer from complete androgen insensitivity syndrome (CAIS). These individuals have a mutation in the gene that contains the androgen receptor protein, so they cannot be influenced by testosterone.[46] SRY instructs them to develop testes and their testes produce testosterone, but it makes no difference in their development because their bodies do not respond to it. Thus they never develop a penis. Though they are XY chromosomally, they develop as females in appearance: "People with androgen insensitivity syndrome develop as normal-appearing but sterile women, lacking a uterus and oviducts and having internal testes in the abdomen."[47]

Now consider some examples of XX DSDs. Some people with XX chromosomes develop as males because one of their X chromosomes contains the SRY gene (which is normally on the Y chromosome). Typically this results from "a translocation of SRY from the paternal Y to the paternal X chromosome."[48] While ordinary cells divide and reproduce identical copies by a process called mitosis (as you may recall from high school biology), the sex cells form by meiosis, in which a 46-chromosome cell produces four 23-chromosome sex cells, either sperm or ova. As sperm are produced by this process in a male, the SRY gene can be translocated from a Y to an X in what's known as meiotic crossover.[49] Because what matters most for male development is the presence of the SRY gene, individuals with SRY on an X chromosome develop for the most part as normal males except for being infertile, since they lack other important genetic material that is located on the Y chromosome.

Other people with XX DSDs develop for the most part as women, though they may also develop some male genitalia in a process known as virilization. For example, some XX people have congenital adrenal hyperplasia (CAH), a disorder that prevents the normal production of cortisol. This results in the overproduction of androgen, the male sex hormone, which in turn can lead to the virilization of the female external genitalia.[50] But internally these individuals develop and function as women.

Let's now consider the parallels between XY DSDs and XX DSDs. An XY without SRY will develop as a female, while an XX with SRY will develop as a male. An XY with SRY but without the ability to respond to androgen (CAIS) will develop as a female, while an XX without SRY but with too much androgen (CAH) will develop as a female with virilized external genitalia. These are just a couple of the ways in which minor genetic or hormonal abnormalities can lead to disorders of sexual development.

In the third general classification of DSDs, the individuals possess cells with both XX and XY genotypes, resulting in a mixture of male and female characteristics. One common cause of this condition is the presence of two sets of DNA in the same person, and therefore two sets of sex chromosomes: XX and XY, or a single X and an XY.[51] When genetic mutations in the developing embryo result in two or more different genotypes in the same person, it's called a "mosaic." When two different embryos combine early in a pregnancy to form one, it's called a "chimera." In both cases, the result is two different sets of DNA, with some of the body's cells being XX (or a single X) and some being XY, and these cells can direct the growth and development of different parts of the same person.[52]

As noted above, DSDs occur in approximately one out of every 5,000 live births, but specific types vary in frequency and in severity. For example, complete androgen insensitivity syndrome (CAIS) occurs in one out of every 20,000 to 64,000 births.[53] The most common form of congenital adrenal hyperplasia (CAH) occurs in one out of every 14,000 to 15,000 births.[54] Ovotesticular DSD occurs in one out of every 100,000 births.[55] The examples of DSDs described here are the more easily understandable varieties. Others have a more complicated etiology and are less well understood. They can result in a more ambiguous body formation, including external genitalia.

The standard treatment for people with DSDs—for example, a newborn baby with ambiguous genitalia—begins with trying to discern the causes of the disorder, which may shed light on the underlying sex of the child. *Pediatric Endocrinology*, a standard desk reference, says that after an "assessment of the anatomy of the sex organs," the decisions regarding a course of treatment should rest "on the likely cosmetic appearance of the reconstructed genitalia, on the potential for normal sex steroid secretion at puberty, on the potential for normal sexual intercourse, and on the potential for fertility."[56] These children do not constitute a third sex; they are either male or female, but with a disorder in their development. The sound medical response is to identify the predominant underlying sex and then take measures to provide health and functioning, as far as possible, through hormones and possibly surgery.

"Disorders" or "Differences"?

Recently, there has been a push to reclassify "Disorders of Sexual Development" as "Differences of Sexual Development." A few clinics have adopted this new terminology, undoubtedly motivated in part by a wish to avoid stigmatizing people. But another reason is the desire to erase the distinction between ordered and disordered development of the human person, at least when it comes to sexuality. Postmodern thinkers seek to undermine the very concept of the normative and to obscure the fact that a natural order exists. Instead of normal versus abnormal human development, there would just be a variety of ways in which humans can develop.

The concern about stigmatizing people is reasonable, but the word "disorder" does convey something important for human well-being. The distinction between ordered and disordered development is based on an understanding of purpose and function in the systems of an organism. To abolish the concept of the normal in human development is to erode the foundations of medical science, for when politics doesn't intrude, we can see that the distinction between order and disorder is operative everywhere in science and medicine.

We'll consider some uncontroversial examples first. The cardiovascular system is meant to circulate blood and thus transport the various nutrients carried in the blood. The respiratory system is meant to take in oxygen and expel carbon dioxide, thus enabling the cardiovascular system to circulate *oxygenated* blood. The digestive system is meant to break down the food we eat, converting it into energy and nutrients for the body. The various organs that constitute these systems are understood to play particular functional roles: the heart to pump blood, the lungs to breathe, and the intestines to digest. This is why we can speak of cardiovascular disorders and heart disease, respiratory disorders and lung disease, digestive disorders and intestinal disease. We don't speak of "differences" in heart development. A heart that doesn't pump blood well isn't "different," it's diseased. A digestive system that doesn't process nutrients is disordered; it isn't ordered to its proper end. A similar logic applies to the reproductive system and the sex organs.

The basic point is that the human body—like other bodies—is a complex matrix of integrated systems. The human body is an organism made up of organs that are organized in various systems to perform various functions. Organs are judged healthy or sick on the basis of how they perform their function within the system of which they are a part. Humans are judged healthy when all of their biological systems fulfill their functions properly. The nomenclature, then, is accurate: there are indeed "disorders of sexual development" when a sex organ or organ system develops in a way that leads to problems with reproductive functioning.

As a biological matter, the disorders of sexual development that we have examined here have little if anything to do with our transgender moment. Most people with a DSD do not identify as transgender, and most people who do identify as transgender do not have a DSD. But the effort to redefine DSDs as "differences" rather than "disorders" has something in common with transgender activism at a philosophical level: a rejection of objective standards of human well-being, in favor of a more fluid or subjective measure. This will become more readily apparent as we turn to the debate over the appropriate treatment for people with gender dysphoria.

CHAPTER FIVE

Transgender Identity and Sex "Reassignment"

G ender dysphoria can occur in anyone. From young children, to people in the prime of life, to the elderly. Sadly, some people find it difficult to identify with their own bodies, and this sense of having been "born in the wrong body" can cause severe distress and debility. In evaluating two hundred peer-reviewed studies on sexuality and gender identity in 2016, Lawrence Mayer and Paul McHugh concluded that people who identify as transgender have an elevated risk for various mental health problems.[1] Most alarming are the statistics on suicide. A study done in 2014 found that 41 percent of people who identify as transgender will attempt suicide at some point in their lives, compared with 4.6 percent of the general population.[2]

Suicide attempts do not spring from nowhere, and people who identify as transgender are more likely to suffer from conditions that too often lead to suicide: depression, anxiety disorders, and substance abuse.[3] These problems do not seem to be alleviated much by sex reassignment procedures. While those measures may bring temporary satisfaction, as we saw in the stories of detransitioners, they do not tend to promote long-term mental health. The poor outcomes can't be blamed on a hostile or bigoted society, since they are reported even in the cultures most accepting of people who identify as transgender.[4] It is true that transgender individuals face discrimination and other kinds of social stress, but the research doesn't show these factors to be solely or chiefly responsible for the relatively poor mental health of transgender subpopulations.[5]

So people are suffering from gender dysphoria; they are not generally finding well-being through sex reassignment procedures; and these poor outcomes cannot be explained solely by social stigma. We need to seek more effective therapies based on scientific evidence, and this requires gaining a clearer understanding of what causes gender dysphoria. Unfortunately, the existing scientific research sheds little light on the development of gender identity in general, and even less on the genesis of a gender identity at odds with one's biological sex.[6] Researchers simply do not understand how people acquire their gender identity, especially when it does not accord with their sex. Without a clear understanding of causes, any discussion of treatment must proceed with caution and humility.

In that spirit, this chapter provides a concise summary of where the science stands today. Among the questions it addresses are: How should we understand the phenomenon of discordant gender identities? Can a boy be born into a girl's body? Can a girl be born with a boy's brain? Does the "consistent, persistent, and insistent" belief that one is a man or a woman settle the matter, regardless of one's anatomy? What are the possible causes of gender dysphoria? Are the treatments promoted by transgender activists effective? Do sex reassignment therapies actually change one's sex? Is sex change even possible? (The subsequent chapter looks at the special case of children.)

Defining Gender Dysphoria

It is hard to get accurate numbers on how many people identify as transgender. One report from 2016 says that somewhere around 0.6 percent of adults in the United States "identify as a gender that does not correspond to their biological sex."[7] Another says: "Gender discordance occurs in 0.001% of biological females and in 0.0033% of biological males."[8] That is a wide statistical spread: more than one in every 200 people at the high end; fewer than one in 20,000 at the low end.

According to new clinical guidelines, however, not all of the people who experience a discordant gender identity have "gender dysphoria," a term that refers more specifically to distress associated with a transgender identity.[9]

In the most recent edition of the *Diagnostic and Statistical Manual of Mental Disorders* (DSM-5), gender dysphoria is defined as "incongruence between one's experienced/expressed gender and assigned gender" in conjunction with "clinically significant distress or impairment in social, occupational, or other important areas of functioning."[10] Immediately we notice some politicized language, in the reference to *assigned gender* rather than *biological sex*. But leave that aside for now. The more pertinent point here is that the APA now says that a patient has gender dysphoria only when there is "significant distress or impairment" arising from the disconnection between bodily sex and internal sense of gender.

This is a change from the previous edition of the DSM, which listed "gender identity disorder" rather than "gender dysphoria," and said that *anyone* who persistently manifests an incongruence between biological sex and experienced gender has this disorder. As Dr. McHugh explains, that earlier clinical definition correctly encompassed the dual nature of the disorder: "This intensely felt sense of being transgendered constitutes a mental disorder in two respects. The first is that the idea of sex misalignment is simply mistaken—it does not correspond with physical reality. The second is that it can lead to grim psychological outcomes."[11] The older clinical guidelines reflected the fact that the incongruence itself—the disconnection between bodily reality and subjective self-understanding—is properly a matter of concern.

Something has changed in psychiatry and other mental health professions, moving them away from objective standards of human well-being and healthy functioning. Dr. Allan Josephson, a professor of psychiatry, observed in an expert declaration to a federal court that the shift in terminology and definitions related to discordant gender identity is a result of politics, not science: "Changes in diagnostic nomenclature in this area were not initiated through the result of scientific information but rather the result of cultural changes fueling political interest groups within professional organizations."[12] Psychiatrists are now in disagreement on "whether gender incongruence reflects a psychopathology or a variant of normal human functioning with concomitant psychiatric distress."[13]

Many psychologists and psychiatrists think of gender dysphoria as similar to other dysphorias, or forms of profound discomfort with one's body. The feelings of discomfort can lead to mistaken beliefs about oneself or about reality, and then to actions in accordance with those false beliefs. Dr. McHugh says that people who identify as transgender "suffer a disorder of 'assumption' like those in other disorders familiar to psychiatrists." The "disordered assumption" of those who identify as the opposite sex, he says, is similar to the faulty assumption of those who suffer from anorexia nervosa, who believe themselves to be overweight when in fact they are dangerously thin.[14] Dr. Josephson describes the phenomenon as a "delusion," which in psychiatry refers to "a fixed, false belief which is held despite clear evidence to the contrary." He too draws a parallel between the beliefs involved in anorexia and the belief that one is the opposite sex "despite overwhelming evidence to the contrary."[15]

Someone who becomes subject to a delusion or a disordered assumption may at first be aware of harboring feelings that are not in line with reality, but over time these feelings generate an alternative reality in their own minds. Some people with anorexia, for instance, may initially *feel* overweight but *know* they are not, so they struggle with their mistaken feelings until the feelings overwhelm them and they come to believe that they actually are fat, and this belief governs their actions. Likewise, some people with gender dysphoria *feel* as if they were the opposite sex but *know* that they are not, so they struggle with their feelings until the feelings overwhelm them and they come to identify as the opposite sex, and act accordingly.

Dr. Michelle Cretella, the president of the American College of Pediatricians—a group of doctors who formed their own professional guild in response to the politicization of the American Academy of Pediatrics—gives other examples of dysphorias that show parallels to gender dysphoria:

> a girl with anorexia nervosa has the persistent mistaken belief that she is obese; a person with body dysmorphic disorder (BDD) harbors the erroneous conviction that she is ugly; a person with body integrity identity disorder (BIID) identifies as a disabled person and feels trapped in a fully functional body. Individuals with BIID are often so distressed by their fully capable bodies that they seek surgical amputation of healthy limbs or the surgical severing of their spinal cord. Dr. Anne Lawrence, who is transgender, has argued that BIID has many parallels with GD [gender dysphoria].[16]

Granted, there are significant differences among these. Most obviously, those with anorexia nervosa and body dysmorphic disorder are trying to get as far away as possible from what they mistakenly believe they are, while those with gender dysphoria want to transform their bodies into what they mistakenly believe their real self is. Yet the similarities suggest that the most effective approach for treating gender dysphoria may be similar to the treatment for other dysphorias. In all cases, the starting point is to recognize that feelings are not the same as reality. "Psychiatrists obviously must challenge the solipsistic concept that what is in the mind cannot be questioned," says McHugh. "Disorders of consciousness, after all, represent psychiatry's domain; declaring them off-limits would eliminate the field."[17] He's right. Mental health professionals must not simply help people survive with whatever beliefs they happen to hold, but help people accept the truth, as they work through the deeper issues beneath the false beliefs.

It is vital to help people accept reality, says Cretella, when their false beliefs "are not merely emotionally distressing...but also life-threatening." Consider what would be involved in medically "affirming" the false assumptions instead: for example, performing a requested amputation on a person with body integrity identity disorder. This might alleviate the emotional distress, for a while, but would do nothing to resolve the underlying psychological problem, and it might lead to the person's death.[18] Cretella suggests that sex reassignment surgery for gender dysphoria should be regarded in the same light. A more genuinely helpful therapeutic strategy would focus on the psychological issues that gave rise to the dysphoric feelings and false beliefs.

"Sex Reassignment" Therapy

The central debate in treating people with gender dysphoria is whether therapies should focus primarily on the mind or on the body. How one answers this question depends not only on scientific and medical evidence, but also on philosophical judgments and worldview. Transgender activists, rejecting the historic understanding of health and well-being, argue that sex reassignment is the proper way to treat gender dysphoria—that hormonal and surgical procedures should be performed to "affirm" one's inner gender identity. Here we will look first at what those procedures entail, and then at their outcomes.

The Endocrine Society published a consensus statement in 2009 on the treatment of people who identify as transgender, recommending that these people be given cross-sex hormones: testosterone to masculinize women, and estrogen to feminize men.[19] In 2017, right as this book went to press, they released an updated statement.[20] Likewise, the World Professional Association for Transgender Health (WPATH) declared in its 2011 *Standards of Care for the Health of Transsexual, Transgender, and Gender Nonconforming People*: "Feminizing/masculinizing hormone therapy—the administration of exogenous endocrine agents to induce feminizing or masculinizing changes—is a medically necessary intervention for many transsexual, transgender, and gender nonconforming individuals with gender dysphoria."[21] WPATH lists the effects of this hormone therapy:

- In FtM [Female to Male] patients, the following physical changes are expected to occur: deepened voice, clitoral enlargement (variable), growth in facial and body hair, cessation of menses, atrophy of breast tissue, increased libido, and decreased percentage of body fat compared to muscle mass.
- In MtF [Male to Female] patients, the following physical changes are expected to occur: breast growth (variable), decreased libido and erections, decreased testicular size, and increased percentage of body fact compared to muscle mass.[22]

Submitting to these changes in one's body is no small matter, yet WPATH endorses this treatment even while admitting that "no controlled clinical trials of any feminizing/masculinizing hormone regimen have been conducted to evaluate safety or efficacy in producing physical transition."[23]

Both the Endocrine Society and WPATH recommend sex reassignment surgery as an appropriate next step after hormone treatment. WPATH acknowledges that many people "find comfort with their gender identity, role, and expression without surgery," but claims that "for many others surgery is essential and medically necessary to alleviate their gender dysphoria."[24] Here's how the society describes these procedures:

> Sex reassignment surgeries available to the MTF transsexual persons consist of gonadectomy, penectomy, and creation of a vagina. The skin of the penis is often inverted to form the wall of the vagina. The scrotum becomes the labia majora. Cosmetic surgery is used to fashion the clitoris and its hood, preserving the neurovascular bundle at the tip of the penis as the neurosensory supply to the clitoris. Most recently, plastic surgeons have developed techniques to fashion labia minora. Endocrinologists

should encourage the transsexual person to use their tampon dilators to maintain the depth and width of the vagina throughout the postoperative period until the neovagina is being used frequently in intercourse. Genital sexual responsivity and other aspects of sexual function should be preserved after genital sex reassignment surgery.... Another major effort is the removal of facial and masculine-appearing body hair using either electrolysis or laser treatments. Other feminizing surgery, such as that to feminize the face, is now becoming more popular.

Sex reassignment surgeries available to the FTM transsexual persons have been less satisfactory. The cosmetic appearance of a neopenis is now very good, but the surgery is multistage and very expensive. Neopenile erection can be achieved only if some mechanical device is imbedded in the penis, *e.g.* a rod or some inflatable apparatus. Many choose a metaidoioplasty that exteriorizes or brings forward the clitoris and allows for voiding while standing. The scrotum is created from the labia majora with a good cosmetic effect, and testicular prostheses can be implanted. These procedures, as well as oophorectomy, vaginectomy, and complete hysterectomy, are undertaken after a few years of androgen therapy and can be safely performed vaginally with laparoscopy.

The ancillary surgery for the FTM transition that is extremely important is the mastectomy. Breast size only partially regresses with androgen therapy. In adults, discussion about mastectomy usually takes place after androgen therapy is begun. Because some FTM transsexual adolescents present after significant breast development has occurred, mastectomy may be considered before age 18.[25]

From this description, you might conclude that modern medicine is quite skilled in turning a man into a woman, and vice versa, or at least in giving patients satisfaction that this result has essentially been achieved. But what is really accomplished by these hormonal and surgical treatments in the long term?

Physical Outcomes

The first observation to make about the outcome of sex reassignment surgery is that it doesn't actually reassign sex. Cosmetic surgery and cross-sex hormones don't change the deeper biological reality, which begins with our DNA and fetal development, unfolding in every bodily system. Recall that sex is understood scientifically on the basis of an organism's organization for reproduction, and that sex differences manifest themselves all the way down to the molecular level. People who have sex reassignment surgery do not become the opposite sex, because they do not change their organismal organization for reproduction; they merely acquire the outward appearance of a change in bodily organization. As the philosopher Robert P. George puts it, "Changing sexes is a metaphysical impossibility because it is a biological impossibility."[26]

Surgeons are becoming more skillful in building and attaching artificial genitalia, but they do not change a person's biological sex with those "add-ons."[27] No matter how technically advanced the plastic surgery becomes, it doesn't create an actual sex organ, but a mere simulacrum. The result is not integrated into the organism as organized for reproduction, and it cannot fulfill the purpose that is central to the organ's definition. The sex organs are necessarily defined in terms of the role they fill "in the overall biological economy of a sexed human being," explains Christopher Tollefsen, a professor of philosophy. And those functions are the result of long preparation in biological history, beginning at conception:

> The penis typically penetrates the vagina but then also deposits sperm, which is in turn capable of procession towards and penetration of the female oocyte; the vagina is typically a receptacle and conduit of sperm to the oocyte, and so on. And both organs' identities are linked not only *forward* in these ways to the functions they might eventually perform, but are also linked *backward* to previous events and functions. For example, the origin of male gametes is to be found in the production of primordial germ cells that occurs many years before sexual intercourse is even possible, but this production occurs *in order that* sperm will eventually be produced which the penis will eventually deposit. An organ lacking this historical role in the biological economy is not a penis.

One cannot therefore make a vagina, say, simply by creating an orifice in a particular place. Absent some relationship to a vagina's larger biological functionality in the organism, no orifice is a vagina. Nor can one create a penis by creating something that will become enlarged on stimulation. One could only genuinely make a penis or vagina by re-creating the entire biological context within which those realities are what they are.

But those larger biological contexts are themselves not freestanding in the organism: The organism is primordially sexed from its very first moment, and its biological development involves the working out through time of capacities that were present at the beginning for the development of those organs in their appropriate contexts.[28]

Plastic surgery on the reproductive organs, no matter how "realistic" the result may appear, does not create the organs of the opposite sex.

A critic might point to the successes of modern medicine in organ transplantation. But transplanting an organ—a heart or a kidney, for example—is fundamentally different from the artificial construction of an opposite-sex sex organ. A heart transplant is successful when the heart is "integrated into a biological matrix that is fundamentally oriented towards that organ's presence," Tollefsen explains. A transplanted heart plays the functional role it is supposed to fill in the cardiovascular system by pumping blood. Nothing like this can happen if an artificial vagina is created for a man, or a penis for a woman. Even a transplant could not "integrate a male sex organ into the biological life of a being whose root capacities are female, or vice versa." On the contrary, says Tollefsen, "every surgical attempt to *change* sex must involve a mutilation of the bodily capacity that identifies one's true sex."[29]

Surgery does not change the organism's organization, and thus it cannot change someone's sex. Tollefsen's philosophical argument finds support from Lawrence Mayer, the epidemiologist and biostatistician: "Scientifically speaking, transgender men are not biological men and transgender women are not biological women. The claims to the contrary are not supported by a scintilla of scientific evidence."[30] So the medical therapy preferred by transgender activists—sex reassignment—does not succeed in actually changing a person's sex, whatever subjective satisfaction it may bring.

Psychological Outcomes

Is there enough subjective satisfaction from sex reassignment procedures to make the case for them? Judging from the evidence available so far, the psychological benefit is not very great, and this isn't surprising when the result is so artificial. "Transgendered men do not become women, nor do transgendered women become men" through hormones and surgery, Dr. McHugh emphasizes. Instead, they become "feminized men or masculinized women, counterfeits or impersonators of the sex with which they 'identify.'"

Their future is problematic, since it is "not easy nor wise to live in a counterfeit sexual garb."[31]

Sadly, just as "sex reassignment" fails to reassign sex biologically, it also fails to bring wholeness psychologically. The medical evidence suggests that it does not adequately address the mental health problems suffered by people who identify as transgender. Even when the procedures are successful technically and cosmetically, and even in cultures that are relatively "trans-friendly," these people still face poor psychological outcomes.[32]

The University of Birmingham's aggressive research intelligence facility (Arif), as noted earlier, evaluated more than one hundred studies on people who had undergone sex reassignment surgeries. Commissioned by the *Guardian* in 2004, this review found no "conclusive evidence that gender reassignment is beneficial for patients," although most of the research "was poorly designed, which skewed the results in favour of physically changing sex." The studies did not assess the effectiveness of other treatments, nor did they examine whether gender confusion might decrease over time. No thorough investigation had been done into the possible complications of hormone therapies and surgery, including deep vein thrombosis and incontinence. "There is huge uncertainty over whether changing someone's sex is a good or a bad thing," said Chris Hyde, the director of Arif. Even if doctors are careful to perform these procedures only on "appropriate patients," there are still large numbers of people who remain deeply troubled after the surgery, many to the point of suicide.[33]

A new review of the scientific literature was done in 2014 by Hayes, Inc., a research and consulting firm that evaluates the safety and health outcomes of medical technologies. Hayes found that the evidence on long-term results of sex reassignment was too sparse to support meaningful conclusions, and gave these studies its lowest rating for quality.[34]

> Statistically significant improvements have not been consistently demonstrated by multiple studies for most outcomes. Evidence regarding quality of life and function in male-to-female (MtF) adults was very sparse. Evidence for less comprehensive measures of well-being in adult recipients of cross-sex hormone therapy was directly applicable to GD patients but was sparse and/or conflicting. The study designs do not permit conclusions of causality and studies generally had weaknesses associated with study execution as well. There are potentially long-term

safety risks associated with hormone therapy but none have been proven or conclusively ruled out.[35]

One rigorous study, conducted by researchers at the University Hospital and University of Bern in Switzerland and published in 2009, looked at quality of life fifteen years after sex reassignment surgery.[36] Using a control group of females who had undergone at least one pelvic surgery, this study found that "postoperative transsexuals reported lower satisfaction with their general quality of health and with some of the personal, physical, and social limitations they experienced with incontinence that resulted as a side effect of the surgery."[37]

The largest and most rigorous academic study on the results of hormonal and surgical transitioning, published in 2011 by Cecilia Dhejne and her colleagues at the Karolinska Institute and Gothenburg University in Sweden, found strong evidence of poor psychological outcomes.[38] For example, the rate of psychiatric hospitalization for postoperative transsexuals was about three times the rate for the control groups, adjusted for previous psychiatric treatment. The risk of mortality from all causes was significantly higher, and so was the rate of criminal conviction. Suicide attempts were nearly five times more frequent, and the likelihood of death by suicide was *nineteen* times higher—again, after adjustment for prior psychiatric illness.[39] It is important to be clear about what the Dhejne study says and does not say. It does not speak to whether sex reassignment was the *cause* of these poor outcomes. What it does suggest is that those procedures may not alleviate the mental health problems associated with transgender identities.[40]

We should therefore be skeptical of claims for the psychological benefits of sex reassignment procedures. While it is imperative to end maltreatment of people who identify as transgender, as Mayer and McHugh stress, it is also essential to gain a better understanding of what contributes to the high rates of suicide and other mental health problems in the transgender population, and to think more carefully about treatment options.[41]

The Causes of Transgender Identities

In focusing heavily on treatments for gender dysphoria without looking into its possible causes, the transgender moment has the cart before the horse. But the causes of gender dysphoria are difficult to find when the very concepts of "gender" and "gender identity" are so murky. While biological sex has a stable and objective meaning, "gender" is a more amorphous concept and "gender identity" is explicitly subjective. So it isn't surprising that when we seek a scientific basis of gender identity we find little clarity. The vast majority of biological males come to understand themselves as men, and the vast majority of biological females come to understand themselves as women, yet scientists do not know exactly how this happens, nor do philosophers have a clear idea of what it means to have a self-understanding as male or female.

Things are even more opaque when people claim a gender identity at odds with their biological sex. This raises metaphysical questions concerning what it could mean to "be" a man in a woman's body, and epistemological questions concerning how a man could know what it is to "feel" like a woman. As the philosopher Thomas Nagel argued back in 1974, no one (other than a bat) can answer the question "What is it like to be a bat?"[42] So, can a man know what it feels like to be a woman? Or vice versa? It is impossible to know experientially what it is like to be something one is not. The claim of a biological male that he is "a woman stuck in a man's body" presupposes that someone who has a man's body, a man's brain, a man's sexual capacities, and a man's DNA can *know* what it is like to *be* a woman. As many feminists have pointed out, no biological male can really experience what it is like to be a woman, for males can have no embodied female experiences. Many of the claims made by transgender activists seem therefore to rely on stereotypes of what "real" men and women are like, of male versus female preferences and interests.

Indeed, Mayer and McHugh criticize the DSM-5 criteria for diagnosing gender dysphoria in children as being too heavily dependent on gender stereotypes. One of the diagnostic criteria is a "strong preference for the toys, games, or activities stereotypically used or engaged in by the other gender."[43] Mayer and McHugh ask, "Should parents worry that their tomboy daughter is really a boy stuck in a girl's body?" What about a son who dislikes guns and violence, and avoids rough play? "There is no scientific basis for believing that playing with toys typical of boys defines a child as a boy, or that playing with toys typical of girls defines a child as a girl," they say. A child might display social traits or behavior more typical of the other sex yet not *identify as* the opposite gender. Moreover, a diagnosis of gender dysphoria may be unreliable even if a child *identifies as* the opposite gender. Some children simply have "psychological difficulties in accepting their biological sex as their gender," perhaps because they are uncomfortable with the expectations linked to gender roles, or because of distressing experiences associated in their mind with their biological sex.[44] (In the next chapter we will see how clinical experts have effectively treated many children suffering from gender dysphoria by helping them develop a more nuanced understanding of gender.)

Even if a three-year-old boy *could* know what it feels like to be a girl, and if scientists could measure that feeling, we would still have little in the way of *biological* explanations for gender identity. In their recent review of the scientific literature, Mayer and McHugh concluded that "almost nothing is well understood" about how biology might cause the sense of having a gender at odds with one's biological sex.[45]

Trapped in the Wrong Body?

One of the most popular claims about people who identify as transgender is that they are simply trapped in the wrong body—that the *real* person is of a gender, or sex, different from what the body indicates. But what, or who, is the "real" self? Again we see philosophical and metaphysical questions lurking beneath the scientific debates.

Robert George detects the scent of ancient Gnosticism, with its body-self dualism, in transgender claims. "The idea that human beings are non-bodily persons inhabiting non-personal bodies never quite goes away," he observes. In the dualistic view, "the person is not the body, but only inhabits it and uses it as an instrument. Perhaps the real person *is* the conscious and feeling self, the psyche, and the body is simply material, the machine in which the ghost resides." If the real me is something other than my body, then the real me—the conscious self—can make use of my body in an instrumental way. To a neo-Gnostic, "the body serves at the pleasure of the conscious self, to which it is subject."[46]

There are profound philosophical difficulties in this notion. What exactly is this real me, the conscious self that is distinct from the body? What is it sensing when it has an "internal sense of gender"? What does it mean for the inner self to have a "gender identity"? What do transgender activists actually mean when they claim that people who identify as the opposite sex really *are* the opposite sex? Professor George asks,

> What is a pre-operative "male-to-female" transgender individual *saying* when he says he's "really a woman" and desires surgery to confirm that fact? He's not saying his *sex* is female; that's obviously false. Nor is he

saying that his gender is "woman" or "feminine," even if we grant that gender is partly or wholly a matter of self-presentation and social presence. It is clearly *false* to say that this biological male is *already* perceived as a woman. He wants to be perceived this way. Yet the pre-operative claim that he is "really a woman" is the premise of his plea for surgery. So it has to be prior. What, then, does it refer to? The answer cannot be his inner *sense*. For that would still have to be an inner sense *of something*—but there seems to be no "something" for it to be the sense *of*.[47]

This goes beyond Nagel's epistemological question to pose an ontological problem: there's nothing really *there* for a person who identifies as transgender to latch on to. This is a problem especially for modern thinkers who long ago gave up on notions of an immaterial soul when they embraced a crude materialism. But even from a traditional Aristotelian and Judeo-Christian perspective, the soul is understood to be the form of the body, not a separate substance. If the soul has an inner sense of something, it is of and through the body. Souls aren't radically detached from bodies; they are the principle that informs them, organizes them, and grounds their root capacities.[48]

Given the philosophical difficulties inherent in the dualistic view of the human person, especially for materialists, it's no surprise that many transgender activists have tried to make the case that transgender identities have a biological basis, and that it can be located in the brain. For example, Robert Sapolsky, a biologist, claims that some people can have a male-type brain in a female body, and vice versa.[49] This neurobiological theory has gained some notice in the scientific community as well as popular attention, although Mayer and McHugh observe that it has "fairly little support in the scientific literature" and it "remains outside of the scientific mainstream."[50] It's worth noting that Sapolsky's arguments were published in a newspaper op-ed.

Mayer and McHugh found that the gender identity studies focusing on the brain "have demonstrated weak correlations between brain structure and cross-gender identification." And the correlations that show up "do not provide any evidence for a neurobiological basis for cross-gender identification."[51] One problem with the existing studies is that their sample sizes are small, nonrandom, and nonrepresentative. Moreover, their conclusions are often "conflicting and confusing."[52]

But perhaps the biggest problem with the existing brain studies on transgender identity is how flat-footed they are. Many of them aim to reveal brain differences between people who identify as transgender and people who do not, but fail to show whether these differences occur between *populations* or just between *individuals*. They do not demonstrate whether any such observed differences are *causes* or *effects* of transgender identification. They do not tell us whether transgender identities are innate and fixed, or subject to environmental forces. They do nearly nothing to tease out the role of biology from the roles of society and psychology in the formation of gender identity. "Neurological differences in transgender adults might be the consequence of biological factors such as genes or prenatal hormone exposure, or of psychological and environmental factors such as childhood abuse, or they could result from some combination of the two," write Mayer and McHugh.[53]

These brain studies don't wrestle with the question of causality or the reality of neuroplasticity—how the brain rewires itself in response to our behavior. If an individual has been self-presenting as the opposite sex for years, that behavior may have produced changes in the brain that differentiate it from the brains of other people of the same biological sex.[54] This means that even if brain scans reveal differences between a transgender population and the control group, they can't tell us whether those differences are cause or consequence of a discordant gender identity. And those differences in brain morphology don't actually tell us much about the roots of a particular trait or behavior. Psychiatrists and neuroscientists recognize the "inherent and ineradicable methodological limitations of *any* neuroimaging study that simply associates a particular trait, such as a certain behavior, with a particular brain morphology." Studies of this kind, Mayer and McHugh conclude, "cannot provide statistical evidence nor show a plausible biological mechanism strong enough to support *causal connections* between a brain feature and the trait, behavior, or symptom in question."[55]

Moreover, contrary to media reports, the existing studies that show some brain differences among individuals have not shown significant differences between *groups*. There are no brain studies demonstrating a "predictive power" in any of the biological differences examined, and this lack of predictive power is a serious weakness for a scientific theory. So there is no warrant for the claims in popular media outlets that biological differences located in the brain determine gender identity.[56]

In short, the brain studies hyped in the popular media do not actually show what transgender activists claim they do. There is no scientific evidence that a transgender identity is biologically determined. In fact, there is some evidence—though by no means conclusive—that other factors must be involved. Professor Paul Hruz cites studies on identical twins, with the same genetic complements and the same prenatal environment, who developed differing gender identities.[57] If transgender identity were innate and independent of nurture, then two children who shared a womb and have identical genetic material would both be transgender, or neither would be. But that isn't what the research indicates.

For example, a study by Milton Diamond published in the *International Journal of Transgenderism* looked at transgender individuals who have an identical twin, and found that the twin also identified as transgender in 20 percent of the cases.[58] That figure suggests some measure of biological predisposition, but far from biological determination. Dr. Quentin Van Meter noted in court testimony that the concordance rate would be close to 100 percent if genes and/or prenatal hormones were the primary causes of transgender identities. Clearly, life experiences play a large role.[59] Neither twin studies nor brain imaging supports the hypothesis that a transgender identity is innate and fixed, or that a person could really be "a man trapped in a woman's body" or "a woman trapped in a man's body."[60] Instead, as Mayer and McHugh conclude, the "consensus of scientific evidence overwhelmingly supports the proposition that a physically and developmentally normal boy or girl is indeed what he or she appears to be at birth. The available evidence from brain imaging and genetics does not demonstrate that the development of gender identity as different from biological sex is innate."[61]

Psychosocial Explanations

Since biological science provides little help in understanding the phenomenon of gender identity at odds with biological sex, various psychosocial explanations have been offered. One starting point for these theories is recognizing that the manifestation of discordant gender identity is different between children and adults, and also between males and females, and among individuals within a demographic group. Thus there is likely to be no one single cause. Current research indicates a variety of possible causes, but these are only hypotheses, given how new the question is as a subject of scientific inquiry. Still, the best evidence available today suggests different causes for adults as compared with children. The next chapter focuses on transgender identity in children; here we will consider one theory that applies specifically to adult males.

Dr. Jon Meyer of Johns Hopkins studied men who had sought a sex change operation there, and Dr. McHugh reports on his colleague's findings:

> Most of the cases fell into one of two quite different groups. One group consisted of conflicted and guilt-ridden homosexual men who saw a sex-change as a way to resolve their conflicts over homosexuality by allowing them to behave sexually as females with men. The other group, mostly older men, consisted of heterosexual (and some bisexual) males who found intense sexual arousal in cross-dressing as females.[62]

Studies at the Clarke Institute in Toronto arrived at a similar conclusion: that discordant gender identity in adult males could arise from homosexuality or from *autogynephilia*, a man's sexual arousal in presenting himself as a woman. This is the research that led McHugh to believe that providing surgical alteration to these people is "to collaborate with a mental disorder rather than to treat it."[63]

Some researchers and doctors who don't share McHugh's judgment as to treatment have nevertheless come to the same view on the likely causes of discordant gender identity in some adult males. J. Michael Bailey and Kiira Triea published a revealing article titled "What Many Transgender Activists Don't Want You to Know, and Why You Should Know It Anyway" in the journal *Perspectives in Biology and Medicine* in 2007.[64] Bailey is a professor of psychology at Northwestern University, and Triea, who unfortunately passed away in 2012, was a patient of John Money's at Johns Hopkins and had a sex change operation. Both have voiced support for sex reassignment procedures, but they dispute the popular idea that males who identify as transgender "are, essentially, women trapped in men's bodies," an idea they call "the standard, feminine essence narrative, and the associated brain-sex theory." This notion, they say, "has little scientific basis" and "is inconsistent with clinical observations."[65] It persists because it corresponds with the beliefs of many transsexual individuals, who consider it helpful in "gaining cultural legitimacy" for their identity.[66]

Bailey and Triea argue that the facts are better explained by the research of Ray Blanchard—the psychologist in Toronto whose work Dr. McHugh also found useful—suggesting that there are two distinct types of male-to-female transsexuals: homosexual and autogynephilic. They favor Blanchard's theory because it is "based on far more data" than other theories; because "no published scientific data in the peer-reviewed literature contradict it; and other investigators in other countries have obtained similar findings."[67]

Bailey and Triea point to studies showing that many men who at some time experience discordant gender identity end up identifying as gay. A small proportion of these men seek out transition procedures, often after having social, romantic, or sexual difficulties, and the choice to transition seems to be largely an effort to improve those areas of their lives.[68] Bailey and Triea call these people "homosexual transsexuals" for two reasons. First, "it emphasizes the fact that homosexual MtFs [male-to-females] are a subset of, and developmentally related to, other homosexual males." Second, "it emphasizes the most efficient and practical way of distinguishing homosexual and autogynephilic transsexuals. Homosexual transsexuals are unambiguously, exclusively and intensely attracted to attractive men; autogynephilic transsexuals have some other pattern of sexual attraction."[69]

Borrowing from Blanchard, they define autogynephilia as "a male's propensity to be attracted to the thought or image of himself as a woman." It may be thought of as "inner-directed heterosexuality." Bailey and Triea say that "autogynephilic males are like heterosexual men, except that their primary sexual attraction is to the image or idea of themselves as women." Because the *idea* of being a woman is erotically arousing to them, they may in turn attempt to *become* a woman.[70] But while these men present themselves outwardly as female, they do not otherwise show interests or behaviors typical of women. Thus it seems "implausible" that all male-to-female transsexuals "have feminine minds that motivate their feminine identification."[71]

Bailey and Triea observe that autogynephilia "appears to be a paraphilia," that is, an "unusual, intense, and persistent erotic interests." According to the American Psychiatric Association, paraphilias occur almost exclusively in males and tend to occur in combination. For instance, autogynephilia appears to be correlated especially with masochism. Advertisements placed by dominatrixes "frequently offer services to cross-dressers, and autogynephilic males are more likely than other males to become sexually aroused to stimuli depicting masochistic themes." Among men who die while practicing autoerotic asphyxia, a highly risky masochistic activity, about one-quarter are cross-dressed, a considerably higher percentage than the proportion of nonhomosexual cross-dressers in the population as a whole.[72]

Bailey and Triea note that "a common aspect of autogynephilia is the erotic fantasy of being admired, in the female persona, by another person."[73] Dr. McHugh has suggested that this might be the case with Caitlyn Jenner:

> I have not met or examined Jenner, but his behavior resembles that of some of the transgender males we have studied over the years. These men wanted to display themselves in sexy ways, wearing provocative female garb. More often than not, while claiming to be a woman in a man's body, they declared themselves to be "lesbians" (attracted to other women). The photograph of the posed, corseted, breast-boosted Bruce Jenner (a man in his mid-sixties, but flaunting himself as if a "pin-up" girl in her twenties or thirties) on the cover of *Vanity Fair* suggests that he may fit the behavioral mold that Ray Blanchard has dubbed an expression of "autogynephilia"—from gynephilia (attracted to women) and *auto* (in the form of oneself).[74]

Whether or not it provides a way to understand Jenner in particular, we may ask why the theory of autogynephilia has generally been dismissed as one explanation for men identifying as women, while the theory of a female brain in a male body has been widely accepted. One reason is that people's own personal narratives often diverge from "the true reasons for their choices and behaviors," as Bailey and Triea remark. Few of the men who identify as transgender would openly link this identification to a history of arousal by the thought of being a woman.[75] One reason for this may be that people fear being regarded as sexually deviant. The "feminine essence" narrative is more appealing because it reinforces the man's desire to imagine himself as a woman, and it makes a better case for sex reassignment therapies. Then too, some people who have transitioned think of themselves as mentors to younger people considering transition, and they may believe that accepting the "feminine essence" concept will help those younger individuals make the transition. For one thing, "parents may be more accepting of a child whom they think of as a female unfortunately born with a male's body than of a son who is erotically aroused by the idea of being female."[76]

Again, these are theories, for even the Endocrine Society admits that the phenomenon of discordant gender identities is not well understood. In its consensus statement on the treatment of people who identify as transgender, the society acknowledged that "neither biological nor psychological studies provide a satisfactory explanation for the intriguing phenomenon of GIDs [gender identity disorders]." While studies have shown correlations, "the findings are not robust and cannot be generalized to the whole population."[77]

"Consensus" and the Purpose of Medicine

The Endocrine Society recommends radical, irreversible treatments for gender identity disorder even while admitting that little is known about its causes. Dr. Van Meter points out that the organization's consensus statement on the subject rests on the flimsiest evidence:

> Of the 22 recommendations contained in the document, only three were supported by scientific proof. These three warned of potential adverse effects of hormonal manipulation. The remaining 19 recommendations were nearly evenly split into a group that was based on very limited scientific evidence and a group that was based on absolutely no scientific evidence at all. The response to these guidelines was an exponential burgeoning of Gender Identity Clinics in the United States from three to over forty-five in a period of seven years.[78]

The Endocrine Society itself acknowledged the low quality of the evidence behind the guidelines: "This evidence-based guideline was developed using the Grading of Recommendations, Assessment, Development, and Evaluation (GRADE) system to describe the strength of recommendations and the quality of evidence, which was low or very low."[79]

Van Meter reveals how the process of formulating a professional "consensus statement" may be skewed toward a particular conclusion from the outset: "Mainstream clinicians and scientists who consider gender discordance to be a mental disorder have been deliberately excluded in the makeup of the steering committees of academic and medical professional societies which are promulgating guidelines that were previously unheard of."[80] It isn't surprising, then, if these committees produce statements that are scientifically dubious.

Dr. Hruz offers more insight into the process of formulating these "consensus" statements. He was present at the national meeting of the Pediatric Endocrine Society where its guidelines were first presented, and at a later meeting that was supposed to offer an "open forum" for discussing the recommendations. He recalls:

The panel selected included only those who supported the emerging practices and attempts by many of the endocrinologists present to raise concerns were muted. Subsequent attempts to engage in respectful dialogue regarding serious medical and ethical treatment concerns with colleagues who are providing hormonal treatment of gender dysphoric children have similarly been rejected.[81]

Beneath the debates over therapies for people with gender dysphoria are two related questions: How do we define mental health and human flourishing? What is the purpose of medicine, particularly psychiatry? Those general questions encompass more specific ones: If a man has an internal sense that he is a woman, is that just a variety of normal human functioning, or is it a psychopathology? Should we be concerned about the disconnection between feeling and reality, or only about the emotional distress or functional difficulties it may cause? What is the best way to help people with gender dysphoria manage their symptoms: by accepting their insistence that they are the opposite sex and supporting a surgical transition, or rather by encouraging them to recognize that their feelings are out of line with reality and learn how to identify with their bodies? All of these questions require philosophical analysis and worldview judgments about what "normal human functioning" looks like and what the purpose of medicine is.

Settling the debates over how to approach a proper response to gender dysphoria requires more than scientific and medical evidence. Medical science alone cannot tell us what the *purpose* of medicine is. Science cannot answer questions about meaning or purpose or worth in a moral sense. Of course, it can tell us things about biological purposes, about the function of the cardiovascular system and the respiratory system, for example. But it can't tell us how human beings and human minds ought to operate. Those are philosophical questions.

While medical science does not answer philosophical questions, every medical practitioner has a philosophical worldview, whether explicit or not. A philosophy that normalizes certain disorders as merely "differences" is likely to influence how they are treated, particularly in mental health. Some doctors may regard feelings and beliefs that are disconnected from reality as a part of normal human functioning and not a source of concern unless they cause distress. Other doctors will regard those feelings and beliefs as dysfunctional in and of themselves, even if the patient does not find them distressing, because they indicate a defect in mental processes. But the way psychiatrists view the matter for purposes of diagnosis and treatment should not dictate the answer to the *philosophical* question: is it good or bad or neutral to harbor feelings and beliefs that are utterly disconnected from reality? Should we accept them as authentic and definitive, or try to understand the causes and correct the error, or at least mitigate the effects?

The current findings of medical science provide arguments against sex reassignment therapies, but we also need to look deeper for philosophical wisdom, starting with some basic truths about human well-being and healthy functioning. Our minds and senses function properly when they reveal reality to us and lead us to knowledge of truth. And we flourish as human beings when we embrace the truth and live in accordance with it. A person might find some subjective satisfaction in believing and living out a falsehood, but that person would not be objectively well off. Someone could make it through life believing and living out a falsehood without experiencing psychiatric distress, but that person would not fully flourish.

This philosophical view of human well-being is the foundation of a sound medical practice. Dr. Cretella emphasizes that mental health care should be guided by norms grounded in reality, including the reality of the bodily self. "The norm for human development is for one's thoughts to align with physical reality, and for one's gender identity to align with one's biologic sex," she says.[82] For human beings to flourish, they need to feel comfortable in their own bodies, readily identify with their sex, and believe that they are who they actually are. For children especially, normal development and functioning require accepting their physical being and understanding their embodied selves as male or female.

Unfortunately, many professionals now view health care in general, and mental health care in particular, as primarily a matter of fulfilling a patient's desires. In the words of Leon Kass, a professor emeritus at the University of Chicago, today a doctor is often regarded as merely "a highly competent hired syringe":

> The implicit (and sometimes explicit) model of the doctor-patient relationship is one of contract: the physician—a highly competent hired syringe, as it were—sells his services on demand, restrained only by the law (though he is free to refuse his services if the patient is unwilling or unable to meet his fee). Here's the deal: for the patient, autonomy

and service; for the doctor, money, graced by the pleasure of giving the patient what he wants. If a patient wants to fix her nose or change his gender, determine the sex of unborn children, or take euphoriant drugs just for kicks, the physician can and will go to work—provided that the price is right and that the contract is explicit about what happens if the customer isn't satisfied.[83]

This modern vision of medicine and medical professionals gets it fundamentally wrong, says Dr. Kass. Professionals ought to profess their devotion to the purposes they serve and the ideals they look up to. Teachers should be devoted to learning, lawyers to justice, clergy to things divine, and physicians to "healing the sick, looking up to health and wholeness." Healing is "the central core of medicine," Kass writes; "to heal, to make whole, is the doctor's primary business."[84]

And yet some doctors are looking more to a false notion of social justice than to health and wholeness. The Dutch doctors who pioneered puberty blocking for children with gender dysphoria defended their approach by saying it was "proof of solidarity of the health professional with the plight of the applicant." In response, Drs. Hruz, Mayer, and McHugh acknowledge that "it is important for physicians to establish a relationship of trust and compassion with their patients," but stress that offering "proof of solidarity" by granting whatever the patient wants, whether or not it's in the patient's best interests, is a standard of practice far removed from the Hippocratic tradition. It is an approach that "surrenders the physician's responsibility to treat patients with their ultimate benefit in mind."[85]

To provide the best possible care, serving the patient's medical interests, requires an understanding of human wholeness and well-being. Mental health care must be guided by a sound concept of human flourishing. The minimal standard of care should begin with a standard of *normality*. Dr. Cretella explains how this standard applies to mental health:

One of the chief functions of the brain is to perceive physical reality. Thoughts that are in accordance with physical reality are normal. Thoughts that deviate from physical reality are abnormal—as well as potentially harmful to the individual or to others. This is true whether or not the individual who possesses the abnormal thoughts feels distress.

> A person's belief that he is something or someone he is not is, at best, a sign of confused thinking; at worst, it is a delusion. Just because a person thinks or feels something does not make it so.[86]

Our brains and senses are designed to bring us into contact with reality, connecting us with the outside world and with the reality of ourselves. Thoughts that disguise or distort reality are misguided. When thoughts and feelings are utterly disconnected from reality, persistently false and unfounded, and idiosyncratic (i.e., not socially or culturally promoted), they can take us from confused to delusional.

Recall that a delusion, in psychiatric terms, is "a fixed, false belief which is held despite clear evidence to the contrary."[87] If this concept applies to anorexia and to body dysmorphic disorder, why should it not apply to gender identity disorder? The answer hinges partly on whether the delusional thoughts are in fact being endorsed socially and culturally. After all, plenty of "cisgender" people believe that when Bruce Jenner announced he is now "Caitlyn," it meant he should be considered a woman. Are these people confused or delusional? I don't know. I do know that they're wrong. Jenner is not a woman. Regardless of which technical labels the experts apply to him, the crucial point is that his feelings and thoughts are misguided and they do not change reality.

Given the sad state of "evidence-based" science in this area today, it is imperative that scientists and clinicians conduct deeper study of discordant gender identity, its underlying causes, and possible treatments—studies that are not clouded by the politics of transgender activism. A good example is the literature review by Mayer and McHugh that I quote frequently in this book. Trans activists responded to their report by attempting to smear the reputation of Dr. McHugh, one of America's most prominent mental health experts. But Mayer and McHugh refuse to be silenced. In 2017 they released another report, this one focusing on children, the subject of the next chapter.

CHAPTER SIX

....

Childhood Dysphoria and Desistance

In 2012, the *Washington Post* ran a provocative piece titled "Transgender at Five."[1] The title actually downplayed things, for the story tells us that little Kathryn declared "I am a boy" when she was only two years old. Her parents at first assumed it was just one of those stages that kids go through, so they didn't worry about their daughter's fixation on being a boy. When the behavior had continued for a year, they tried to explain to Kathryn that she was, in fact, their daughter: "'See? You're a girl. You have girl parts,' Jean told her big-eyed daughter. 'You've always been a girl.'" But Kathryn didn't see it that way.

Over time, Jean came to see things the way her daughter did, the *Post* reports: "Her little girl's brain was different. Jean could tell." Jean had heard about people "who are one gender physically but the other gender mentally." Indeed, nearly everyone knew about the transformation of Chastity Bono into Chaz Bono, who was featured on *Dancing with the Stars* in the autumn of 2011. When Kathryn was four, Jean broached the subject with her husband, telling him, "I'm pretty sure Kathryn is transgender. She's not just a tomboy." Jean thought it might be best to start letting their daughter refer to herself as a boy.

They took Kathryn to a psychologist, who gave her a diagnosis of gender dysphoria and a treatment plan consisting of social transition: a new name, Tyler, new pronouns, a new wardrobe, and a new persona. Her older sister was quite casual about this change, explaining to her second-grade classmates:

"It's just a boy mind in a girl body." Their private school would allow "Tyler" to begin kindergarten as a boy. There would be no mention of Kathryn. The *Post* says, "Tyler doesn't really like to talk about Kathryn or even acknowledge she existed. 'I'm not transgender,' he fumes when he hears the word, often spoken by his mom as she explains things. 'I. Am. A. Boy.'"

When this story was published, the issue of transgender identities wasn't nearly as politicized as it would become over the next few years, so the *Post* could accurately report that "children have been openly transitioning genders for probably less than a decade" in the United States. "There is very little to go on, scientifically, to support that approach, and the very idea of labeling young children as transgender is shocking to many people." Today there is still very little to go on scientifically in support of transitioning, yet doctors are telling parents that the best chance of happiness for their children is to affirm the belief that they are the opposite sex. Jean looked into the experiences of other parents in a similar situation, learning about "their painful decision to allow their children to publicly transition to the opposite gender." The *Post* reports:

> Some of what Jean heard was reassuring: Parents who took the plunge said their children's behavior problems largely disappeared, schoolwork improved, happy kid smiles returned. But some of what she heard was scary: children taking puberty blockers in elementary school and teens embarking on hormone therapy before they'd even finished high school.[2]

Three years later, the *Post* ran a follow-up story on Tyler at age eight, and the decision to go on puberty blockers. If medical tests revealed that Tyler was beginning to develop into a woman—in bone growth and mineral density, in estrogen levels, in soft-tissue growth on the chest—then "it would be time for the medical part of becoming Tyler." The only question that remained was what method to employ in blocking puberty:

> [Tyler] and his parents would have to decide whether to visit the doctor monthly for shots or use a surgical implant to inject drugs to stop puberty and keep his body from looking like that of a young woman. "The implant. Definitely the implant," the third-grader told the doctor. And Tyler is certain about one other thing: "I'm a boy," he says.[3]

In essence, an eight-year-old child was treated as an authority on whether and how to block puberty. A third-grader was "definitely" sure that the implant was right.

By this time, Bruce Jenner had made headlines with his *20/20* interview, in April 2015. The journalist for the *Post* who three years earlier had admitted that there was no good science to support "gender-affirming" procedures was now confident that they involve no risks:

> Medically, the puberty blockers Tyler is certain he wants appear to do no harm. Normal development can resume anytime in the tween's life simply by stopping them. Doctors who specialize in trans kids said the puberty blockers can be lifesaving, helping kids integrate during the toughest times of teendom. They also prevent costly and dangerous surgery later in adulthood, if gender reassignment surgery is the path taken. Eventually, some older teens also begin taking hormones of the gender they identify with. So Tyler would get testosterone shots. Those hormone injections, which typically begin at 16, would be a much tougher choice because they make the child sterile.[4]

This reporting follows the mold of what Jesse Singal, who writes the "Science of Us" column for *New York* magazine, calls "mainstream journalistic treatments" of children who identify as transgender: "The child knows from a very young age they were born in the wrong body, the parents (perhaps after a brief period of reflection or resistance) agree, and the kid transitions, blossoming into their true self as a result." This is what sometimes happens with childhood gender dysphoria, Singal writes, but many other cases "are far more complicated, and that's where the debate comes in."[5]

The *Washington Post*'s account leaves out the debate. Nowhere does it quote a cautious voice, let alone a skeptical one. Nowhere does the reporter consider the fact that an eight-year-old normally isn't considered the best judge of which medical procedures to undergo. There is no acknowledgment that the vast majority of children with gender dysphoria—80 to 95 percent—naturally grow out of it, if they aren't encouraged to transition.[6] The reporter does not mention that blocking puberty may interfere with the developmental mechanisms that help children accept their bodies, or that virtually *none* of the children put on puberty blockers grow out of their gender dysphoria.

Neither does the reporter mention the long-term health risks of puberty blockers. And it is simply wrong to say that "normal development can resume anytime" in an adolescent who stops taking puberty blockers, since development at age sixteen that was supposed to occur at age ten is not normal.

Children with gender dysphoria are in a particularly vulnerable situation. Even doctors and activists who are generally supportive of transgender identities admit that children are different from adults. So why should their gender dysphoria be approached in the same way, as though a young child had a mature understanding of the issues? "Adolescents and kids are *different* from adults in vital ways," Singal observes. "We recognize this in every other conversation about human behavior, and we should recognize it here." He laments that a much-needed "public conversation" on the subject of gender dysphoria in children is stifled by the insistence that these children will necessarily remain transgender over the long term. This has become a popular belief, which "renders a complicated subject simple" and makes important questions harder to ask. And this "doesn't help anyone."[7]

The Activists' Treatment Plan

Transgender activists maintain that when a child identifies as the opposite sex in a manner that is "consistent, persistent, and insistent," the appropriate response is to support that identification. This means, first, a social transition: giving the child a new wardrobe, a new name, new pronouns, and generally treating the child as if he or she were the opposite sex.

Second, a child approaching puberty will be placed on puberty blockers to prevent the normal process of maturation and development. This means there will be no progression of the pubertal stage, and a regression of sex characteristics that have already developed. In girls, breast tissue will weaken and may disappear altogether; in boys, testicular volume will decrease.[8]

Third, around age sixteen, comes the administration of cross-sex hormones: boys will be given feminizing hormones such as estrogen, and girls will be given masculinizing hormones such as androgens (testosterone). The purpose is to mimic the process of puberty that would occur in the opposite sex. For girls, testosterone treatment leads to "a low voice, facial and body hair growth, and a more masculine body shape" along with enlargement of the clitoris and atrophying of the breast tissue. For boys, estrogen treatment results in the development of breasts and a body shape with a female appearance. These patients will be prescribed cross-sex hormones throughout their lives.[9]

Finally, at age eighteen, these individuals may undergo sex reassignment surgery: amputation of primary and secondary sex characteristics, and plastic surgery to create new sex characteristics. To summarize these procedures (described in detail in the previous chapter): Male-to-female surgery involves removing the testes and constructing "female-looking external genitals." It may include breast enlargement if estrogen therapy has not produced satisfactory growth of breasts. Female-to-male surgery often begins with mastectomy. The uterus and ovaries are often removed as well. Some patients will undergo phalloplasty, the surgical construction of a penis, but many do not, because the results are variable in quality and functionality.[10]

This four-stage course of treatment is the current standard of care promoted by transgender activists. But the ages for each phase to commence are getting lower. In July 2016, the *Guardian* reported that "a doctor in Wales is prescribing cross-sex hormones to children as young as 12 who say they want to change sex, arguing that if they are confident of their gender identity they should not have to wait until 16 to get the treatment."[11] There are no laws in the United States prohibiting the use of puberty blockers or cross-sex hormones for children, or regulating the age at which they may be administered.

This course of treatment is founded upon a questionable set of beliefs. The first is that very young children can possess a gender identity that may be discordant with the body. Trans-affirming clinicians, moreover, are confident that they can accurately identify which kids are "really transgender," not just going through a phase that they'll eventually grow out of, so they believe that these children should be helped to make a transition as soon as possible. But there is no reliable scientific evidence to support the view that professionals can actually know whether a child will persist in a transgender identity into adulthood.[12]

Another belief underlying the trans-affirming treatment regime is that puberty may be an "undesirable" and unhealthy condition for children with gender dysphoria. "The experience of full biological puberty, an undesirable condition, may seriously interfere with healthy psychological functioning and well-being," claims the Endocrine Society. For an individual to look female while living as a male, or vice versa, "creates difficult barriers with enormous lifelong disadvantages."[13] No doubt. But it isn't clear why the remedy would be to change the body rather than address the disconnection at the psychological level.

A third belief supporting this treatment plan is that we should have no *a priori* preference either for allowing puberty to occur naturally or for blocking it, as neither option is morally neutral, nor is one to be considered more normal than the other. "Neither puberty suppression nor allowing puberty to occur is a neutral act," according to the WPATH *Standards of Care for the Health of Transsexual, Transgender, and Gender Nonconforming People.*[14] But the balance may be tipped by the dubious belief that blocking puberty is reversible, while allowing it to proceed is not. The point of puberty blockers, says WPATH, is to prevent "the development of sex characteristics that are difficult or impossible to reverse."[15] The Endocrine Society agrees on blocking the "irreversible" development of "undesirable sex characteristics" in transgender adolescents during puberty.[16] At the same time, activists claim that the effects of blocking puberty with drugs are fully reversible. This turns things upside down, for virtually every part of the body undergoes significant development in sex-specific ways during puberty, and going through the process at age eighteen can't reverse ten years of blocking it.

Activists claim that blocking puberty allows children "more time to explore their gender identity, without the distress of the developing secondary sex characteristics," as the Dutch doctors who pioneered this treatment put it.[17] This is an odd argument, say Drs. Paul Hruz, Lawrence Mayer, and Paul McHugh. "It presumes that natural sex characteristics interfere with the 'exploration' of gender identity, when one would expect that the development of natural sex characteristics might contribute to the natural consolidation of one's gender identity."[18] The rush of sex hormones and the bodily development that happens during puberty may be the very things that help an adolescent come to identify with his or her biological sex. Puberty blockers interfere with this process. In fact, *every one* of the children placed on puberty blockers in the Dutch clinic persisted in a transgender identity, and they generally went on to begin cross-sex hormone treatment at around age sixteen. Perhaps the Dutch doctors correctly identified the kids who would naturally persist in a transgender identity, but it's more likely that the puberty blockers reinforced their cross-gender identification, making them more committed to taking further steps in sex reassignment.[19]

Transgender-Affirming Therapies and Desistance

There are good reasons to be seriously concerned about the transgender-affirmative approach to treating gender dysphoria in children, starting with the fact that it encourages and promotes a child's false assumption. It diminishes the chances that a child will naturally grow out of a gender-discordant stage, as the vast majority otherwise do. "All competent authorities agree that between 80 and 95 percent of children who say that they are transgender naturally come to accept their sex and to enjoy emotional health by late adolescence," stated McHugh, Hruz, and Mayer in an amicus brief they submitted to the U.S. Supreme Court in early 2017 for a pending case involving "gender identity" policies in schools.[20]

Some scholars have tried to refute this statistic, but honest brokers admit that it's true. "Every study that has been conducted on this has found the same thing," writes Jesse Singal. "At the moment there is strong evidence that even many children with rather severe gender dysphoria will, in the long run, shed it and come to feel comfortable with the bodies they were born with." The critiques of these findings on desistance, he says, "don't come close to debunking what is a small but rather solid, strikingly consistent body of research."[21] Thank God for honest liberals willing to report the truth even when it's politically inconvenient.

Researchers have found that a young child's gender identity is both "elastic" and "plastic." It can change over time, and it responds to outside forces, including the approval or disapproval of parents, as well as messages received from the broader culture. This means that transgender-affirming treatments may cause some children to persist in a transgender identity when they would otherwise have grown to accept their natal sex. Those children may then go on to subject themselves to unnecessary surgeries and ongoing hormonal treatments.[22]

For this reason, some therapists who do not oppose transition treatment in general still think it's a bad idea for children. Dr. Kenneth Zucker and his protégé Devita Singh are concerned about how the transgender-affirming approach, beginning with social transitioning, serves to reinforce dysphoria during a stage of development when children are normally learning behavior and consolidating an identity in harmony with their biological sex. Singh has predicted that rates of transgender persistence will increase over time as more children are encouraged to begin a social transition after their first visit to a transgender-affirmative clinic. As more children find their way to these clinics, the desistance rate is likely to decrease.[23]

Parents may come to play a role in discouraging desistance if they accept the diagnosis and treatment plan offered by the clinic, Singal writes. First they become "champions" of their child's transgender identity to teachers and other parents, and often they become advocates for transgender ideology more generally. These efforts are bound to influence the child's sense of self, one clinician told Singal. If the dysphoria begins to fade, the child then faces a dilemma: "either sticking with a gender identity that no longer feels like it fits or telling their parents, as the clinician put it, 'This whole life that you've created for yourself as an advocate, I don't want to be part of that anymore.'" Schools and other family members will also have become involved in the transitioning process, so they would need to reverse course as well if the child detransitions. Initiating a transition too early could therefore "limit a child's future options because of the social or familial costs of transitioning back."[24] The problem is magnified when serious medical procedures interfere with the child's developmental process.

Activists dismiss these concerns first by saying that they can accurately identify which children will inevitably persist in their transgender identity. For example, Dr. Johanna Olson-Kennedy, a transgender-affirmative clinician at Children's Hospital Los Angeles, insists that "it's clear, it's clear. I think that once you see hundreds and hundreds of kids you get a feeling for kids that are and kids that aren't."[25] But Dr. Singh, who wrote her dissertation on the patients treated at Dr. Zucker's clinic in Toronto, argues that it really isn't so clear. It might seem reasonable to say that "consistent, persistent, and insistent" identification with the opposite sex distinguishes a child who will persist in transgender identity from those who will desist in the future, but there's very little in the way of careful long-term studies on why some children eventually desist while others do not. Singal reports:

> While there's some early, emerging evidence that severity of childhood gender dysphoria can predict persistence, some of it from Singh's dissertation, she also found in her research that plenty of GIC clients who exhibited rather severe gender dysphoria later went on to desist. So in the view of her and other GIC clinicians, there's nowhere near enough data

for anyone to be making big decisions based solely or primarily on how insistent a 5-year-old is that they were born the wrong gender—especially given that these clinicians can also point to specific examples from their own professional experience of kids who appeared to be quite gender dysphoric at a specific point in time, but later grew up to be cisgender.[26]

So doctors have no reliable way of knowing whether a particular child is among the 5 to 20 percent who will persist in transgender identification into adulthood or among the 80 to 95 percent who will eventually come to identify with their bodies—if they aren't socially and medically encouraged to maintain a transgender identity.

Dr. Michelle Cretella argues that putting a child on a path of social transition and pubertal suppression is a "self-fulfilling" protocol, for it points to an "inevitable" and irreversible outcome. Citing what science now knows about neuroplasticity, she notes that for a boy with gender dysphoria "the repeated behavior of impersonating a girl alters the structure and function of the boy's brain in some way—potentially in a way that will make identity alignment with his biologic sex less likely." On top of this behavioral effect, the medical suppression of puberty "prevents further endogenous masculinization of his brain," so that he remains "a gender non-conforming prepubertal boy disguised as a prepubertal girl." Meanwhile, his peers are developing normally into men or women, so the boy is even more isolated and less able to identify as male. "A protocol of impersonation and pubertal suppression that sets into motion a single inevitable outcome (transgender identification) that requires life-long use of synthetic hormones, resulting in infertility, is neither fully reversible nor harmless," Dr. Cretella concludes.[27]

The course of treatment promoted by transgender activists is, in short, self-reinforcing. Anything that would encourage a child to persist in identifying as transgender should give us pause, given the risks and difficulties inherent in transitioning, and the high probability that those difficulties could be avoided with a different course of treatment. The "greatest lifelong benefit" comes from accepting a gender identity concordant with one's biological sex, Dr. Hruz says. "Any intervention that interferes with the likelihood of resolution is unwarranted and potentially harmful."[28]

The reality of desistance in children is slighted or ignored in the dominant media narrative about gender dysphoria. So are the stories of detransitioners, who found that transitioning was not the remedy for their distress. The desisters and detransitioners refute the theory that "gender dysphoria is always a mark of a stable, deep-seated identity," as Singal remarks. He calls out his liberal colleagues for their shoddy journalism on this subject: "Unfortunately, many progressive media outlets have done a poor job covering desistance and detransition. Vice and Vox and ThinkProgress have all written misleading articles falsely claiming that desistance is a 'myth' (or close to it), that detransitioners are nothing more than pawns for transphobic bigots to make it harder for people to transition, or both."[29]

The prevailing media message puts a heavy burden on parents who may be doubtful that a young child—however strong-willed and insistent—can have a firm, fixed gender identity at odds with the body and immune to outside influences. Singal quotes one mother saying, "I feel like sometimes there's no middle ground. You're either trans or you're not, and you can't be this kid who is just kind of exploring." Parents of desisters haven't coalesced into an interest group, Singal says, because "desisting isn't an identity-politics lodestone in the way persisting is." Another mother said, "We're quieter. There are a bunch of us scattered around, and we're not acting collectively." Singal concludes that today's politics have no place for the parents who "don't fit neatly into the binary in which trans identities are either accepted or rejected, full stop."[30]

Is Puberty-Blocking Therapy Safe?

Transgender activists insist that a child's discordant gender identity must be accepted as who the child really is, and affirmed with social transition followed by puberty blockers. They claim that blocking puberty is a cautious and prudent measure, allowing the child time to "explore" his or her "gender identity" without the "undesirable" changes of puberty. But what do we actually know about the effects of puberty blockers as a treatment for gender dysphoria?

Activists and some medical professionals are suggesting that a drug developed and tested to help prevent the *early* onset of puberty—what's known as precocious puberty—can be safely used to delay puberty indefinitely. Precocious puberty is often caused by the early production of a hormone known as GnRH (gonadotropin-releasing hormone), which is naturally released by the hypothalamus in bursts, stimulating the pituitary to release other hormones called gonadotropins, which in turn stimulate the growth of the gonads (ovaries and testes). Physicians treat precocious puberty not by blocking GnRH, but by providing more constant levels of a synthetic form called a GnRH analogue. This has the effect of desensitizing the pituitary gland to GnRH and reducing its secretion of gonadotropins, thus slowing down the maturation of the gonads and their secretion of androgens and estrogens, and thereby preventing the premature development of secondary sex characteristics.[31] This outcome is beneficial in the case of precocious puberty, since developing too early can cause psychological, social, and physical problems. Administering GnRH analogues to push back the start of puberty to its normal biological schedule is medically appropriate.

The same cannot be said about the use of GnRH analogues to suppress normal puberty indefinitely. Judging from the treatment guidelines produced by transgender activists, one might think there's a firm scientific consensus that it is safe and effective for treating gender dysphoria. But this is far from the reality, as Hruz, Mayer, and McHugh point out: "Whether puberty suppression is safe and effective when used for gender dysphoria remains unclear and unsupported by rigorous scientific evidence." Instead of regarding puberty blocking as a "prudent and scientifically proven treatment option," parents should view it as a "drastic and experimental measure."[32]

The use of any experimental medical treatment on children calls for "especially intense scrutiny," they emphasize, "since children cannot provide legal consent to medical treatment of any kind...to say nothing of consenting to become research subjects for testing an unproven therapy." The rapid acceptance of puberty suppression as a treatment for gender dysphoria with little scientific scrutiny should raise concerns about the welfare of the children who receive this treatment. In particular, we should question the claim that it is both physiologically and psychologically "reversible."[33]

All of the major activist groups, and many professional groups, perpetuate the claim that puberty suppression is reversible.[34] But doctors don't know whether this is true or not, because few people have sought to have it reversed (perhaps because of its self-reinforcing effect). Thus, "there are virtually no published reports, even case studies, of adolescents withdrawing from puberty-suppressing drugs and then resuming the normal pubertal development typical for their sex." Without such studies, we cannot really know how "normally" an adolescent will develop after the artificial suppression of puberty.[35] So if an eighteen-year-old goes off of the GnRH analogues, perhaps puberty will commence. Or perhaps not. Or at least not in a normal way.

The claim for the reversibility of puberty-blocking treatment is purely speculative, and it is also inherently misleading, for in developmental biology "it makes little sense to describe anything as 'reversible,'" Hruz and colleagues explain. There is a normal sequence in which many things happen as the body matures, and when some things happen out of phase, the developmental process is not normal. "If a child does not develop certain characteristics at age 12 because of a medical intervention, then his or her developing those characteristics at age 18 is not a 'reversal,' since the sequence of development has already been disrupted."[36]

Allowing the developmental sequence to proceed without interruption is vital not just for physical maturation—the proper ordering of growth spurts and organ development and the formation of secondary sex characteristics, etc.—but also for psychological development. That's because the two are linked in complex ways. "Gender identity is shaped during puberty and adolescence as young people's bodies become more sexually differentiated and mature," say Hruz and colleagues. How this normally happens is not well understood, so it's imperative to be cautious about interfering with the process.[37] But far from being cautious and prudent by using puberty blockers to treat gender dysphoria, doctors are conducting a giant experiment that does not come close to the ethical standards demanded in other areas of medicine.

No one really knows all the potential consequences of puberty blocking as a treatment for gender dysphoria, but there are some known effects of puberty suppression on children who are physiologically normal, and these carry long-term health risks. Children placed on puberty blockers have slower rates of growth in height, and an elevated risk of low bone-mineral density.[38] Some other possible effects are "disfiguring acne, high blood pressure, weight gain, abnormal glucose tolerance, breast cancer, liver disease, thrombosis, and cardiovascular disease."[39] And, of course, all of the children who persist in their transgender identity and take puberty blockers and cross-sex hormones will be infertile. Given what we already know about puberty blocking and how much remains unknown, it isn't surprising that the use of GnRH analogues for puberty suppression in children with gender dysphoria is not FDA-approved. But the off-label prescription of these drugs is legal.

Even if the long-term risks never materialize, the near-term outcome of blocking puberty will be a man or a woman trapped in adolescence, looking like a boy or a girl. Dr. Hruz and his colleagues offer a thought experiment:

Imagine two pairs of biologically and psychologically normal identical twins—a pair of boys and a pair of girls—where one child from each pair undergoes puberty suppression and the other twin does not. Doctors begin administering GnRH analogue treatments for the girl at, say, age 8, and for the boy at age 9. Stopping the gonadal hormone pathway of puberty does not stop time, so the puberty-suppressed twins will continue to age and grow—and because adrenal hormones associated with puberty will not be affected, the twins receiving GnRH analogue will even undergo some of the changes associated with puberty, such as the growth of pubic hair. However, there will be major, obvious differences within each set of twins. The suppressed twins' reproductive organs will not mature: the testicles and penis of the boy undergoing puberty suppression will not mature, and the girl undergoing puberty suppression will not menstruate. The boy undergoing puberty suppression will have less muscle mass and narrower shoulders than his twin, while the breasts of the girl undergoing puberty suppression will not develop. The boy and girl undergoing puberty suppression will not have the same adolescent growth spurts as their twins. So all told, by the time the untreated twins reach maturity, look like adults, and are biologically capable of having children, the twins undergoing puberty suppression will be several inches shorter, will physically look more androgynous and childlike, and will not be biologically capable of having children.[40]

Is it any wonder that children undergoing this treatment feel different from their peers? And is it prudent to allow children and adolescents, like "Tyler" at the beginning of this chapter, to make the choice to expose themselves to these effects?

"Locking In" Transgender Identities

Even if puberty suppression were "reversible" in a physical sense, it sets children on a course with its own momentum, each step reinforcing the trajectory. Blocking puberty runs the risk of reducing the chances of a child coming to terms with his or her biological sex, and thus it increases the likelihood that further transitioning steps will be taken.

The Endocrine Society recommends initiating a schedule of cross-sex hormones at age sixteen, to induce the pubertal development of the desired sex. That is deemed an appropriate age to be making life-changing medical choices, because sixteen-year-olds in many countries are considered "legal adults with regard to medical decision making," and because "most adolescents" at that age "are able to make complex cognitive decisions."[41] Seriously. The Endocrine Society's guidelines don't even address the question of how doctors can depend on the self-diagnosis of preteens who think they should go on puberty blockers. But as we saw in the last chapter, the guidelines themselves say they are based on evidence of "low or very low" quality.[42]

Neuroscientists often tell us that "the adolescent brain is too immature to make reliably rational decisions," Hruz and colleagues observe, yet "we are supposed to expect emotionally troubled adolescents to make decisions about their gender identities and about serious medical treatments at the age of 12 or younger."[43] In their amicus brief for the Supreme Court, they list some consequences of medical choices that adolescents are said to be competent to make for themselves at or before the age of sixteen:

> Puberty suppression hormones prevent the development of secondary sex characteristics, arrest bone growth, decrease bone accretion, prevent full organization and maturation of the brain, and inhibit fertility. Cross-gender hormones increase a child's risk for coronary disease and sterility. Oral estrogen, which is administered to gender dysphoric boys, may cause thrombosis, cardiovascular disease, weight gain, hypertriglyceridemia, elevated blood pressure, decreased glucose tolerance, gallbladder disease, prolactinoma, and breast cancer. Similarly, testosterone administered to gender dysphoric girls may negatively affect their cholesterol; increase their homocysteine levels (a risk factor for heart disease); cause hepatotoxicity and polycythemia (an excess of red blood cells); increase their risk of sleep apnea; cause insulin resistance; and have unknown effects on breast, endometrial and ovarian tissues. Finally, girls may legally obtain a mastectomy at sixteen, which carries with it its own unique set of future problems, especially because it is irreversible.[44]

At age eighteen, the gonads can be removed, and this step can never be reversed. The organs that normally produce the androgens and estrogens crucial for sexual development will no longer exist.

Just a few years ago, the *Washington Post* reported that this kind of treatment for gender dysphoria in children was a novelty, that it was shocking to many people, and that it had little scientific basis. Today there is still virtually no serious scientific evidence to demonstrate that it is beneficial, as Dr. Cretella stresses:

> There is not a single large, randomized, controlled study that documents the alleged benefits and potential harms to gender-dysphoric children from pubertal suppression and decades of cross-sex hormone use. Nor is there a single long-term, large, randomized, controlled study that compares the outcomes of various psychotherapeutic interventions for childhood GD with those of pubertal suppression followed by decades of toxic synthetic steroids. In today's age of "evidence-based medicine," this should give everyone pause.[45]

If science doesn't support this course of treatment for children, why are these "drastic and experimental measures" now being promoted as the norm?

One reason is that it's hard to develop effective treatments for a condition whose causes are not well understood.[46] Some will argue that knowing the cause of a disorder isn't necessary for treating it—that a doctor doesn't need to know how a bone was broken, for example, in order to fix it. But things really aren't that simple. Whether a bone broke from an accident (perhaps because of a balance problem), an assault (perhaps because of an abusive family situation), or a pathology (perhaps osteoporosis) has implications for what treatment will best serve the patient's health in the long term. The same is even more true for mental health. As we gain knowledge of the causes of gender dysphoria, or at least the contributing factors, doctors can tailor their recommendations for each patient accordingly. With a better understanding of how the gender dysphoria arose in the first place, it will be possible to offer better therapies.[47]

Where knowledge is lacking, ideology steps in. The main reason for the wide acceptance of transitioning treatment for children today is politics, Singal remarks:

> It has simply been decided, in some quarters, that firm childhood statements of gender dysphoria are signals of real, meaningful identity, and need to be respected as such. In a sense, this is understandable: For decades trans adults have faced the potent, dehumanizing obstacle of

denialism, of people telling them they aren't *really* who they say they are, that they're actually mentally ill or perverted or whatever else. The problem is that there's solid scientific evidence—not infallible, but solid—to suggest that kids really *are* a different category.[48]

Because of an ideological commitment to the view that adults who identify as transgender should be affirmed in their identity, activists want to treat children the same way, taking their gender dysphoria to be a manifestation of a deep and permanent reality. This is why over forty-five gender clinics popped up in the United States from 2007 to 2017.[49] It's why the United Kingdom saw a 50 percent increase in the number of children referred to gender clinics in just one year, from 2011 to 2012.[50] Transgender activists, school counselors, and the mainstream media tell parents that if they don't put their child on puberty blockers they will be rejecting the truth about their child—thus rejecting *their child*—and will make future transition procedures more difficult. They claim that the child will be more likely to commit suicide—a claim not supported by the data.

It's hard to avoid the sense that an underlying motive for promoting social transition followed by puberty blockers is to "lock in" a transgender identity. But if parents instead choose a therapeutic approach that explores the reasons for the gender dysphoria, there's a great likelihood that the child will come to identify with his or her body, and be spared a lifetime of hormone treatment and all of the physical and psychological turmoil that comes with identifying as transgender. We'll now see what this kind of therapy looks like.

A Better Approach

Earlier we saw that some mental health professionals liken gender dysphoria to other dysphorias, such as anorexia, body dysmorphic disorder, and body integrity identity disorder. All of these involve false assumptions, or feelings that solidify into mistaken beliefs about the self. Dr. McHugh finds that other psychosocial issues usually lie beneath the false assumptions. In children with gender dysphoria, there may be anxieties about "the prospects, expectations, and roles that they sense are attached to their given sex." Much like patients with anorexia nervosa, these children mistakenly believe that a drastic change of their bodies will solve or minimize their psychosocial problems. But adjusting the body through hormones and surgery doesn't fix the real problem any more than liposuction cures anorexia nervosa. An effective treatment strategy would "strive to correct the false, problematic nature of the assumption and to resolve the psychosocial conflicts provoking it," McHugh says.[51]

In the case of gender dysphoria, unfortunately, the mistaken belief is often encouraged by school counselors who, "rather like cult leaders, may encourage these young people to distance themselves from their families and offer advice on rebutting arguments against having transgender surgery." What these young people need is to be removed from this "suggestive environment" and be presented with a different message.[52] The proliferation of gender clinics in America and gender identity programs in the schools makes it less likely that children will get the help they need to work out their issues. Instead, they find "gender counselors" who encourage them to maintain their false assumptions.[53]

This is contrary to standard medical and psychological practice, as McHugh, Hruz, and Mayer emphasize in their amicus brief. Normally, a child is not encouraged to persist in a belief that is discordant with reality. A traditional form of treatment for gender dysphoria would "work with and not against the facts of science and the predictable rhythms of children's psychosexual development." A prudent and natural course of treatment would enable children to "reconcile their subjective gender identity with their objective biological sex," avoiding harmful or irreversible interventions.[54]

That is the approach taken by Dr. Kenneth Zucker, perhaps the world's leading expert on treating discordant gender identity in children. Recall that Zucker ran the Centre for Addiction and Mental Health in Toronto and its Gender Identity Clinic for some thirty years before his politically charged ousting. He thinks that gender dysphoria in adults is frequently best treated by hormones and surgery.[55] But he doesn't think that's the case for children, in view of what he and his colleagues have discovered in their work.

In 2012, Zucker and three colleagues published "A Developmental, Biopsychosocial Model for the Treatment of Children with Gender Identity Disorder" in the *Journal of Homosexuality*. This article presents the results of forty years' worth of clinical experience and study on the treatment of children with gender identity disorder. One of their key findings is that this condition in children is usually not permanent:

> For children who present clinically with the diagnosis of GID, long-term follow-up studies suggest that their gender identity is not necessarily fixed. The majority of children followed longitudinally appear to lose the

diagnosis of GID when seen in late adolescence or young adulthood, and appear to have differentiated a gender identity that matches their natal sex.

The second main finding is that a variety of factors, including "biological factors, psychosocial factors, social cognition, associated psychopathology, and psychodynamic mechanisms," play into the development of gender identity. In this multifactorial model,

> biological factors (e.g., possible genetic factors, prenatal sex hormones, temperament) are conceptualized as possible predisposing factors for the expression of a particular gender identity phenotype. They are not conceptualized as fixed factors leading to invariant gender identity differentiation across developmental time. The other parameters can be conceptualized as predisposing, precipitating or perpetuating factors.[56]

In short, biological factors may be predisposing but they are not determining, while nonbiological factors can contribute in various ways. Zucker examined some of those nonbiological factors in an earlier article: "the role of temperament, parental reinforcement of cross-gender behavior during the sensitive period of gender identity formation, family dynamics, parental psychopathology, peer relationships and the multiple meanings that might underlie the child's fantasy of becoming a member of the opposite sex."[57] We will consider some of those predisposing factors.

Biological Predisposing Factors

Zucker and his colleagues do not think there is scientific evidence to support the proposition that a boy could be trapped in a girl's body, or that a girl's brain could be located in a boy's head. The majority of children at their clinic who were diagnosed with gender identity disorder eventually developed a gender identity concordant with their biological sex.[58] This suggests that biology does not *determine* a gender-discordant identity, though biological factors might predispose someone to it.

For example, one part of our biological constitution is temperament, and one aspect of temperament is "activity level" (AL), or "the propensity for intense physical energy expenditure and the proclivity for rough-and-tumble play." Zucker and colleagues observe that this is "a sex-dimorphic trait, with likely genetic and prenatal hormonal influences."[59] Boys on average are more physically active than girls, but children with a discordant gender identity have inverted activity levels—the boys have lower AL and the girls higher. Zucker hypothesizes that the idiosyncratic activity levels may lead these children over time to identify more closely with the opposite sex.

A boy with a low activity level might find the typical behavior of girls more compatible with his own temperament than that of other boys. He might therefore be inclined to join the girls at playtime, which in turn could make him more interested in the toys and activities that girls tend to prefer. This could have a "feedback effect on the child's gender identity, especially during early development when cognitive reasoning is fairly rigid and black and white."[60] A young boy has a simple understanding of the difference between boys and girls: boys enjoy rough-housing and girls enjoy playing house. His thought process might look like this: "Because I don't enjoy rough-housing, and because most of my friends are girls who also don't enjoy rough-housing, and because I enjoy playing house, as do my friends who are girls, I must be a girl too."

One such boy was Frank, who met the diagnostic criteria for gender identity disorder when he was brought to the clinic at age seven:

> In contrast to his two brothers, Frank was described by his parents as more sensitive and emotional. He had a long history of an avoidance of rough-and-tumble play, complaining that other boys were both mean and aggressive. Indeed, one of his brothers, who had a history of severe disruptive behavior, had often been mean and aggressive towards him. The problematic relationship with his brother appeared to generalize to Frank's view of all boys, as he complained that all boys were mean. He affiliated primarily with girls and, with them, engaged in a variety of stereotypical feminine activities. By age 5, he began to voice the wish to be a girl, stating that if he were a girl, then all of his problems would be solved.

If his sensitive temperament was understood as a predisposing factor in Frank's wish to be a girl, then an appropriate therapy could be designed to help him realize that not all boys are mean and aggressive. Frank could be exposed to other boys with a temperament similar to his own, so he might "develop a more nuanced understanding of gender: that there are different ways to be a boy, that one does not have to be a girl as a fantasy solution to cope with his difficulties with his aggressive brother or the more boisterous boys in the school environment, and so on."[61]

A sensitive temperament—an aspect of biology—might predispose a boy to identify with girls, but the remedy is *not* to tell him that he actually is a girl, dress him as a girl, give him a feminine name, and eventually put him on puberty blockers and cross-sex hormones. Rather, an effective therapy would help him see that it's perfectly normal for a boy to be sensitive.

Social Cognition

Young Frank's activity level was one predisposing factor, and it worked in conjunction with a problem of social cognition: a belief that boys must be rough and boisterous. Young children tend to have simplistic ideas about what is proper and natural for boys and girls to do. Until they are about five or perhaps seven years of age, most children "conflate gender identity with surface expressions of gender behaviors." For this reason, says Zucker, it isn't really unusual for a girl at age four "to express the belief that, if she wore boys' clothes and engaged in boys' activities, then this would mean that she was a boy."[62] His team found that children with a discordant gender identity are typically slower to develop a mature understanding of gender than other children, and this developmental lag can be a predisposing or perpetuating factor in gender dysphoria.

Here are some examples of children who went to Zucker's clinic expressing inflexible ideas of what it means to be a boy or a girl:

> [W]hen asked why he wanted to be a girl, one 7-year-old boy said that it was because he did not like to sweat and only boys sweat. He also commented that he wanted to be a girl because he liked to read and girls read better than boys. An 8-year-old boy commented that "girls are treated better than boys by their parents" and that "the teacher only yells at the boys." His view was that, if he was a girl, then his parents would be nicer to him and that he would get into less trouble at school. One 5-year-old boy talked about having a "girl's brain" because he only liked Barbie dolls. In this particular boy's treatment, he created drawings of his own brain, writing in examples of what made his brain more like a girl's brain and what made his brain more like a boy's brain (e.g., when he developed an interest in Lego). Over time, the drawings of the size of his girl's brain shrunk and the size of his boy's brain expanded.[63]

These are real children who were brought to a clinic because their gender dysphoria was quite pronounced. Had they been brought to a different clinic—like the typical gender clinic today—their parents might have been counseled to initiate a social transition and then put the children on puberty blockers. Thankfully, these children were instead helped to develop a better understanding of what it means, and doesn't mean, to be a boy or a girl, and thus to be more comfortable with who they are.

Co-occurring Psychopathologies

Zucker and his colleagues have found that other psychopathologies can function as predisposing factors for a discordant gender identity. One example is autism spectrum disorder, especially at the high-functioning end.[64] A team of researchers from the UK, in a literature review published in 2016, also saw a considerably higher rate of autism spectrum disorder among children and adolescents with symptoms of gender dysphoria than in the general population.[65]

To show how the two syndromes might be linked, Zucker and colleagues begin by noting that "children with GID generally show intense, if not obsessional, interests, in cross-gender activities." A co-occurring autism spectrum disorder (ASD) could amplify the intensity of those interests. Both GID and ASD involve a "predisposition for obsessional or focused interests and extreme rigidity in thinking," accompanied by "intense anxiety" in response to any interference with the obsession. Parents commonly describe serial obsessions—for example, "with a particular color, with a particular book that must be read over and over in ritualistic fashion, with specific objects, such as washing machines, vacuum cleaners," and so on. Gender can be a focus of obsessional thinking, and this obsession might be essentially a "magnification" of interests that a typical child would have at a similar stage of development.[66]

They illustrate the co-occurrence of GID and ASD with the case of David, age five, who had previously exhibited a variety of obsessional interests. His parents had tried to ignore his fixations, but when he became obsessed with the idea of being a girl, they bought girls' toys for him and let him wear his mother's clothes regularly. At school, when boys and girls lined up separately, he joined the girls' line. Then, while the assessment was in progress, David's mother reported that his obsessiveness had found a new focus: "He now thinks that he is a computer." She considered this a preferable sort of obsession. By the time David was twelve, the symptoms of gender dysphoria had disappeared, though now he was obsessed with heavy metal rock stars and trying to emulate them in appearance.[67]

As he matured, David was able to reflect on the reasons for his former wish to be a girl:

> David discussed his experience of bullying from peers for his gender atypical areas of interest. He speculated that, in many ways, his desire to become a girl may have been an effort to avoid the bullying from peers. David again reiterated the very reinforcing aspects of many of his female-typical interests. Finally, he reflected on his negative feelings about himself and his behavior and we considered his gender dysphoria as an effort to cope with these feelings.[68]

He was still displaying "a tendency towards preoccupations," but the clinicians were providing him with ongoing therapy to help manage them and improve his social skills.

Family Dynamics

Problems in family dynamics can play a role in causing a discordant gender identity, and addressing them can help resolve the identity conflict. One example is the case of Tom, age four, who had displayed "pervasive cross-gender behavior, including the repeated wish to be a girl," for about a year before he came to Zucker's clinic. His discordant gender identity had emerged after the arrival of a baby sister into a home with a narcissistic mom and a largely absent dad.

> Tom's mother was an intense, volatile, and extremely anxious woman, with strong narcissistic personality traits. She viewed Tom as a perfect child, until he began to express the desire to be a girl. She then experienced Tom as less than perfect, which, for her, was a severe narcissistic injury. Tom's father played little role in his day-to-day life, working 18-hour days, 7 days/week.

Tom's little sister had been born shortly before his third birthday, and Zucker's team understood his gender dysphoria in the context of that change in the family:

> He felt abandoned by his mother, who seemed to transfer much of her psychologic investment to the sister. She adorned the baby sister in pink

(in early therapy sessions with Tom, he only used the color pink in his numerous drawings). In part, we conceptualized Tom's GID as the result of feeling an intense psychologic abandonment by his mother and an intense jealous rage towards his sister ("If you could be a girl like Suzie, then mom would pay more attention to you").[69]

Tom's wish to be a girl began as a fantasy solution to the loss of his mother's attention, though it didn't work as he may have expected. He was a boy going through family problems, not a girl trapped in a boy's body. Zucker's clinic helped him work through his gender identity conflict by making him aware of his jealousy toward his sister and of how those feelings affected his family life.

Tom's story is just one of many that illustrate how relationships with parents can influence a child's self-understanding. One of Zucker's students found that about three-quarters of young boys with gender identity disorder had "an insecure attachment relationship to the mother," and unpublished data suggest a similar percentage for girls. Zucker also reports that approximately half of the mothers of boys with GID had two or more diagnoses of a mental disorder, and about one-quarter had at least three such diagnoses.[70]

Abuse suffered by one parent may influence how that parent relates with the child, and what the child learns about gender. One example was a girl named Rose, who came to the clinic at age nine wearing a boyish haircut and clothes. She had "a long history of cross-gender behavior, including the strong desire to be a boy." When she was four years old, Rose found her mother's body at the bottom of a staircase. She had been murdered by her boyfriend. With no biological relatives who could take care of her, Rose was adopted at age six. But the trauma of her mother's death stayed with her, and it fueled her fantasy of being a boy.

During the assessment, Rose commented that she wanted to be a boy because boys were stronger than girls. She told her adoptive mother that when they walked down the street together that her mother need not be afraid, because "I look like a boy and no one will hurt you." Rose acknowledged that she has had the recurring thought that, had she been a boy, then she would have been able to protect her mother from the boyfriend because "boys are stronger than girls."

Zucker and his colleagues viewed Rose's desire to be a boy as a symptom of post-traumatic stress disorder, in combination with "rigid normative social cognitions about gender." On that basis, she had created a fantasy solution to the problem that took her mother's life.[71]

An Effective Therapy Plan

More than four decades of experience in treating children with discordant gender identity is the basis for the course of treatment that Zucker and his colleagues recommend. We have seen some aspects of it already. Here is the general protocol:

a) weekly individual play psychotherapy for the child;
b) weekly parent counseling or psychotherapy;
c) parent-guided interventions in the naturalistic environment; and
d) when required for other psychiatric problems in the child, psychotropic medication.[72]

Play psychotherapy should be "tailored to the child's developmental level and cognitive sophistication."[73] The aim is to understand *why* the child thinks that he or she is the opposite sex, and focus on the likely underlying causes of the dysphoria, whether those be family dynamics, problems in cognitive development, or co-occurring psychopathologies. Zucker has found that cross-gender behavior is often part of a "fantasy solution" to some associated problem, as we saw in the stories of Tom and Rose: the child imagines being "happier or more valued" as a member of the opposite sex. Therapy is designed to explore the underlying issues, including "cognitive gender confusion, rigid gender schemas, idealization of the opposite sex and devaluation of one's own sex, anxiety in relation to same-sex peers, the connections between separation anxiety and gender, representations of the parents, and triggers that fuel the cross-gender behavior."[74]

Therapy sessions give the child an opportunity to talk about gender identity issues, to play them out, "to make sense of their internal representational world," and "to master various developmental tasks" that may be difficult for them.[75] Sometimes a child is forthcoming in therapy, and the process moves forward quickly. One very intelligent girl, age four, had asked her parents to take her to a therapist "because she was confused about why she wanted to be a boy." She was able to discuss her gender feelings easily in therapy. Other children are more reticent. One little boy "was never able to talk about his day-to-day life" in two years of treatment. Instead, he would enact scenarios from his family life. But eventually, as with the girl, his gender dysphoria went into full remission.[76]

Treatment also involves the parents, first by addressing anything they might be doing to cause or perpetuate a discordant gender identity. In one family, a father needed help in dealing with his "rage toward his child." In another family, the mother had been date-raped, and she admitted that she hated men as a consequence, and that she "wanted little to do with" her son. She needed help in developing a healthier relationship with men so that she could be a better mother to her boy.[77]

The second way that parents become involved is in setting appropriate limits on the child's cross-gender behavior. Setting limits is "an effort to alter the GID from the 'outside in,' while individual therapy for the child can explore the factors that have contributed to the GID from the 'inside out.'" If parents do not establish limits, they are essentially tolerating or even reinforcing the discordant gender identity. A therapist can explore why they tolerated or encouraged the child's cross-gender behavior in the first place. For some parents, it's because they believed or were told that the behavior was "only a phase," or that "all children" engage in similar behavior. For others, the reasons are more complex, and it may be necessary to deal with the parents' underlying issues before they will be comfortable in changing their approach to their child's gender dysphoria.[78] Parents might overreact in either direction: by overindulgence of the child's fantasies, or by excessive strictness. Calling a gender-dysphoric girl by male pronouns can be counterproductive, but so can forcing her to wear dresses. Zucker and his colleagues recommend helping parents to strike the right balance, and to recognize that the surface behaviors are symptoms of a deeper problem.[79]

Striking the right balance is also crucial in guiding children toward activities that might help them identify with their biological sex. Parents can encourage gender-typical or neutral activities that would appeal to their children. They can also provide a great benefit by helping their children find same-sex friends who share their particular interests, not just stereotypical boy or girl interests. Parents can arrange "play dates" for their children with same-sex peers of similar temperament, or enroll them in activities where they could meet compatible peers: in drama clubs, gymnastics programs, or team sports, for example. Having compatible same-sex friends can greatly help children to realize that there are "many ways to be a boy or many ways to be a girl," and to be more comfortable in their own bodies.[80]

Let's Not Attack Good Medicine

Transgender activists are fiercely opposed to Dr. Zucker's therapeutic approach for children, as we know, and they got him fired and his Toronto clinic shuttered. But at least he is still legally allowed to practice good medicine in Canada. The same is not true in several U.S. states. As of May 2017, eight states had enacted laws that bar health-care facilities from employing practices aimed at changing the sexual orientation or gender identity of minors, a practice often referred to as "conversion therapy." For instance, a New Mexico bill signed into law in April 2017 defines "conversion therapy" as "any practice or treatment that seeks to change a person's sexual orientation or gender identity, including any effort to change behaviors or gender expressions." The law explicitly permits "counseling or mental health services that provide acceptance, support and understanding of a person without seeking to change gender identity or sexual orientation."[81]

This means that a doctor who helps a young boy socially and hormonally transition into a "girl" does not violate the law, but a doctor who helps a young boy identify with and accept his body might be acting unlawfully. It's an Orwellian abuse of language to say that helping a child be comfortable in his own body is "conversion therapy," but transforming a boy into a "girl" is simply allowing the child to be "her" true self. Of course, the doctors who use the former approach don't think they're doing "conversion" at all, but activists believe it's an effort to suppress the child's "real" gender identity.

Not surprisingly, it's the most liberal states that have passed laws against so-called "conversion therapy": New Jersey, California, Oregon, Illinois, New York, Vermont, New Mexico, and Connecticut.[82] It is unclear, however, if all the states that outlaw "conversion therapy" actually ban *all* therapies intended to help children overcome gender dysphoria without transitioning. The label "conversion therapy" has become associated with certain abhorrent methods of trying to change sexual orientation, and the objections to that discredited approach have tarnished the image of beneficial therapies to help people with same-sex attractions live chastely, or to help people with gender dysphoria come to accept their bodily nature.

Pressure by activists has led some professional associations to issue statements against any practice designed to help individuals embrace reality and accept their bodily selves. For example, the American Psychoanalytic Association declares:

> Psychoanalytic technique does not encompass purposeful attempts to "convert," "repair," change or shift an individual's sexual orientation, gender identity or gender expression. Such directed efforts are against fundamental principles of psychoanalytic treatment and often result in substantial psychological pain by reinforcing damaging internalized attitudes.[83]

The Human Rights Campaign has a website collecting dozens of statements from professional associations condemning "conversion therapy" for LGBT people.[84] HRC asserts that "conversion therapy" consists of "a range of dangerous and discredited practices that falsely claim to change a person's sexual orientation or gender identity or expression," and that these practices "have been rejected by every mainstream medical and mental health organization for decades."[85] But a close reading of the statements posted on the website reveals that the vast majority of those professional associations have not said what HRC and other transgender activists claim. These statements speak of attempts to change *sexual orientation*, but most do not mention therapies directed at *gender identity*. Except, of course, for the statements from transgender activists. In its most recent *Standards of Care*, WPATH (the World Professional Association for Transgender Health) says: "Treatment aimed at trying to change a person's gender identity and expression to become more congruent with sex assigned at birth has been attempted in the past without success.... Such treatment is no longer considered ethical."[86] To back up the claim that therapy of this kind has been unsuccessful, WPATH cites two studies from the 1960s. So much for cutting-edge research.

Apart from the alleged lack of success, what could make that kind of treatment unethical? Zucker quotes one expert who argues that "attempting to change children's gender identity seems as ethically repellant as bleaching black children's skin in order to improve their social life among white children."[87] This, of course, gets the analogy exactly backward. It's the transgender activists who favor the equivalent of skin-bleaching, in the radical effort to "reassign" a person's sex chemically and surgically. In response, Zucker says that "it is as legitimate to want to make youngsters comfortable with their gender identity (to make it correspond to the physical reality of their biological sex) as it is to make youngsters comfortable with their ethnic identity (to make it correspond to the physical reality of the color of their skin)."[88] Just so.

Children need our protection and guidance as they navigate the challenges of growing into adulthood. We need medical professionals who will help them mature in harmony with their bodies, rather than deploy experimental treatments to refashion their bodies. And we need a culture that cultivates a sound understanding of gender and how it is rooted in biology, a culture that respects our differences without imposing restrictive stereotypes. The next chapter examines gender theory and considers how to think about the social relevance of our sexual identity.

CHAPTER SEVEN

Gender and Culture

Part of an effective treatment plan for gender dysphoria in children is to cultivate a mature and nuanced view of gender, so the child understands that there are various ways to be real boys and real girls—that we don't all have to conform to a stereotype. But this does not require adopting the view that gender norms are entirely artificial, mere "social constructs." Indeed, that notion is hard to square with the belief that a boy could have a compelling inner sense of being female, contrary to what society has told him. Then again, transgender ideology doesn't stop at a gender binary; it offers numerous gender options and unlimited gender fluidity. The promotion of transgender identities is just one application of what has been called "gender ideology." Formulating an effective response to this ideology begins with understanding how our culture arrived at a place where our leading social network, Facebook, lists fifty-six gender options for users, and where schoolchildren must locate their "gender identity" along a spectrum.

The deconstruction of gender started with a denial of the biological basis for sex differences, and this is where some seemingly contradictory ideas have a common root. That denial is also the historical link between the transgender movement and radical feminism. While these two movements don't have the same objectives and are sometimes at odds, they have drawn inspiration from each other in problematizing gender and detaching it from biology. To correct the cultural errors that have led to the transgender moment, we need to recover a sound understanding of gender and of why it's important for our society to respect the fundamental differences between male and female.

Getting Gender Right, and Wrong

A couple of recent news items illustrate how our culture has lost clarity on the realities of sex differences. In March 2017, Karen Pence, the wife of the vice president, set off a minor scandal by telling the *Washington Post* that her husband had a policy of not eating dinner alone with other women, or drinking alcohol at public events when his wife wasn't with him.[1] For the next week, Mike Pence was denounced in the media as a misogynist whose social practice rested on a stereotype of women as seducers. His critics claimed that it resulted in holding back female employees in their careers, depriving them of mentorship and opportunities, since all the important business of the nation's capital (they said) happens over dinner and drinks. Thus, Pence was discriminating against women. The prominent liberal website *Vox* ran an article titled "Vice President Pence's 'never dine alone with a woman' rule isn't honorable. It's probably illegal."[2] The article was written by a law professor who teaches employment law.

Mike Pence follows a version of what is known as the Billy Graham Rule, after the evangelist's practice of avoiding situations that might carry temptation or invite suspicion. Regardless of whether any of us would adopt the rule for ourselves, it is entirely reasonable, defensible, and admirable. Pence, like Graham, takes the differences between the sexes seriously, and he strives to protect the goods that those differences make possible—marriage and family life—while avoiding the traps they can create. Pence himself first mentioned this policy to a reporter in 2002, when he was a young congressman representing an Indiana district in Washington, D.C. Sexual scandal had recently been swirling around many powerful men in politics, from President Bill Clinton and Senator Ted Kennedy to Speaker Newt Gingrich. This failing was clearly bipartisan. So it's understandable why some men would follow the Graham Rule, and why some women would want their husbands to do so. Such a rule can help protect husbands from infidelity by creating a barrier to romance and temptation; it can give wives peace of mind; it can guard reputations from media speculation and scandalmongering; and it lets female employees know their boss is committed to keeping work relationships professional and avoiding any confusion about it. This is one way for a culture to recognize and respect sex differences.

After the *Post*'s profile of Karen Pence had sparked a ritual denunciation of the vice president, a former staffer of his, Mary Vought, wrote a defense of him that ran on the *Post*'s website. In response to the charge that he discriminated against women, she wrote: "Pence's personal decision to not dine alone with female staffers was never a hindrance to my ability to do my job well, and never kept me from reaping the rewards of my work. In fact, I excelled at my job because of the work environment created from the top down."[3] After all, one can value the expertise and insights of female staffers without sharing dinner or drinks. And there are many ways to advance in your career that don't involve one-on-one dinners with the boss. (Apparently, Pence has not made a practice of dining one-on-one with male staffers either.) Vought explained that Pence's personal rule on dining and drinking was just one small part of a larger policy of taking marriage and family seriously. For example, he would hurry home after his official duties to share dinner with his wife and children whenever he could. In various ways, "he modeled for male and female staffers alike that it was possible to serve in a public role with excellence while being wholly dedicated to his family." Pence should be commended, said Vought, for his commitment to "work-life balance, the importance of family time, and respect in the workplace: values we can all get behind."[4]

You might think we could all support those values. But you'd be wrong. Some feminists believe that certain choices about marriage, family, and work-life balance should not be tolerated, or even be legal. A week before the Karen Pence profile ran in the *Post*, a columnist for the *Daily Telegraph* wrote an op-ed titled "It should be illegal to be a stay-at-home mum." Sarrah Le Marquand argued that feminism shouldn't be about giving women choices, but rather about making women equal to men, with "equal" understood as acting the same—regardless of what any woman might want. Le Marquand is willing to tolerate moms staying home for the first couple of years in a child's life, but she isn't willing to tolerate that choice when children are old enough to attend school, and she wants her preference to be enforced by law. "Rather than wail about the supposed liberation in a woman's right to choose to shun paid employment," she wrote, "we should make it a legal requirement that all parents of children of school-age or older are gainfully employed."[5]

That might sound a bit extreme, yet decades ago the founder of second-wave feminism, Simone de Beauvoir, proposed the same policy in more unqualified terms: "No woman should be authorized to stay at home to raise her children. Society should be totally different. Women should not have that choice, precisely because if there is such a choice, too many women will make that one."[6] This way of thinking is common in a certain strain of feminism, which holds that freedom isn't sufficient for women's liberation because they might make the "wrong" choices. They might choose to be different from men, and thus remain "unequal." In Le Marquand's view, "Only when the tiresome and completely unfounded claim that 'feminism is about choice' is dead and buried (it's not about choice, it's about equality) will we consign restrictive gender stereotypes to history."[7] Choice leaves women free to perpetuate outdated patriarchal stereotypes, so women should not be permitted that choice: "Only when the female half of the population is expected to hold down a job and earn money to pay the bills in the same way that men are routinely expected to do will we see things change for the better."[8] What Le Marquand views as equality could more accurately be called an enforced *sameness*.

Feminism originally sought to liberate women from a restrictive understanding of gender and free them to be themselves, but it turned into a movement seeking to make women the same as men. Our culture has gone from the error of exaggerated and rigid sex stereotypes, to the opposite error of denying that there are any important differences between the sexes. From that error comes a culture of androgyny and gender confusion. The feminist aim of erasing all differences between men and women might seem contrary to the transgender insistence that the inner sense of a distinctly male or female gender identity cannot be altered by therapy, though beneath it all is a delinking of gender from our biological nature.

Historically, "gender" was primarily a linguistic and grammatical term. But when the word "gender" was used to mean a personal attribute, it was synonymous with a person's sex—until recently. The term has now acquired another meaning, related to sex though distinct from it—and in some people's opinion, separable from it. Here is how the American Psychological Association sets out the difference between "sex" and "gender":

> *Sex* is assigned at birth, refers to one's biological status as either male or female, and is associated primarily with physical attributes such as chromosomes, hormone prevalence, and external and internal anatomy. *Gender* refers to the socially constructed roles, behaviors, activities, and attributes that a given society considers appropriate for boys and men or

girls and women. These influence the ways that people act, interact, and feel about themselves. While aspects of biological sex are similar across different cultures, aspects of gender may differ.[9]

Some activists go further than the APA and argue that gender is merely a social construct. That idea should be rejected, but this doesn't mean we need to jettison the concept of gender altogether. Sex is a bodily, biological reality, and gender is how we give social expression to that reality. Gender properly understood is a social manifestation of human nature, springing forth from biological realities, though shaped by rational and moral choice. Human beings are creatures of nature and of culture, but a healthy culture does not attempt to erase our nature as male or female embodied beings. Instead, it promotes the integrity of persons, in part by cultivating manifestations of sex differences that correspond to biological facts. It supports gender expressions that reveal and communicate the reality of our sexual nature.

Gender is socially shaped, but it is not a mere social construct. It originates in biology, but in turn it directs our bodily nature to higher human goods. A sound understanding of gender clarifies the important differences between the sexes, and guides our distinctly male or female qualities toward our well-being. A misguided concept of gender, on the other hand, conceals, denies, and distorts the realities of our nature and hinders human flourishing.

Feminism and Gender Ideology

Many cultures throughout history have cultivated false ideas about women, underestimating their capabilities, holding them to rigid stereotypes, and limiting their opportunities. The first wave of feminist thinkers contested those untrue stereotypes and unfair limitations. It began in 1792 with *A Vindication of the Rights of Woman*, where Mary Wollstonecraft asserted that the liberal arguments of the day for the natural rights of man should apply equally to woman—that natural rights have no sex. Women are fully rational animals, like men, and thus they should receive a similar education. Almost a century later, John Stuart Mill, in "The Subjection of Women," criticized the way that women were taught to accept a subordinate status: "All women are brought up from the very earliest years in the belief that their ideal of character is the very opposite to that of men; not self will, and government by self-control, but submission, and yielding to the control of other."[10] He argued that women should have the same rights as men and be self-governing like men.

First-wave feminists took aim at a system in which women lost their own legal identity once they were married.[11] Full legal equality and citizenship for women was the goal of these feminists, including Elizabeth Cady Stanton and Susan B. Anthony, who emphasized the similarities between men and women. Another strand of early feminism, highlighting the distinctively feminine attributes of women, was developed by Hannah More, Frances Willard, and Clare Boothe Luce—names largely forgotten today, but more popular and prominent in their own time than the feminists who are now better known.[12]

The first wave of feminism achieved some notable successes, particularly gaining for women the legal right to own property and the right to vote. But natural rights and legal equality were insufficient for second-wave feminists, who disapproved of the ways that some women exercised their rights. These feminists contended that society was conditioning women to internalize their own subjugation. Simone de Beauvoir inaugurated this line of thinking in *The Second Sex* (1949). Recall these memorable lines from the book: "One is not born, but rather becomes, a woman. No biological, psychological, or economic fate determines the figure that the human female presents in society; it is civilization as a whole that produces this creature, intermediate between male and eunuch, which is described as feminine."[13] In other words, society and culture teach girls to think of themselves as the "second sex," defined by their subordination to the first sex.[14] Women are socialized to accept the drudgery of domestic life—childbearing and rearing, cooking and housekeeping—as their lot. According to Kate Millett, a radical follower of Beauvoir's, the "social construction" of gender by the patriarchy is done so inconspicuously that it can pass itself off as simply a matter of nature.[15]

These themes were extended by Betty Friedan, who wrote in *The Feminine Mystique* (1963) that "American women are kept from growing to their full human capacities" as the country keeps producing "millions of young mothers who stop their growth and education short of identity."[16] As a result, the typical woman "has no goal, no purpose, no ambition patterning her days into the future, making her stretch and grow beyond that small score of years in which her body can fill its biological function," and this is "a kind of suicide." Thus, Friedan said, "the feminine mystique has succeeded in burying millions of American women alive."[17]

At the heart of this argument is the idea that the female body, particularly in its capacity for bearing children, is at odds with women's freedom. While other female mammals have the same reproductive role, Beauvoir remarks, the female human is "the most deeply alienated" among them all, "the one that refuses this alienation the most violently; in no other is the subordination of the organism to the reproductive function more imperious nor accepted with greater difficulty." A woman thus rebels against her destiny by "affirming herself as an individual."[18] Beauvoir doesn't consider the possibility that a woman's individuality and her bodily nature might be "in *direct and positive* relation to each other," as Margaret McCarthy puts it. The theory of gender as a "social construct" arises from a deep discomfort with the female body, a sense that a woman's body "opposes her existence as a person," and therefore she must resist her own body.[19] Here again is a modern form of the ancient Gnostic heresy, wherein the real person is the self/mind/will, which must transcend and liberate itself from the body.

Shulamith Firestone took Beauvoir's ideas about the oppressiveness of the female body to their logical (if dystopian) conclusion in *The Dialectic of Sex* (1970). The book uses Marxist terms in calling for a "feminist revolution" by the sexual "underclass," with the aim of eliminating not just "male privilege" but any distinction at all between the sexes. To this end, women need to seize control of reproduction and change it fundamentally, Firestone declares, in a futuristic vision that merits quoting at length:

> [J]ust as to assure elimination of economic classes requires the revolt of the underclass (the proletariat) and... their seizure of the means of *production*, so to assure the elimination of sexual classes requires the revolt of the underclass (women) and the seizure of control of *reproduction*: not only the full restoration to women of ownership of their own bodies, but also their (temporary) seizure of control of human fertility—the new population biology as well as all the social institutions of childbearing and childrearing. And just as the end goal of socialist revolution was not only the elimination of the economic class *privilege* but of the economic class *distinction* itself, so the end goal of feminist revolution must be, unlike that of the first feminist movement, not just the elimination of male *privilege* but of the sex *distinction* itself: genital differences between human beings would no longer matter culturally. (A reversion to an unobstructed *pansexuality*—Freud's "polymorphous perversity"—would

probably supersede hetero/homo/bi-sexuality.) The reproduction of the species by one sex for the benefit of both would be replaced by (at least the option of) artificial reproduction: children would be born to both sexes equally, or independently of either, however one chooses to look at it; the dependence of the child on the mother (and vice versa) would give way to a greatly shortened dependence on a small group of others in general and any remaining inferiority to adults in physical strength would be compensated for culturally. The division of labor would be ended by the elimination of labor altogether (through cybernetics). The tyranny of the biological family would be broken.[20]

Let that sink in for a moment. Firestone calls for bringing an end to "the sex distinction itself," with the help of biotechnology. Sexual differences between human beings "would no longer matter" if we implemented a radically new form of procreation, rightly described as "artificial reproduction," and somehow make children have less need of mothers or of any nurturing by adults. Then, at last, "The tyranny of the biological family would be broken." Beauvoir spoke approvingly of Firestone's book and said its thesis was "correct, because women will not be liberated until they have been liberated from their children and by the same token, until children have also been liberated from their parents."[21] Beauvoir too believed that "the family must be abolished."[22]

Feminists may have been justified in criticizing unfair limitations placed on women because of their capacity to bear children—inferior legal status, restrictive social roles, limited opportunities, and little political power—but then they basically threw the baby out with the bathwater. The average feminist today doesn't generally speak of abolishing the family or envision a future where "artificial reproduction" replaces the natural kind. Instead, feminists focus monomaniacally on abortion. Feminism today boils down simply to abortion, says the conservative lawyer Cleta Mitchell, and this principle is absolute and unqualified: "No limits, no debate, no conversation. No nuances, no caveats, no *tolerance*. Wear your 'pussyhat' and don't ask questions."[23] The hat she referred to is, of course, the suggestive pink knitted cap worn by nearly everyone at the Women's March on Washington, in January 2017, but trans activists faulted it for excluding "women without vaginas."

The feminist and transgender movements aren't always on the same page, but they have taken inspiration from each other. Many second-wave feminists sought evidence in science for the view that sex-based differences in social roles and expectations have no basis in biology, and they believed they found it in research on disorders of sexual development.[24] Specifically, they cited John Money, the psychiatry professor whose work with "intersex" children at Johns Hopkins led him to conclude that our social concept of male and female, or "gender," is entirely separable from biological attributes. Robert Stoller, who founded the Gender Identity Center at the University of California, Los Angeles in 1965, endorsed Money's work as evidence that "gender role is determined by postnatal forces, regardless of the anatomy and physiology of the external genitalia," and that the latter might "contribute to the sense of maleness" (or femaleness) but are not "essential" for it.[25] Money later claimed that transsexuals provide clear evidence that "the gender identity gate is open at birth for a normal child no less than for one born with unfinished sex organs" and that it remains open for at least a year thereafter.[26] Second-wave feminists embraced Money's theory of gender identity because it suggested that our bodies do not pull us toward any fixed norms of femininity or masculinity, and because it eroded male supremacy and traditional roles by "problematizing the biological basis of identity," as Scott Yenor puts it.[27]

For some radical feminists, to say that gender is socially constructed and not naturally linked to the body doesn't go far enough. Thus, Judith Butler maintains that even the body is a "social construct." In her view, a conception of the body as something fixed and indisputable is pernicious because it "successfully buries and masks the genealogy of power relations by which it is constituted."[28] In short, "the body" conceived as something in particular is all about power.

Butler takes issue with sex reassignment therapy, and even surgery for people with disorders of sexual development, since these treatments presuppose a particular bodily form that is correct or optimal. She suggests that "mixed genital attributes might be accepted and loved" instead of being transformed into "a more socially coherent or normative notion of gender," and she notes that opposition to "idealized gender dimorphism" is growing within the transsexual movement.[29] Butler doesn't think there's a gender identity inside of us, waiting to be found. Gender in Butler's view, as McCarthy explains, isn't a noun or an adjective—*man* or *woman, masculine* of *feminine*—but rather "a *verb* that *constructs*."[30]

In a word, Butler thinks of gender as a "performance."[31] The performance of gender can become part of a "struggle to rework the norms by which bodies are experienced," and to "contest forcibly imposed ideals of what bodies ought to be like."[32] Transgender activists may be participants in this "struggle," but it isn't only about transgender identities; it's about what is to be considered reality for all of us. The deep political importance of the transgender movement for Butler lies in its challenge to the concepts of "normative human morphology" that "give differential 'reality' to different kinds of humans," and its role in altering "what norms govern the appearance of 'real' humanness."[33] Individuals who are "drag, butch, femme, transgender, transsexual," Butler argues, "make us not only question what is real, and what 'must' be, but they also show us how the norms that govern contemporary notions of reality can be questioned and how new modes of reality can become instituted." For this process to happen, the body must be understood not as "a static and accomplished fact," but instead as "a mode of becoming" that "reworks the norm, and makes us see how realities to which we thought we were confined are not written in stone."[34]

Following the trajectory of radical feminist ideology and thinking about the human body, one might see how we arrived at the concept of gender fluidity and dozens of gender options from which children are obliged to choose. Gender has come to be regarded as something of one's own making, a domain of the "disembodied will," which "chooses" an "identity" without needing to justify the choice. In McCarthy's words, gender ideology is founded on "a view of the body as a problematic limit to freedom—freedom conceived as pure self-initiating self-determination."[35] And that is a problematic understanding of the body and of freedom.

Our Bodies, Our Selves

Is a human being essentially a will that can freely remake the body into whatever it chooses? Is the self fundamentally separable from the body? We do not generally live as though our body were nothing in particular, or as though we could separate our *self* from it. We attend to its needs for water, nourishment, rest, and so on. We may try to improve it, but can we willfully change what it fundamentally is? Can we treat certain bodily characteristics, particularly our bodily sex, as irrelevant to who we are, how we live, and how we structure our society? The evidence says it isn't so easy.

We know that science has revealed a wide range of sex-based biological differences, including brain structure and function, body size and shape, and susceptibility to physical and psychological disease. We have seen how sex-based differences in behavior and preferences are apparent virtually from the moment of birth: that one-day-old girls direct their attention more to faces, and one-day-old boys to mechanical objects. In early childhood play, boys tend to favor balls while girls favor dolls, for the most part, and behavioral differences can be seen through adolescence into adulthood. Of course there is individual variation: some girls think that boys have cooler toys, while some boys are drawn more to creative arts than to rough sports. But a general pattern of sex-based differences shows up consistently in academic research. It is simply natural.

Some feminists have pressured schools and toy companies to counteract these demonstrated preferences, on the grounds that children have been "socialized" into them, and in the belief that gender-neutral toys and activities might undo or prevent this effect. One kindergarten teacher decided to forbid boys from using Legos in their free-play time because she was displeased to see girls playing with dolls or crayons while the boys rushed to the blocks and began building things. One way or another, she was determined to get the girls building with Legos, even if it meant denying that opportunity to the boys.[36] One toy company produced a catalogue showing "little boys playing with a Barbie Dream House and girls with guns and gory action figures." These efforts at social engineering inevitably fail, for even when boys and girls are given the same toys, they are likely to use them in different ways. The Hasbro toy company tried to produce a gender-neutral playhouse, and found that girls were likely to dress the dolls and kiss them, and generally "play house." By contrast, the boys would take the tiny baby carriage and catapult it from the roof of the house. Noticing this pattern, a Hasbro manager came to a startling conclusion: "Boys and girls are different."[37]

As Christina Hoff Sommers puts it, "boys and girls, on average, do not have identical interests, propensities, or needs." Academic research consistently shows sex-based differences in children's play, across cultures and even across species:

> The female preference for nurturing play and the male propensity for rough-and-tumble hold cross-culturally and even cross-species. Among our close relatives such as vervet and rhesus monkeys, researchers have found that females play with dolls far more than their brothers, who prefer balls and toy cars. It seems unlikely that the monkeys were indoctrinated by stereotypes in a Top-Toy catalog.[38]

The Lego company, recognizing that boys and girls are different, sought to capitalize on this fact by creating new sets of Legos that would be especially appealing to girls. Known as "Lego Friends," these sets increased Lego's customer base by 25 percent.[39] Jonathan Last described the Lego Disney Castle as "a Death Star for girls," and as "a big, 4,080-piece step toward gender equality."[40] Lego sets had always been created on the assumption that typical male interests and preferences are the norm, and the new sets corrected that mistake.

We should be comfortable acknowledging that it's natural for boys and girls, on average and for the most part, to have different preferences in toys and games. This is a sound understanding of gender, but the qualifier "on average and for the most part" is important. If a particular boy tends to be more interested in stereotypically girl toys, we shouldn't jump to the false conclusion that he must be a girl trapped in a girl's body—or vice versa. We need to avoid the extremes of forced androgyny on the one hand, and inflexible stereotypes on the other. In play and in other respects, we need to allow boys and girls to express their sex-based differences *and* their individuality.

A sound theory of gender would likewise accommodate the demonstrated differences between men and women in "work-life" preferences. As a descriptive matter, men and women tend to prefer different ways of arranging their lives professionally and domestically. A study published in the *Journal of Personality and Social Psychology* in 2008 looked at data from fifty-five countries and found that across the world, "women tend to be more nurturing, risk averse and emotionally expressive, while men are usually more competitive, risk taking, and emotionally flat," as Hoff Sommers reports the findings. But what may be especially surprising is that these differences are most pronounced in "the more prosperous, egalitarian, and educated societies."[41] That's right: the most developed countries show the greatest gender differences in various measures of personality and disposition. The explanation is unlikely to be patriarchy and male power, then. Rather, it appears that "prosperity and equality bring greater opportunities for self-actualization," Hoff Sommers concludes. "Wealth, freedom, and education empower men and women to be who they are."[42]

Today there are more women than men earning doctoral degrees, particularly in the humanities and social sciences, and even in biology and health sciences.[43] Some feminists complain that women still earn fewer doctoral degrees in hard sciences like physics and math, and they regard it as a sign either of overt discrimination or of internalized cultural stereotypes. But Hoff Sommers suggests that the real reason is most likely that women have the opportunity to pursue careers in the fields they find most interesting.[44] We should be comfortable with their freedom to make those choices.

The difference in men's and women's preferences is especially marked in what is now called "work-life balance." According to a recent Pew study, more than three-quarters of married moms would rather *not* work full-time (preferring part-time work or full-time homemaking), while more than three-quarters of married dads prefer to work full-time. W. Bradford Wilcox refers to this pattern as the "neo-traditional" family model: Fathers do considerably more child care and housework than they did in the 1950s, and most married moms today have paying jobs. But most husbands still do the larger share of the breadwinning, and wives generally do more of the childrearing. American men and women prefer neither a strict alikeness in domestic and breadwinning responsibilities, nor a "1950s-style 'Leave It to Beaver' model of family life."[45] And it appears that young Millennials in particular favor something in between, viewing ideal family arrangements in a more traditional way than did the Generation Xers or the baby boomers.[46]

Wilcox and Samuel Sturgeon suggest that differences in how men and women choose to strike a work-life balance reflect young women's realization that they have equal opportunity and they have choices. Many young women—and young men—are now adopting a "choice feminism," accepting the idea that mothers can stay at home or hold part-time jobs as long as it's their own decision. These young adults "support an ethic of equal opportunity for women in the public sphere, even as they embrace an ethic of gender specialization in the private sphere."[47] Rather than decry these preferences— or outlawing stay-at-home moms—we should honor them, and respect the choices that women make for their own lives. Hoff Sommers remarks that "American women today are as independent-minded and self-determining as any in history." Thus it is "condescending to suggest that they have been manipulated when they choose home and family over high-octane careers."[48] *Vive la différence.*

Gender and Human Flourishing

The previous section was largely descriptive, reporting on the preferences that boys and girls, men and women, tend to show. What follows is prescriptive:

How *should* we order our society in view of demonstrated sex differences? A healthy culture will recognize and try to accommodate our complementary ways of being equally human. It will strive to arrange our social life in a way that respects both male and female preferences and allows both men and women to flourish according to their nature.

A basic principle of sound ethical reflection is that there is *natural* goodness for natural kinds, not merely conventional or willfully created "goodness."[49] If we have houseplants, we therefore provide them with proper soil and the levels of sunlight and water suitable to their nature. We cannot willfully make them flourish in darkness or drought. If we have a pet dog and we understand its nature, we provide it with physical nourishment and exercise, along with games of fetch and belly-rubs, and all the things we know are beneficial for a dog. We do not arbitrarily choose what shall be good for our houseplants or our pets, but acknowledge that there is a *natural* goodness for their kind.

The same is true for human lives. A human being has a particular nature set by the human form. We have an integrated rational animal nature, a personal bodily nature. Certain things are good for our nature, and other things are not. Human persons are naturally directed toward certain ends, in order to fulfill the type of creature they are. Some activities contribute to our well-being and perfect our nature, while others detract from our flourishing and defile our given nature.[50] A healthy culture builds upon a sound understanding of what human nature is and what human flourishing requires.

Human culture grows out of the basic truths of our nature as embodied beings, male and female. Because these truths are universal and inescapable, every society has some understanding of gender that arises from our nature and then, in turn, influences our behavior and gives structure to social relations. Gendered social structures are universal because they are inextricably tied to our nature, as J. Richard Udry explains:

> Humans form their social structures around gender because males and females have different and biologically influenced behavioral predispositions. Gendered social structure is a universal accommodation to this biological fact. Societies demonstrate wide latitude in this accommodation—they can accentuate gender, minimize it, or leave it alone. If they ignore it, it doesn't go away. If they depart too far from the underlying sex-dimorphism of biological predispositions, they will generate social

malaise and social pressures to drift back toward closer alignment with biology. A social engineering program to de-gender society would require a Maoist approach: continuous renewal of revolutionary resolve and a tolerance for conflict.[51]

In short, a society cannot attempt to erase sex differences without serious consequences. Building a society on a sound understanding of gender is simply good for our nature.

Engendered and Engendering Bonds

The deepest way in which our sexual embodiment shapes our society and our personal relationships is in our capacity to be husbands and wives, mothers and fathers. This capacity lies at the very heart of the concept of gender, as the word's etymology makes clear. The root of the word "gender" is *gen*, which also gives us *generate*, meaning "to produce" or "to beget," and its noun form, *generation*, referring to offspring or kin.[52] Sister Mary Prudence Allen tells us that this concept of *gen* "was commonly used in both philosophy in Athens and theology in Jerusalem" for over a millennium. Tracing the continuation of the concept in the English language, she finds these related words in *The Oxford Dictionary of English Etymology*:

> gender, genealogy, generate, generous (nobly born), genesis, genetic, gene, genial (nuptial, productive, joyous), genital (external generative organs), genitive (grammatical possessor or source), genius (innate capacity, person possession prevalent disposition of spirit), genocide, gens, gentleman, gentlewoman, genuine, and the suffix, -geny (e.g. progeny).

This etymology, she concludes, gives us one kind of evidence that "the radical separation of the concept and word 'sex' from the concept and word 'gender' suggested by some 20th century authors is artificial indeed."[53]

Our sexed nature has profound implications for how we should structure the formation of young people to prepare them for marriage and family life, and how husbands and wives interact with each other and with their children as moms and dads. It also has implications for how we form same-sex and opposite-sex friendships. Again, a sound theory and expression of gender will reveal relevant sex differences and channel them to human goods, not conceal or distort them.

Margaret McCarthy highlights three derivations from the root *gen*, saying that we should understand ourselves as "engendered, gendered, and generous." First, as engendered beings, we are "brought into existence through the sexual process, through *generation*."[54] This gives us an immediate relationship to a mother and father and to a family. Second, as gendered beings, we are embodied in a sexual way, as male and female, standing in relation to one another as potential husband and wife. Third, we are to be generous, "in the *generosity* of the act specific to the sexes."[55] Our legal and philosophical traditions have long called this the *generative* act.[56] When engaged in as a free and loving expression of spousal commitment, the generative act is also the *marital* act—and it can make husband and wife into father and mother. Our embodiment as male or female situates us within society and sets us on a certain trajectory:

> [T]o have a sexual body is to find ourselves already in relations we do not simply choose and, even more, in relations that define us—constitutive relations. To have a sexual body places us before three such relations. Being sexual, we are born and as such are children, sons and daughters, owing our existence to others, being, effectively an "inheritance." Then, being sexual, we are already poised toward the opposite sex. To say "male" or "female" is already to have the other in view. Finally, being sexual, we are potentially mothers or fathers. All of this, then, situates our freedom, and dramatically so, whether we like it or not.[57]

McCarthy's three-fold series of gender relations entails that boys should understand themselves as sons and potential husbands and fathers, girls as daughters and potential wives and mothers. This understanding should shape how we relate to each other. The prescriptive sense of gender tells us how we *ought* to approach marriage, family life, and friendship. We are volitional agents when it comes to our gender, which deeply influences how we prepare for marriage, how we interact with nonmarital friends, and how we relate to our children as mothers and fathers, but it doesn't all come automatically. We need to be nurtured and educated in a right understanding of gender, a right way of understanding and perfecting our nature. This process of nurture is not a mere "social construct" or an "alien imposition," as McCarthy comments, but something that "belongs to human nature. It is what human nature demands."[58]

A "social construction" is not by definition at odds with nature, for it emerges from our nature and serves human needs. Our nature requires a sound social construction, including a social concept of gender that reveals our sex differences and highlights their potential for marriage and children. We have seen that biological sex is a coherent concept only in relation to the organizational capacity for sexual intercourse and procreation, and thus a sound understanding of gender would promote our "orientation towards the one form of the marital good (husband or wife), and one form of parenting (father or mother), that one's sex makes possible," writes the philosopher Chris Tollefsen. Communicating these truths about our embodied nature is crucial "because of the massive significance of the good of marriage and family for personal and social well-being."[59]

Amy Kass, as a professor at the University of Chicago, found that young people didn't understand what marriage is or why it matters, and they had no idea how to get or stay married. When she asked her students what would be the most important decision they'd ever make in life, nearly all of them gave answers that touched on career preparation. But one student answered differently: "Deciding who should be the mother of my children." The other students attacked him—the men for his willingness to put family above career, and the women for his judging a potential wife on her suitability for motherhood. Kass, on the other hand, thought his answer "revealed an admirable seriousness about life and the life cycle," an awareness of "the supreme importance of finding the right person with whom they might make a life, both for themselves and for those who would replace them."[60]

A healthy culture fosters an atmosphere in which boys and girls come to understand themselves, in significant part, in terms of their potential to be husbands and wives, fathers and mothers. This means replacing the hookup culture with a revived marriage culture. It means cultivating modesty and self-respect in girls as they grow to womanhood, and it means teaching boys to respect women and to discipline their impulses.

Cultivating Boys and Girls

The way we educate boys and girls must begin with the awareness that our social concept of gender grows out of nature and cannot be understood apart from it. Anthony Esolen observes that the very concept of "masculinity" is rooted in physical nature, and therefore our social norms of masculinity need to work *with* nature:

There is no human masculinity out there, free-floating in the space of ideals; it is always grounded upon the physical and psychological basis of the human male. Nor is there a physical human maleness that is not already oriented towards its social flourishing and fulfillment.... When a man is a man, he is not simply playing a role. He is fulfilling his being.

When we raise boys and girls, we raise them at once in accord with the sexual nature they possess already and with the flourishing of that nature that we hope to see as they become husbands and wives, fathers and mothers. We must always have that aim in mind. The boyishness of the boy is to come to flowering in manhood and fatherhood. The girlishness of the girl is to come to flowering in womanhood and motherhood. That is what the sexes are for. We want no longer to deny reality. We want to work in harmony with it.[61]

The way to guide a boy into manhood is not the same as the way to lead a girl into womanhood. Boys and girls on average have differences in brain structure and functioning, in interests and proclivities. They have different trajectories as they flower into adulthood, and the sexual dynamics between males and females influence how they interact. For these reasons, it is valuable to set aside some time for single-sex education and activities, in order to help boys and girls mature into men and women without the complications of opposite-sex dynamics. This was one reason for the founding of the Boy Scouts and Girl Scouts, as well as fraternities and sororities.

The careful formation of boys is especially crucial when our culture seems to be having a crisis of manhood, Esolen says. "A girl grows into womanhood more naturally than a boy grows into manhood, because the potential for motherhood is expressed so obviously in the form of her body," while a boy "must be *made into* a man." A boy's "physical, psychological, and intellectual development is more protracted" than a girl's.[62] Yet the organizations that once existed to help boys navigate this development into manhood have all disappeared or been radically transformed by an ethos of androgyny. There is no longer a Young Men's Christian Association or a Boys' Club of America. The Boy Scouts of America still exist, but they "do not believe there is such a thing as *boyhood* that is to become *manhood*. They do not know what boys *are,* or they pretend they do not. They might then be called the Physically Immature Male Scouts of America."[63] Esolen wrote those lines before the Boy Scouts announced that they would now be open to girls.[64]

The main reason that boys need activities and organizations of their own, Esolen explains, is because boys act differently when girls are around:

> Boys sense that they cannot be themselves in the company of girls. More particularly, they do not form close friendships with one another in the company of girls. Boys who are shy or unathletic or slower to develop are hurt the most by the prohibition against this feature of normal boyhood, because the early grower, the tall boy, the athlete, will be admired no matter what; everyone else will be scorned or ignored. But when boys *are* alone, they work out a kind of natural hierarchy that gives everyone a place, and they establish *rules* that transcend them all and that unite them.[65]

Contrary to what girls might imagine, boys are less aggressive among themselves when girls are not present, and even their fighting is more restrained. But things change in mixed company:

> When the girls are around, then they have to show off, they grow nervous and suspicious of one another, and they will try to win points with the girls by displays of dominance over their weaker fellows, a dominance that is accompanied not by grace, or by honoring the courage of a boy who lacks the stature and strength to win a fight, but by contempt and dismissal.[66]

Boys need opportunities to learn how to temper their own aggression and rivalry, even as they learn how to interact with girls, too. Giving boys and girls what they need to blossom into men and women requires knowing when co-education is appropriate and when single-sex education is best. Single-sex sports teams, clubs, and friendships provide valuable opportunities for boys and girls to develop. We need to avoid the androgyny mistake, pretending that boys and girls are the same, and the opposite mistake of thinking they are so different that they must always be educated separately.

Can't We Just Be Friends?

Adults need to acknowledge that their own interactions with the opposite sex are likely to be different from those with the same sex. This doesn't mean that men and women *can't* be friends—Harry in *When Harry Met Sally* got it wrong—but that these friendships are likely to be different from same-sex friendships. Men generally share interests with other men that can form the basis of friendships among themselves, and it's likewise for women. Trying to eliminate male-only associations and activities in a misguided spirit of egalitarianism can be damaging to men, and to the women they care about.

Men and women need both same-sex and opposite-sex friendships, but they need to approach them in different ways, for the latter bring complications that the former do not. C. S. Lewis noted how easily and naturally a male-female friendship may pass into erotic love.[67] He also wrote about the misunderstandings that arise from differing assumptions, since "what is offered as Friendship on one side may be mistaken for Eros on the other, with painful and embarrassing results. Or what begins as Friendship in both may become also Eros."[68]

Several years ago, *Scientific American* reported on an academic study that provided evidence of differing assumptions and a pattern of misunderstanding in male-female "platonic" friendship. Using real-life pairs of friends, the study found large differences in how the men and the women experienced the friendship:

Men were much more attracted to their female friends than vice versa. Men were also more likely than women to think that their opposite-sex friends were attracted to them—a clearly misguided belief. In fact, men's estimates of how attractive they were to their female friends had virtually nothing to do with how these women actually felt, and almost everything to do with how the men themselves felt—basically, males assumed that any romantic attraction they experienced was mutual, and were blind to the actual level of romantic interest felt by their female friends. Women, too, were blind to the mindset of their opposite-sex friends; because females generally were not attracted to their male friends, they assumed that this lack of attraction was mutual. As a result, men consistently *overestimated* the level of attraction felt by their female friends and women consistently *underestimated* the level of attraction felt by their male friends.

Men, it appears, find it difficult to be "just friends" with women, for they "seem to see myriad opportunities for romance in their supposedly platonic opposite-sex friendships." According to this study, "we may think we're capable of being 'just friends' with members of the opposite sex, but the opportunity (or perceived opportunity) for 'romance' is often lurking just around the corner, waiting to pounce at the most inopportune moment."[69]

This reality is the main reason why Billy Graham established for himself the "rule" that Mike Pence too finds prudent. The underlying principle has even been endorsed by Ta-Nehisi Coates, the progressive best known for his writing on race and his call for reparations.[70] Coates recognizes that setting up guardrails around our natural impulses is not a partisan issue:

> I've been with my spouse for almost 15 years. In those years, I've never been with anyone but the mother of my son. But that's not because I am an especially good and true person. In fact, I am wholly in possession of an unimaginably filthy and mongrel mind. But I am also a dude who believes in guard-rails, as a buddy of mine once put it. I don't believe in getting "in the moment" and then exercising will-power. I believe in avoiding "the moment." I believe in being absolutely clear with myself about why I am having a second drink, and why I am not; why I am going to a party, and why I am not. I believe that the battle is lost at Happy Hour, not at the hotel. I am not a "good man." But I am prepared to be an honorable one.[71]

The kind of guardrails that Coates describes are part of a sound culture designed to govern human nature. How we structure our own guardrails may vary, but the need for them is unquestionable.

Mothering and Fathering

Guardrails are one way to promote a happy marriage, which most of us say we want. Indeed, the most important consequence of the distinctly male and female forms of embodiment is the possibility for the one-flesh union known as marriage.[72] The fruit of marriage is procreation and childrearing, to which mothers and fathers contribute differently, and not out of mere preference. We have seen that mothers and fathers typically *do* make different choices with respect to childrearing, and because of their distinct bodily natures and capacities they ordinarily *should* make different choices.

There is no such thing as generic "parenting." There is mothering, and there is fathering, and children do best with both. While many mothers and many fathers have raised children alone out of necessity, and have done so successfully, it remains true that mothers and fathers bring different strengths to the task. A variety of parenting skills "tend to be distributed in sex-specific ways," as W. Bradford Wilcox found in reviewing the research in psychology, sociology, and biology. This research shows that "men and women bring different gifts to the parenting enterprise" and that "children benefit from having parents with distinct parenting styles." This is one reason why family breakdown is so harmful to children and society.[73] Mothers and fathers are not interchangeable, and it bears emphasizing that mothers cannot replace fathers. "The burden of social science evidence supports the idea that gender-differentiated parenting is important for human development and that the contribution of fathers to childrearing is unique and irreplaceable," writes David Popenoe.[74] Men and women are "different to the core, and each is necessary—culturally and biologically—for the optimal development of a human being."[75]

These differences are not the result of gender stereotypes. They are a matter of what comes naturally to moms and dads. Mothers have a greater understanding of infants and children, and a special ability to nurture and comfort children. Fathers do especially well in the areas of "discipline, play, and challenging their children to embrace life's challenges," as Wilcox puts it.[76] The concerns of fathers are directed more toward the child's "long-term development," while mothers concern themselves more with the child's "immediate well-being," Popenoe observes. Fathers are typically firm in discipline, while mothers tend to be more responsive. The "flexibility and sympathy" of mothers is valuable for children's healthy development, but so is the "predictability and consistency" provided by fathers.[77] Both sons and daughters benefit from the distinct and complementary attention of a mother and a father.

With sons, it is fathers who tend to engage in rough-and-tumble play, which has the benefit of channeling masculine energy while teaching the proper limits of aggression: headlocks, okay, but no biting, pulling hair, or gouging eyes. Boys learn self-control "from playing with and being disciplined by a loving father," and also by watching their father "handling frustration, conflict, and difficulty without resorting to violence," Wilcox says. Boys who lack this kind of discipline and example will be more inclined to display "compensatory masculinity," seeking always to "prove their masculinity by engaging in domineering and violent behavior." This explains the strong statistical correlation between fatherlessness and crime. One study, for example, found that "boys raised outside of an intact nuclear family were more than twice as likely as other boys to end up in prison, even controlling for a range of social and economic factors." Another found that "70 percent of juveniles in state reform schools, 72 percent of adolescent murderers, and 60 percent of rapists grew up in fatherless homes."[78] When there are no fathers around to guide boys into manhood, the social costs are high.

Fathers also make distinct contributions to the development of daughters. Because they were once boys themselves, fathers know what the wrong sort of boy might want from their daughter, so they are more likely to police her dating, and naturally better equipped to scare away bad boyfriends. A father who loves and respects his wife can model for his daughter how a man is supposed to treat a woman. A father who is "affectionate and firm" with his daughter plays a crucial role in her development into womanhood, as Wilcox explains:

> The affection that fathers bestow on their daughters makes those daughters less likely to seek attention from young men and to get involved sexually with members of the opposite sex. Fathers also protect their daughters from premarital sexual activity by setting clear disciplinary limits for their daughters, monitoring their whereabouts, and by signaling to young men that sexual activity will not be tolerated.

Even on a biological level, Wilcox adds, a father's presence affects his daughter, as the pheromones released from his body slow down her sexual development. That makes her less likely to experience early puberty and less likely to be sexually active before marriage. The rate of teenage pregnancy is far lower among girls who have had a father at home throughout their childhood and adolescence than among those whose father has left the home sometime before they turn eighteen, and this effect is greater the longer a father sticks around.[79]

The best sociological evidence available, controlling for other factors including poverty and even genetics, indicates that both boys and girls fare best on virtually every indicator examined—educational achievement, emotional health, familial and sexual development, and delinquency—when they are raised by their wedded biological parents.[80]

Marriage and "Work-Life Balance"

A sound understanding of gender requires spouses to take seriously their embodiment and their distinct parenting gifts as they negotiate "work-life balance." Only a mother can carry a child in her womb for nine months. Only a mother can breastfeed. Mothers are uniquely positioned to care for infants. Husbands are well suited to provide support and protection to their wives during pregnancy, labor, and recovery. This suggests that it's a natural choice—not the only legitimate choice, but one that often fits the needs of young families—for a father to focus his efforts on paid labor outside the home, while a mother focuses her energy, at least for a time, on unpaid labor inside the home.

Unfortunately, our culture doesn't value the choice of a mother to devote herself for a time to childcare and homemaking. As Anthony Esolen writes, "the phrase 'stay-at-home mom' is patronizing and faintly derogatory, like 'stick-in-the-mud mom' or 'sit-in-the-corner mom.'"[81] Two decades ago, Christopher Lasch noticed this hostility toward mothers who make homes, observing that feminists recognized only one choice for families: both husband and wife must work full-time in the marketplace. This model was seen as an inevitable result of social development, making old ways obsolete. "The two-career family represents 'progress,' and laggards have to fall in line," according to this view.[82] Around the same time, Leon Kass remarked that modern women were "compelled to regard private life, and especially marriage, homemaking, and family, as lesser goods, to be pursued only by those lesser women who can aspire no higher than 'baking cookies.'"[83] (He was referring to Hillary Clinton's notorious comment that she wasn't the sort of woman who would have "stayed home and baked cookies and had teas.")

The two-career family model rests on the belief that mothers and fathers and day-care workers are all functionally interchangeable—that caring for babies and young children can be done just as well by any adult. Another underlying belief is a form of patriarchal androgyny that defines "work"— valuable work—by typically male norms, discounting the work that is more distinctively female. "Naturally, women have always worked and always will," Margaret McCarthy points out. The question is "whether or not the work specific to them counts for work," and what relation it has to other kinds of work they might do.[84]

G. K. Chesterton praised the vocation of mother and homemaker as *greater* than paid employment in the modern marketplace, noting especially the broad range of responsibilities it involves. In her own domain, a homemaker is like the Queen, "deciding sales, banquets, labors and holidays";

she is like Whiteley, the great retailer, "providing toys, boots, sheets, cakes and books"; she is like Aristotle, "teaching morals, manners, theology, and hygiene." Chesterton remarked:

> I can understand how this might exhaust the mind, but I cannot imagine how it could narrow it. How can it be a large career to tell other people's children about the Rule of Three, and a small career to tell one's own children about the universe? How can it be broad to be the same thing to everyone, and narrow to be everything to someone? No. A woman's function is laborious, but because it is gigantic, not because it is minute.[85]

Today, Esolen echoes Chesterton, saying that our culture has gotten this backward. If a woman works full-time in the modern economy, specializing in one task—perhaps cooking, arranging flowers, or performing music—then society praises her. But if she "*can do all these things* and in fact does them for the people she loves and for those whom she welcomes into her home (and she is not afraid of guests, because her home is always just a whisk or two away from hospitality), we shake our heads and say that she has wasted her talents." On the contrary, Esolen says, she has put her talents to use. Instead of "preferring the specialist who amputates and cauterizes and does one thing well, for herself primarily and sometimes even at the expense of the family," we must renew our respect for "the woman of many talents and many tasks in the home."[86] Like Chesterton, we must acknowledge that the dignity of work does not depend on pay, and that the work done inside the home is just as important as the work done outside of it, and perhaps more so.[87]

At the same time, we should recognize that modernity has diminished the range of activities done in the typical home. What we think of as the "traditional family" was an entirely novel creation of the Industrial Revolution, with its specialization of the workforce and the shifting of manufacture from cottage industries into large factories. In 1938, Dorothy Sayers, the famous Dante translator and novelist, described how "women's work" used to be understood, and how industrialization took many "pleasant and profitable activities" away from women:

> It is a formidable list of jobs: the whole of the spinning industry, the whole of the dyeing industry, the whole of the weaving industry. The whole catering industry and—which would not please Lady Astor,

perhaps—the whole of the nation's brewing and distilling. All the preserving, pickling and bottling industry, all the bacon-curing. And (since in those days a man was often absent from home for months together on war or business) a very large share in the management of landed estates. Here are the women's jobs—and what has become of them? They are all being handled by men. It is all very well to say that woman's place is the home—but modern civilisation has taken all these pleasant and profitable activities out of the home, where the women looked after them, and handed them over to big industry, to be directed and organised by men at the head of large factories. Even the dairy-maid in her simple bonnet has gone, to be replaced by a male mechanic in charge of a mechanical milking plant.

Because of industrialization, "women's work" became more narrowly defined, so that "the home contains much less of interesting activity than it used to contain." Sayers chided those who would fault women for seeking to regain more interesting kinds of work: "It is perfectly idiotic to take away women's traditional occupations and then complain because she looks for new ones. Every woman is a human being—one cannot repeat that too often—and a human being *must* have occupation."[88]

When Betty Friedan wrote in 1963 that domestic life was burying women alive, she was referring to the *modern* form of homemaking and motherhood, with its relatively constricted domain, which denied women opportunities to flourish in meaningful work. Even the physical dwelling itself had shrunk, lacking enough land for growing food or space for the old activities of preserving it, to say nothing of room for a cottage industry. The suburban home, distant from the old hubs of community life, had become a "comfortable concentration camp," filled with ennui, loneliness, and "nameless dissatisfaction."[89]

McCarthy lists other things that are missing from the average home in the twenty-first century, a lonely place with "nobody home" and very little happening:

There is no nursing a baby (in the well-appointed nursery), no taking walks to the park, no witnessing first steps (which happen at the "wrong time"), no informal neighborhood clubs after school, no gathering of teenage friends under watchful eyes, no real cooking (in the gourmet kitchen), no dinners with friends (in the non-existent dining rooms), no neighborly charity for sick friends or new mothers. In short there is no time together.[90]

One remedy is to repopulate the home with meaningful activities, perhaps reviving some of the work that used to be done there. We can encourage the flowering of new home businesses, facilitated by technology. We should also respect a woman's choice to devote herself fully to homemaking and childrearing, even while recognizing that those women who seek other kinds of work aren't simply rebelling against the way things have always been.

Another remedy is to find better ways to balance and harmonize the work done inside and outside the home. Even the phrase "work-life balance" suggests that something is out of order. "Work is not something you are supposed to balance against the claims of your family," Esolen remarks.[91] Work is best done in the service of our families. "We live in comforts that the richest of aristocrats not very long ago could never have dreamed of, and yet we claim that we are too poor to have more than a child or two. The truth is the reverse: we are too rich to have more than a child or two, too committed to work for work's sake and to the purchase of prestige."[92] One imperative, then, is to reorder our loves, to get our priorities straight.

This resetting of priorities requires changing the workplace to make it more hospitable to women. We'll need to begin by acknowledging that men and women really are different, and taking those differences seriously in how we structure the workplace, rather than promoting a policy of sameness. Steven Rhoads has observed that "encouraging more equal patterns of male and female parenting and work" in academia has failed to help women get ahead in their careers. "Gender-neutral" policies in tenure extension have actually worked to the disadvantage of female faculty members, apparently because "many men had used the stopped clock to conduct research, while the women concentrated on parenting duties." This result is not surprising, since "pregnancy and childbirth are not gender-neutral activities."[93] And it can take many months after childbirth for a woman to regain the physical capacity she had before pregnancy. For this reason, says Rhoads, "Preferential treatment of women is justified even if one considers only the requirements of pregnancy, childbirth, and breastfeeding. It would certainly be reasonable to grant only female professors a semester of paid leave after the birth of a child. Male professors in highly unusual situations could petition for exceptions to this general policy."[94] This policy would respect the bodily nature of women and their unique capacity to bear life.

Workplace policies should also recognize that a mother is not interchangeable with other adults, especially when children are young. Rhoads recounts the case of a Ph.D. student in economics at Harvard who was told that the university would cover the cost of day care for her child, but would not provide a research assistant to do coding for her so she could focus on analyzing data when she had time. Never mind that the research assistant she requested would have been cheaper than full-time day care.[95] The preference to outsource mothering rather than coding is problematic, to say the least. A healthy society would recognize a mother's preference to care for her child not only as her personal wish but as what's best for her child and for society.

Cultures Cultivate

Our transgender moment arose in part from a rebellion against the idea of innate differences between the sexes in disposition and preferences, on average and for the most part. We have seen efforts to stamp out those differences, in the belief that they are a product of social conditioning, artificial and unjust. A strain of radical feminism intersects with transgender ideology in the shared premise that gender has no real connection to biology and can be nullified or changed at will.

An effective cultural response to transgender ideology entails recovering a sound cultural understanding of gender and sex differences. First, we must reject the concept of gender fluidity wherein every child has to *choose* a gender among numerous options—a burden that introduces confusion when children need clarity and guidance. Trying to make boys and girls the *same*, in a coercive androgyny, can also result in confusion and resentment. On the other hand, we needn't adopt the overly rigid stereotypes that might lead a boy to think he should be a girl because he is sensitive and artistic, or a girl to think she might really be a boy because she prefers sports over dolls. Acknowledging the richly diverse ways of being male and female can help children more readily identify with and accept their own embodiment.

Getting the balance right is the work of an entire culture. For children, developing into a healthy understanding of their bodies and their sexuality is a delicate enterprise, fraught with difficulties even in the best circumstances.

Transgender ideology makes the process much more difficult by destabilizing what David Cloutier calls the "sexual ecology." It challenges the normality of congruence between sex and gender simply because a small number of people have trouble reconciling themselves with their bodily sex. "To destabilize [the] default position of body/soul congruence," writes Cloutier, "is to allow exceptional cases to reshape the entire ecology."[96]

We should be tolerant—indeed, loving—toward those who struggle with their gender identity, but also be aware of the harm done to the common good, particularly to children, when transgender identity is normalized.[97] Transgender activists are not merely asking for tolerance or kindness; they are demanding affirmation, not just from adults but from children and adolescents who are already challenged by the normal process of sexual development. Cloutier observes that "affirming and accommodating the transgender identity of one child will affect other children, in much the same way that gender stereotypes about alpha males and compliant females affect them."[98] In a culture where transgender identities are not only affirmed but celebrated, everyone will be compelled to construct their own gender identity, unaided by a common understanding of sex differences and why they matter.

The transgender moment has been brought about by activists waging an "assault on a fragile ecology of sexual development," using state power to favor one view of gender identity over an understanding that others support and favor.[99] The next chapter details how this assault is being waged under a new interpretation of Title IX of the Education Amendments of 1972, a law banning discrimination on the basis of sex in federally funded education programs. Then it proposes a better approach to public policy surrounding gender identity.

CHAPTER EIGHT

Policy in the Common Interest

O n New Year's Eve in 2016, a group of Roman Catholic nuns breathed a sigh of relief just before the clock struck twelve. A federal judge had put a hold on a new transgender mandate right before it was to go into effect at midnight. The mandate from the Department of Health and Human Services (HHS) would have forced all health-care plans regulated under the Affordable Care Act (Obamacare) to cover sex reassignment procedures, and it would have forced all relevant health-care workers to perform them. It would have applied to the hospital operated by the nuns and to the insurance plan they provide to their employees.

The judge placed a nationwide injunction on the mandate because it was likely to be a violation of religious liberty—like the contraception mandate that Hobby Lobby and the Little Sisters of the Poor challenged all the way to the Supreme Court—and because it was likely to be unlawful: contrary to the very words of the statute it purported to implement. Whereas the law forbids discrimination on the basis of sex, HHS redefined the word "sex" to mean "gender identity," without legal authority to do so. Medical professionals and health-care organizations would thus be penalized for believing—as a matter of faith, moral conviction, or professional judgment—that maleness and femaleness are biological realities to be respected, not defects to be corrected.[1]

On the same day that the HHS regulation was finalized, May 13, 2016, the departments of Justice and Education sent a "Dear Colleague" letter to the nation's schools setting forth policy on gender identity, defined as "an individual's internal sense of gender." The accompanying press release announced that schools must allow students "to participate in sex-segregated activities and access sex-segregated facilities consistent with their gender identity," because these federal agencies would now "treat a student's gender identity as the student's sex for purposes of enforcing Title IX."[2] When it was passed in 1972, Title IX of the Education Amendments was intended to protect women and girls from harassment and discrimination, to ensure that they have equal opportunities in education, but forty-four years later the Obama administration was unlawfully rewriting it to say that schools must allow boys unfettered access to girls' bathrooms, locker rooms, dorm rooms, hotel rooms, and shower facilities, if they claim to identify as girls. Anything less than full access to the sex-specific intimate facility of one's choice would be deemed a transphobic denial of civil rights and equality.

The Obama administration explicitly rejected compromises such as single-occupancy facilities. According to the guidelines, a school "may not require transgender students to use facilities inconsistent with their gender identity or to use individual-user facilities when other students are not required to do so." When it comes to campus housing or hotels during off-campus trips, a school "must allow transgender students to access housing consistent with their gender identity and may not require transgender students to stay in single-occupancy accommodations."

To be granted these and other accommodations, a student would need only to declare an "internal sense of gender" contrary to biological sex. The press release noted that a school "may not require transgender students to have a medical diagnosis, undergo any medical treatment, or produce a birth certificate or other identification document before treating them consistent with their gender identity." In other words, sheer say-so makes it so. The Obama administration, in essence, completely gave in to the demands of transgender activists that we reviewed in Chapter 2.

Prior to this time, parents, teachers, and local school administrators had been weighing how best to accommodate the dignity, privacy, and safety concerns of students who identify as transgender while also respecting the dignity, privacy, and safety concerns of other students. Schools facing this issue were sensitive to the feelings of embarrassment and discomfort that students who identify as transgender might experience were they to be required to share bathrooms or locker rooms with persons of the same biological sex. But they recognized that students of the other biological sex also had important concerns. Schools found solutions that balanced these competing concerns and that were tailored to the age of their students, from kindergarten to graduate school. No one assumed that a one-size policy would fit every educational institution.

The solution that many schools settled upon was to give the student who identified as transgender limited access to other facilities—such as faculty bathrooms or locker rooms—or to provide single-occupancy restrooms for any student who did not feel comfortable using a multiple-occupancy facility. They found a way to accommodate both the student who identified as transgender and the rest of the students. These nuanced solutions existed long before the recent surge in media coverage of transgender issues; they were worked out at the local level without generating much controversy. But when activists attacked these reasonable compromises as "transphobic," the departments of Justice, Education, and Health and Human Services all capitulated to their demands.

A few months later, on September 20, the Department of Housing and Urban Development (HUD) finalized a new "Gender Identity Rule" for equal access to HUD's housing programs. It revised the 2012 "Equal Access Rule" as it pertained to gender identity by eliminating the exemption for single-sex emergency shelters with common sleeping areas or bathrooms. Shelters for the homeless and for battered women, along with other emergency shelters, would be required to "provide all individuals, including transgender individuals and other individuals who do not identify with the sex they were assigned at birth, with access to programs, benefits, services, and accommodations in accordance with their gender identity," no documentation needed, no "intrusive" questions asked.[3] The new rule offered no religious exemption, and it gave no consideration at all to the particular vulnerabilities of people who need emergency shelters—women fleeing domestic abuse, or homeless people who themselves suffer from higher rates of sexual abuse and mental health problems.

Examples of political overreach in this area can be multiplied, but these are sufficient to illustrate how government agencies have attempted to impose a radical agenda on citizens by redefining "sex" to mean "gender identity" in longstanding laws and policies against discrimination. When Congress passed Title IX, no one thought that "sex" meant "gender identity." It wasn't the same thing then, and it isn't the same thing now. Federal bureaucrats have unlawfully tried to rewrite federal law in order to broaden the scope of unlawful discrimination, but they have not clarified what counts as discrimination on the basis of gender identity. The result is that commonsense policies regarding bodily privacy and sound medicine are now being labeled discriminatory. Title IX has been turned on its head, putting the safety and privacy concerns of girls and women behind the wishes of biological males who say they identify as female. While the Trump administration has begun to remedy this abuse of antidiscrimination law, the transgender policy agenda continues to insinuate itself into the nation's schools.

Ideology

Gender identity policies are not just about allowing citizens who identify as transgender to live as they choose, but about coercing the rest of us to go along with a radical ideology. Schools are a major front in this campaign, as we saw earlier in the guidelines produced by the National Education Association and the ACLU along with various LGBT groups. The aim of protecting students who identify as transgender from bullying and respecting their dignity is reasonable in itself, but that's not what these policies are about. They're about a larger program of indoctrination in gender ideology.

The first step is making teachers get with the program. For instance, in May 2016, a public school district in Oregon paid a $60,000 settlement to a teacher in response to a formal complaint about colleagues' refusal to refer to the teacher as "they." The teacher, Leo Soell, does "not identify as male or female but rather transmasculine and genderqueer, or androgynous." In the complaint, Soell said that other teachers had engaged in "harassment," in part by "refusing to call me by my correct name and *gender* to me or *among themselves*" (emphasis added).[4]

Gender identity policies can quickly generate politically correct speech codes in schools and workplaces. "Antibullying" programs can turn into antidisagreement programs. Dissent is equated with bigotry and hate, so no dissent will be tolerated. All students must accept gender ideology, and their parents will have no say in the matter.

A public charter school in Minnesota, Nova Classical Academy, became roiled with controversy in late 2015 after administrators informed parents that an incoming kindergartner was "gender non-conforming" and that the school would be supporting the child's gender identity. As part of this program, all K–5 students would read *My Princess Boy*, a book about "a boy who expresses his true self by dressing up and enjoying traditional girl things." School officials claimed that they were obligated by law to meet the demands of the transgender child's parents, but pushed aside the concerns and objections of other children's parents. Nova's board of directors approved a new "gender inclusion" policy, allowing students to choose their own gender at will. The school would work together with any student who identifies as transgender to "create a tailored gender transition plan." Students could demand to be addressed by a "preferred name" and pronouns, and would be entitled to use bathrooms and locker rooms of the opposite sex, as well as sleeping facilities on overnight trips.[5]

This was not enough to suit the child's parents, who filed a complaint against the school, alleging that it had not adequately protected their five-year-old from "gender-based bullying and hostility." They complained that the school was unwilling to use "effective materials" on gender identity, such as *I Am Jazz*, a children's book about Jazz Jennings, a biological male who, as we saw in Chapter 1, came out as transgender at age five and now has a reality TV show on TLC. But most of all, they faulted the school for giving other parents the choice of opting their children out of transgender instruction. The complaint says that the school would not "conduct gender education, whether proactive or corrective, without first introducing delay and inviting or encouraging families to 'opt out,'" and would not "inform our child's classmates of her preferred name and pronouns, without first delaying for days and inviting or encouraging families to 'opt out' of this information."[6]

Because the school was not willing to impose a radical worldview on other five-year-old children without first notifying parents of their right to opt out, it was sued. It's worth noting that the father of the child at the center of this lawsuit was working toward a Ph.D. in educational psychology at the University of Minnesota, with a focus on "the creation and implementation of gender inclusive policies and practices in K–12 public schools.'"[7]

Even with the opt-out concession, some parents found Nova's "gender inclusion" policy so disturbing that they opted out of the school entirely. One mother, Emily Zinos, wrote about having to face the possibility that her children would be "sharing locker rooms with the opposite sex, learning bogus theories in science class about gender existing on a spectrum, and being punished for violations of 'preferred' pronoun use." The school had previously been very careful in choosing curriculum, even sometimes creating its own textbooks, she said, but under the new policy, "unsubstantiated claims of bullying were used to pressure committees to approve materials and policies that were anti-scientific and that supplanted parental authority." It all added up to "ideological indoctrination." Eventually she pulled her children out of Nova.[8]

Zinos elaborated on what is at stake when schools adopt policies that promote gender identity as something unrelated to biological sex:

> First, schools will teach children to accept an ideology that is predicated on the lie that biological sex plays second fiddle to a self-proclaimed, subjective gender identity, and that the sex of one's body is mutable or even irrelevant. This isn't just an idea that you can tuck away in a unit study or an anti-bullying presentation. It will inevitably find its way into every aspect of a school and make a deep impression on the developing minds of children. For example, girls, under the regressive mandates of anti-bullying and gender inclusion policies, would have to agree to call boys in their locker room "girls," effectively losing their rights to free speech and to privacy from males. And science—particularly biology—would die a quick death at the hands of a concept that necessarily eradicates observable facts about human sexuality. Gender ideology in the curriculum is a lie enshrined as truth.[9]

Parents are right to be concerned about whether the lessons their children learn in school about sex and gender are grounded in fact, and whether the schools respect parental authority or undermine it.

The larger question is whether children are helped or harmed by a school's "gender-inclusive" policies. The danger may be greatest to the children with gender dysphoria themselves, since affirming young children in a transgender identity may prolong and solidify their dysphoria when they might otherwise have come to accept their bodies naturally as they matured. Drs. Paul McHugh, Paul Hruz, and Lawrence Mayer made this point in the amicus brief they submitted to the Supreme Court concerning "gender identity" policies in schools. Their brief describes the "well-recognized" phenomenon of neuroplasticity, where repetition affects brain structure and function. Thus, "a child who is encouraged to impersonate the opposite sex may be less likely to reverse course later in life," because the child's "brain is likely to develop in such a way that eventual alignment with his biological sex is less likely to occur." This means that transgender-affirmative policies may prevent some gender-confused children from coming to accept their true sex.[10] Instead, they may end up attempting to change their sex through surgery.[11]

In an expert declaration to a federal district court, Dr. Hruz stressed that there is currently no basis to make an accurate prediction of which prepubertal children with gender dysphoria will persist in a transgender identity and which will revert to an identity consistent with their biological sex, as the vast majority do naturally.[12] But policies that mandate "social affirmation" run the risk of interfering with the natural process of gender resolution. "Any activity that encourages or perpetuates transgender persistence for those who would otherwise desist can cause significant harm, including permanent sterility, to these persons."[13]

Policies such as the one adopted by Nova run the risk of prolonging the struggles of students with gender dysphoria rather than alleviating them. Recognizing this problem, Emily Zinos posed these questions to other parents:

- Will we allow our young and vulnerable children to be fed a false anthropology rather than teaching them to speak the truth boldly?
- Will we consent to our children's sterilization rather than patiently guiding them toward an appreciation of their bodies?
- Will we treat our children's mental health issues with double mastectomies rather than demand that doctors provide a true remedy?[14]

Privacy

Even if one agreed with transgender activists' claims about gender identity, and if they could actually predict which gender-dysphoric children would not desist naturally, it does not follow that the public policies favored by the activists are good policy. The transgender policy agenda entirely ignores competing interests and considerations, including the privacy and safety of others, particularly girls and women, and it disregards the requirements of true equality.[15] We'll look first at the question of privacy.

Sex-specific intimate facilities exist in order to provide bodily privacy. This is something that people on both sides of the political spectrum once understood. For example, writing for the majority in the Supreme Court ruling that forced the Virginia Military Institute to become coeducational in 1996, Justice Ruth Bader Ginsburg noted that this change "would undoubtedly require alterations necessary to afford members of each sex privacy from the other sex in living arrangements."[16] Ginsburg has been consistent on this principle over the years. In 1975, while she was a law professor at Columbia University, she defended the proposed Equal Rights Amendment (a predecessor of Title IX that never became law) against the criticism that it would require unisex intimate facilities. Ginsburg wrote that a ban on sex discrimination did not necessitate such an outcome: "Separate places to disrobe, sleep, perform personal bodily functions are permitted, in some situations required, by regard for individual privacy. Individual privacy, a right of constitutional dimension, is appropriately harmonized with the equality principle."[17] The claims of equality do not override the right to bodily privacy.

Many courts have defended the bodily privacy rights of people in a variety of settings, including jails and prisons. The Fourth Circuit Court of Appeals has ruled that prisoners have a right not to be seen in a state of undress by guards of the opposite sex, unless there is a true emergency. The court based its ruling on "society's undisputed approval of separate public restrooms for men and women based on privacy concerns."[18] When the U.S. Department of Justice sued the State of North Carolina in 2016 over its House Bill 2 (HB2, the "bathroom bill"), the state reminded the DOJ of its own prison regulations with respect to bodily privacy, including the requirement that prison policies generally "enable inmates to shower, perform bodily functions, and change clothing without nonmedical staff of the opposite gender viewing their breasts, buttocks, or genitalia."[19]

The federal government evidently regards privacy as an important concern when it comes to people incarcerated for crime. But what about schoolchildren? With the "Dear Colleague" letter from the Justice and Education departments, the Obama administration instructed schools that they may not even *notify* students (or their parents) about whether they will have to share a bedroom, shower, or locker room with a student of the opposite biological sex. The privacy of transgender students is held to be paramount; the privacy of all other students irrelevant. Such a skewed notion of privacy rights has drawn ire from both sides of the political spectrum. The Women's Liberation Front (on the left) and the Family Policy Alliance (on the right) jointly submitted an amicus brief to the Supreme Court in which they said, "It is truly mind-boggling that informing women as to which men have the 'right' to share a bedroom with them is an 'invasion of privacy,' but it is *not* an invasion of privacy to invite those men into women's bedrooms in the first place."[20]

It is entirely reasonable not to want to see persons of the opposite sex in a state of undress, even if they "identify as" the same sex. Likewise, it is entirely reasonable not to want to be seen in a state of undress by persons of the opposite sex, even if they "identify as" the same sex. This is why laws mandating sex-segregated restrooms and changing rooms in the workplace appeared in the late 1800s, as women began to enter the workforce. The Alliance Defending Freedom (ADF), a public interest law firm, notes that most of the states had enacted such laws by 1920. "Because of our national commitment to protect our citizens, and especially children, from the risk of being exposed to the anatomy of the opposite sex, as well as the risk of being seen by the opposite sex while attending to private, intimate needs, sex-separated restrooms and locker rooms are ubiquitous in public places," says ADF.[21] The privacy concern is particularly heightened for children and for adolescents as they go through puberty. Minors "have a fundamental right to be free from State compelled risk of exposure of their bodies, or their intimate activities."[22]

In response to the federal transgender regulations, several families made declarations to the Supreme Court expressing concerns about the privacy of their children at school. For instance, the parents of "C.K.," a girl in middle school in the Charlotte-Mecklenburg district of North Carolina, said that curricular activities required her to change clothes, which meant "undressing in front of other students within a large open single-sex locker room." The district's new policy of allowing students to use facilities on the basis of gender identity was causing her emotional distress:

> She experiences anxiety, discomfort, and embarrassment at the thought of having to change in front of a boy or a man, and the fact that a male may profess a female gender identity does not reduce her anxiety. She also fears that some men may profess a female identity as a pretense to access the locker room where she is changing.
>
> C.K. has been afraid and anxious about returning to school this year because of the school system's new policy regarding sex-specific restrooms, locker rooms, and changing facilities. Her anxiety has been slightly allayed because the new policy is currently on hold as a result of a recent Supreme Court ruling, but nonetheless the thought that she will have to undress in the presence of males, and to be subject to males

undressing in front of her, once that policy goes back into effect, is deeply distressing to her.[23]

Another declaration was submitted by a fourteen-year-old girl who had attended a public middle school in Illinois. From there, students generally go on to a high school that had started permitting males to use female restrooms if they "profess a female gender identity," and has allowed a student "access to locker rooms formerly reserved for the opposite sex." The district adopted this policy without notifying parents. The girl told the court how disturbing this was to her:

> The idea of permitting a person with male anatomy—regardless of whether he identifies as a girl—in girls' locker rooms, showers and changing areas, and restrooms makes me extremely uncomfortable and makes me feel unsafe as well.
>
> Even the idea that a boy or man is allowed in those areas makes me anxious and fearful, regardless of whether I ever encounter them in any of those places.
>
> I feel unsafe because I am concerned that a boy or man can access the girls' facilities by just professing a female identity, and that would allow them to take advantage of the school's policies in order to see me and my friends as we have to undress for school. They could take pictures of us with their phones and then post them to the internet.
>
> I would feel especially violated in the event that the school district's policy enabled a person with male genitalia, regardless of what gender that person professes, to see me partially or fully undressed. I also do not want to be exposed to male genitalia in any way while in facilities formerly designated for girls only.[24]

Bodily privacy is a great concern to young people as they develop into adults. It is also highly important to women who have been victims of sexual abuse. For these women, seeing a naked male body can be a traumatic trigger. Whether the naked male body they suddenly see in front of them belongs to a man who "identifies as" a woman is of no moment to survivors of sexual abuse.

Safe Spaces for Women, a group that "provides survivors of sexual assault with care, support, understanding and advice," submitted an amicus brief to the Supreme Court emphasizing how the vulnerable women it serves are harmed by policies that mandate allowing biological males who identify as female to have access to women's facilities. The organization expressed deep concern that "survivors of sexual assault are likely to suffer psychological trauma as a result of encountering biological males—even those with entirely innocent intentions—in the traditional safe spaces of women's showers, locker rooms, and bathrooms."[25] The Obama administration had issued its guidance on transgender policy "without giving those affected a voice in the process" and had "improperly circumvent[ed] the notice and comment process when that process was needed most."[26]

The Safe Spaces for Women amicus brief includes the testimony of a woman in the state of Washington concerning a new administrative regulation from the state's Human Rights Commission "allowing men who gender identify as female to enter women's locker rooms, spas, and restrooms." She described how this policy had already harmed her:

> As a survivor of childhood molestation and rape, the passage of this law left me feeling vulnerable and exposed in areas [where] I should be protected. I worked for many years to heal from the emotional, physical, and spiritual effects of the trauma inflicted by my childhood attacker. Depression, panic attacks, suicidal thoughts, Post Traumatic Stress Disorder, and physical phantom pains are a legacy of my past abuse.
>
> I had been panic-attack free for over a decade when Washington's law went into effect. Now, using a public bathroom is very difficult and has led to many panic attacks. I have not entered a public women's locker room in over a year. Before Washington's law was passed, if I encountered a man in the woman's bathroom or locker room, management, staff, police and the general public would all have been there to protect my privacy and safety. This is no longer the case. To be in a position where I am left exposed, separate from others and no longer have a voice is the same position I was in as a child of eight.[27]

These testimonials illustrate why an interest in bodily privacy has long been recognized in American law. If this is true even for prisoners, who do give up certain rights upon incarceration, why would it not also be true for women who have broken no laws, or for schoolchildren?

Some people on the political left still understand this principle. Maya Dillard Smith, former head of the American Civil Liberties Union of Georgia, resigned from her position with the ACLU after it came out on the wrong side of this issue. She recounted the unsettling experience of being in a women's restroom with her daughters, who were elementary-school age, when "three transgender young adults over six feet with deep voices" entered the facility. Her daughters were "visibly frightened, concerned about their safety and left asking lots of questions" that she felt unprepared to answer. Smith commented: "I believe there are solutions that can provide accommodations for transgender people and balance the need to ensure women and girls are safe from those who might have malicious intent."[28] As Jeannie Suk Gersen of Harvard Law School has remarked, if some women and girls are uncomfortable being in restrooms with people who are biologically male, that feeling "is not easy to brush aside as bigotry."[29]

Safety

In addition to guarding privacy, sex-specific intimate facilities exist to serve the related purpose of protecting girls and women from male predators. The concern is not that people who identify as transgender will engage in inappropriate acts (as some activists have mockingly said), but that predators will abuse gender identity policies to gain easier access to victims. Law enforcement experts have given testimony on precisely this problem.

Tim Hutchison, retired sheriff of Knox County, Tennessee (which includes Knoxville and the University of Tennessee), points out what every local law enforcement official knows: "Public restrooms are crime attractors, and have long been well-known as areas in which offenders seek out victims in a planned and deliberate way." That was true even before access to restrooms and dressing rooms was based on gender identity, and these new policies create more safety risks for women and children. In a court declaration, Hutchison says that criminal incidents enabled by gender identity access policies "are already occurring."[30]

Another crime expert who submitted a court declaration on the subject is Kenneth V. Lanning, a veteran of forty years in law enforcement, specializing in preventing and solving sex crimes. For twenty years he worked in the Behavioral Science Unit and the National Center for the Analysis of Violent Crime at the FBI Academy in Quantico. He has consulted on thousands of sex crimes and has published an essential book on the subject, *Child Molesters: A*

Behavioral Analysis (now in its fifth edition).[31] Lanning makes it clear that the problem with "gender-identity-based access policies" (GIBAPs) in terms of potential sex offenses is not that transgender persons are likely to commit such crimes, but that males who are not transgender will "exploit the entirely subjective provisions of a GIBAP…to facilitate their sexual behavior or offenses."[32] If a man can have unlimited access to women's facilities simply by claiming to be a transgender woman, this creates "an additional risk for potential victims in a previously protected setting and a new defense for a wide variety of sexual victimization."[33]

The "new defense" for perpetrators derives from the fact that the prosecution of some sex crimes depends on establishing criminal intent, which is harder to do if biological males have a legal right to be in women's restrooms and changing rooms. Predators can "use the cover of gender-identity-based rules or conventions to engage in peeping, indecent exposure, and other offenses and behaviors," Lanning says, and it may be difficult to prove that the actions were not simply misinterpreted.[34] Hutchison notes that women will be compelled to ask themselves: "Is a biological male who displays his private parts to a woman while coming out of a women's restroom stall a flasher or transgendered? What about the biological male whose eyes wander while in a women's locker room?"[35] The existing laws against sex crimes are inadequate to address the potential for abuse of GIBAPs by male sex offenders, he says, "because the specific types of illegal conduct most likely to be encouraged by the policies are intent-based offenses."[36] Those who are pushing for the adoption of GIBAPs "do not see (or maybe do not want to see) the problem."[37]

The difficulty of proving intent in suspected sex crimes is compounded by the lack of a clear and objective standard for who belongs where under gender-identity policies. Without such a standard, law enforcement officers may hold back from pursuing investigations for fear of opening themselves up to charges of discrimination, Lanning says:

> Law enforcement officers and prosecutors will be less likely to record, investigate, or charge indecent exposure or peeping offenses in a GIBAP environment, because there is no objective standard for determining whether someone born a male can lawfully be present in a women-only facility. It would be more difficult to prove lascivious intent when self-reported gender identity drives access rights, and easier to accuse law enforcement personnel of discrimination. This is made even more

difficult when that self-reporting need not be corroborated in any way whatsoever.[38]

The prospect of being accused of bigotry or discrimination can also make women more hesitant to report certain forms of sexual misconduct, such as peeping and indecent exposure. "Most women are already afraid to report suspected crime or suspicious activity if they think that people will label them for making a report," says Hutchison. The fear of being accused of bigotry and transphobia will make this problem worse.[39] Lanning points to the same problem, saying that worries about being accused of bigotry might make a woman unwilling to report an exhibitionist, for instance. Women "would be forced to consider whether the exposure was merely the innocent or inadvertent act of a transgendered individual."[40] Children are even more hesitant to report abuse, often waiting until they are adults before telling anyone what they have suffered, says Hutchison. Gender identity access polices will make girls more vulnerable to sex crimes and very possibly more reluctant to report them.[41] Hutchison and Lanning both predict that the number of sex offenses in public facilities will increase, while the reporting of those offenses decreases.[42]

Anecdotal evidence already demonstrates the worrisome potential for predators to abuse the new access policies:

- In Toronto, a man posing as a transgender woman ("Jessica") sexually assaulted and criminally harassed four women—including a deaf woman and a survivor of domestic violence—at two women's shelters. Previously, he had preyed on other women and girls ranging in age from five to fifty-three.[43]
- In Virginia, a man presented himself as a woman in a long wig and pink shirt to enter a women's restroom at a mall, where he took pictures of a five-year-old girl and her mother.[44]
- In Seattle, a man used a women's locker room at a public swimming pool to undress in front of young girls who were changing for swim practice. When staff asked him to leave, the man said: "the law has changed and I have a right to be here."[45]
- At the University of Toronto, two separate occurrences of voyeurism took place on campus after a policy of gender-neutral bathrooms was implemented. In both cases, individuals used their phone

cameras to film women showering. These incidents prompted the university to revise its new policy.[46]

- In Duluth, Minnesota, a biologically male high school student who identifies as female was allowed access to the girls' locker rooms, where the student danced "in a sexually explicit manner— 'twerking,' 'grinding,' and dancing like he was on a 'stripper pole' to songs with explicit lyrics." He also flashed his underwear while dancing.[47]
- In Milwaukie, Oregon, Thomas Lee Benson was arrested for dressing as a woman to enter the women's locker room at an aquatic park. Benson had previously been convicted of sexual abuse, purchasing child pornography, and unlawful contact with a child.[48]
- In Everett, Washington, a man wearing a wig and a bra was arrested for entering the women's bathroom at Everett Community College. The man, Taylor Buehler, admitted under police questioning that he was the suspect in an earlier reported incident, when he had gone into a girls' locker room to take a shower, for voyeuristic purposes.[49]

Similar incidents have been reported at several Target stores since April 2016, when the company announced its policy of allowing access to bathrooms and fitting rooms in accordance with gender identity rather than biological sex.

- In July 2016, Sean Patrick Smith, a biological man wearing a wig and a dress, was charged with secretly recording an eighteen-year-old girl changing into swimwear in a Target fitting room in Ammon, Idaho.[50] Although Smith claims to be transgender, he admitted to police that he had recorded women undressing in the past for the "same reason men go online to look at pornography."[51]
- In September 2016, customers saw a man taking pictures of women changing in the stall next to him at a unisex Target dressing room in Brick, New Jersey.[52]

In a report for the Heritage Foundation, Melody Wood and I documented over 130 examples of men charged with using bathroom, locker room, and shower access to target women for voyeurism and sexual assault.[53] Intimate facilities are already places where woman can feel unsafe, so why remove essential safeguards?

The safety risks in "gender identity" policies owe partly to the nebulous character of the concept. The Obama administration's guidelines provide no legal definition of "gender identity," nor any legal criteria for determining who is a "transgender" person. Recall that the administration's "Dear Colleague" letter to schools defines "gender identity" as "an individual's internal sense of gender," and that the guidelines forbid schools from requiring a medical diagnosis or any other documentary evidence of a student's gender identity.

Other institutions require evidence for determining gender identity and deciding who shall be treated as transgender. The U.S. Department of State, for instance, "requires a statement from an attending physician stating that he or she has a doctor/patient relationship with the subject, and stating that the subject has completed or is in process of appropriate clinical treatment for gender transition," Lanning observes.[54] So do athletic organizations, as we will see. Objective standards are no less important in law enforcement.[55] Hutchison remarks that successful prosecution of sex offenders will be "difficult if not practically impossible" if any male can enter a public women's facility to do mischief, and then claim that his gender identity is female.[56]

Equality

Many women worry that the original purpose of Title IX—working toward women's equality in education—is threatened when "sex" is redefined to mean "gender identity." The law was intended to remedy a history of disadvantages, and this aim is necessarily compromised by policies that make the category of "woman" ambiguous and fluid. Allowing anyone who *identifies* as a woman to be *regarded* as a woman in public policy erases the very meaning of womanhood in law.

An amicus brief submitted to the Supreme Court on behalf of the Women's Liberation Front highlights the strange transformation of Title IX into a means to *deny* privacy, safety, educational opportunity, and equality to women. This is happening because "the sex-class comprising women and girls now includes men, with all the physiological and social characteristics that come with being male (and vice-versa)." When government agencies adopt "gender identity" policies, people can be whatever they claim to be.[57] Women thus lose the protections that rest on acknowledging the differences between men and women. "The idea that women and girls must surrender their rights and protections under Title IX—enacted specifically to secure women's access to education—in order to extend Title IX to cover men claiming to be women is a jaw-dropping act of administrative jujitsu."[58]

The Women's Liberation Front also submitted a joint amicus brief with the Family Policy Alliance. These two organizations are generally poles apart on political issues, but both recognize that the reinterpretation of "sex" to mean "gender identity" in Title IX and other antidiscrimination policies marks a "truly fundamental shift in American law and society."[59] They emphasize the importance of maintaining the legal category of "woman" as something specific and unambiguous: "When the law requires that any man who wishes (for whatever reason) to be treated as a woman *is* a woman, then 'woman' (and 'female') lose all meaning. With the stroke of a pen, women's existence—shaped since time immemorial by their unique and immutable biology—has been eliminated by Orwellian fiat."[60]

While the bureaucratic redefinition of male and female poses new dangers to women's privacy and physical safety, it also "undercuts the means by which women can achieve educational equality."[61] The joint amicus brief notes that Title IX was intended as "a remedial statute for the benefit of women," and points specifically to scholarships designated for women only, which could now become available to biological men who identify as women. This is one respect in which "granting Title IX rights to men who claim they are women *necessarily violates* the rights Congress gave women in this law."[62]

Whether or not one believes that women today still need scholarships for "remedial" purposes, there are more permanent reasons why genuine equality requires maintaining the legal category of "woman" as distinct from "man." Most obvious are the bodily differences that can raise questions of fairness in competitive athletics, since biological males have natural physical advantages over women in many sports. In Alaska, high school girls have already lost medals in track competitions because they had to compete with a male who identifies as a girl. One of the girls who raced against this athlete commented, "It's not fair scientifically—obviously male and female are made differently. There are certain races for males, and certain races for females, and I believe it should stay that way."[63]

Girls are also on the losing end when they have to compete against girls who identify as transgender and are taking male hormones as part of a transitioning process. In February 2017, a biological girl taking testosterone for that purpose won the Texas state championship in girls' wrestling, completing an undefeated season of competition against girls who were not taking testosterone supplements.[64]

Relying on an entirely subjective measure of gender can be damaging to real equality between men and women. That's why prominent athletic organizations require objective standards for determining whether an athlete is to compete with men or with women. For example, the National Collegiate Athletic Association (NCAA) stipulates that a man who identifies as a woman may compete on a women's team only "if the athlete obtains a doctor's certification of the subject's intention to transition to a woman, and that hormone therapy has actually begun."[65] The International Olympic Committee requires men who identify as women to "demonstrate that their testosterone level has been below a certain cutoff point for at least one year before their first competition."[66] These rules are an effort to make reasonable accommodations for people who identify as transgender, allowing them a chance to compete in athletics, without forcing biological girls to compete on an uneven playing field against biological males or against biological girls who are taking male hormones.

Guaranteeing meaningful equality, as well as privacy and safety, depends on recognizing real sex differences, and working *with* them rather than trying to erase them. As Justice Anthony Kennedy remarked, "To fail to acknowledge even our most basic biological differences...risks making the guarantee of equal protection superficial, and so disserving it."[67]

Unlawful Redefinition of Legal Terms

The "Dear Colleague" letter to schools instructing them on transgender policy under cover of Title IX and the HHS mandate to provide sex reassignment procedures under the Affordable Care Act both entailed redefining "sex" to mean "gender identity." The Obama administration simply tried to rewrite federal law as it wished the law had been written. Since the health-care law incorporates the antidiscrimination language of Title IX, the debate over the meaning of "sex" in Title IX has implications for medical practice as well as for education. When Congress passed that law, the phrase "gender identity" did not even exist outside of some esoteric psychological publications, and the use of the word "gender" to mean something quite distinct from "sex" was a recent coinage. Contrary to what the administration wanted to believe, the term "sex" is not ambiguous and cannot legitimately be redefined by agencies of the executive branch.[68]

In the original text of Title IX, "sex" clearly refers to the biological and physiological differences between men and women. Federal courts agree that this meaning is not ambiguous. In his opinion on the "Dear Colleague" guidance, Judge Reed O'Connor stated that the reinterpretation of "sex" to mean "gender identity" was directly contrary to the original intent and meaning of Title IX, as is evident in its implementing regulations. Referring to the section in the Code of Federal Regulations that pertains to "comparable facilities," Judge O'Connor observed that the Department of Education had clearly complied with congressional intent by stipulating that an educational institution "may provide separate toilet, locker room, and shower facilities on the basis of sex" as long as the facilities are "comparable." He remarked that "biological differences between male and female" are what defined "the common understanding of the term [sex] when Title IX was enacted," and that same understanding guided the regulatory process that led to the provision on comparable facilities.[69] Title IX was expected to be implemented on the basis of biological sex, and the implementing regulations take account of the privacy concerns related to the differences between the sexes.

Another federal judge, Kim R. Gibson, has similarly made clear that Title IX was never intended to include protections on the basis of gender identity, saying that the law "does not prohibit discrimination on the basis of transgender itself because transgender is not a protected characteristic under the statute."[70] Therefore, the University of Pittsburgh was not violating Title IX by "requiring students to use sex-segregated bathroom and locker room facilities based on students' natal or birth sex, rather than their gender identity."[71] Judge Gibson pointed to the plain language of the law, and noted that only Congress could expand its scope:

> On a plain reading of the statute, the term "on the basis of sex" in Title IX means nothing more than male and female, under the traditional binary conception of sex consistent with one's birth or biological sex.... The exclusion of gender identity from the language of Title IX is not an issue for this Court to remedy. It is within the province of Congress— and not this Court—to identify those classifications which are statutorily prohibited.[72]

This reasoning is correct. Title IX was intended to prevent discrimination on the basis of sex, not gender identity. Congress alone—not courts or federal agencies—has authority to change the statute, but unless and until it does so, gender identity protections cannot be considered to fall within the scope of Title IX.

In his dissenting opinion on a Fourth Circuit ruling that schools must provide access to facilities according to gender identity, Judge Paul Niemeyer said that the court's majority had misconstrued the plain meaning of Title IX. The result was a ruling that, "for the first time ever, holds that a public high school may not provide separate restrooms and locker rooms on the basis of biological sex."[73] Judge Niemeyer wrote:

> This holding completely tramples on all universally accepted protections of privacy and safety that are based on the anatomical differences between the sexes.... [S]chools would no longer be able to protect physiological privacy as between students of the opposite biological sex.
>
> This unprecedented holding overrules custom, culture, and the very demands inherent in human nature for privacy and safety, which the separation of such facilities is designed to protect. More particularly, it also misconstrues the clear language of Title IX and its regulations.[74]

These redefinitions of statutory terminology are often defended with the claim that modern science shows that sex *is* gender identity. But science, as we have seen, shows no such thing. "There is no scientific basis for redefining sex on the basis of a person's psychological sense of 'gender,'" said Dr. Hruz in a court declaration. Opinion should not be treated as medical fact, nor should the normal be redefined on the basis of pathological variation, he stressed. "The prevailing, constant and accurate designation of sex as a biological trait grounded in the inherent purpose of male and female anatomy and as manifested in the appearance of external genitalia at birth remains the proper scientific and medical standard."[75]

The history of language does not support the redefinition of "sex" to mean "gender identity," since the latter was coined precisely in contradistinction to the former.[76] Recent legislative and executive actions also distinguish between "sex" and "gender identity." Congress and the executive branch apparently know how to make policy on the basis of "gender identity" when they want to do so. Congress has specifically included "gender identity" as distinct from (and alongside) "sex" in two bills: the Violence Against Women Reauthorization Act of 2013 and the Matthew Shepard and James Byrd, Jr., Hate Crimes Prevention Act of 2009.[77] By specifying protection on the basis of gender identity *and* on the basis of sex, these laws show that Congress, at least as late as 2013, did not think of gender identity as falling under the definition of sex. If Congress had intended to include gender identity protections in Title IX, it could have so specified, but it did no such thing.

President Barack Obama similarly showed that he understood "sex" and "gender identity" to be different categories. In his executive order barring federal contractors from discriminating on the basis of "sexual orientation and gender identity," he replaced existing protections on the basis of "sex" with protections on the basis of "sex, sexual orientation, gender identity."[78] Evidently he did not assume that legal protections on the basis of "sex" included protections on the basis of "gender identity" by definition.

Just as Congress knows how to include "gender identity" protections explicitly in legislation, it also knows how to reject such provisions and has done so dozens of times. For example:

- The Employment Non-Discrimination Act (ENDA), which would prohibit employment discrimination both on the basis of sexual orientation and on the basis of gender identity, has been introduced in almost every Congress since 1994 but has never been enacted.[79] Title VII of the Civil Rights Act of 1964 already bans discrimination on the basis of sex in employment. Would members of Congress keep trying to pass a law for over two decades if its provisions were already covered in existing law?
- The so-called Equality Act, which would go beyond ENDA and add "sexual orientation and gender identity" (SOGI) to more or less every federal law that prohibits discrimination on the basis of race, has never been enacted by Congress.[80]
- The Student Non-Discrimination Act, championed by the Human Rights Campaign, would "prohibit public schools from discriminating against any student on the basis of actual or perceived sexual orientation and gender identity," but it has never become law.[81]

None of these bills attempting to establish legal protections on the basis of gender identity has been authorized by Congress. The administrative redefinition of sex to include gender identity goes against congressional precedent, for Congress has been clear on when it does and does not intend to establish protection on the basis of gender identity. The burden is on transgender advocates to prove that statutory terms carry the meaning they prefer, and they have failed.

Enforcing Orthodoxy through Antidiscrimination Law

Policies that prohibit discrimination on the basis of gender identity often start with existing civil rights laws that guarantee protection on the basis of sex or race, and simply add the term "gender identity." The resulting policies lack the nuance and specificity needed for the problems they are supposed to remedy. There are both conceptual and practical reasons why the established paradigm of policy responses to racism and sexism is not appropriate to the policy needs of people who identify as transgender.

Conceptually, gender identity is unlike race and sex in important ways. Gender identity is not an objective, verifiable trait, but an expressly subjective one. As we saw regarding law enforcement concerns, there are no reliable standards for determining who falls into the protected class. At the same time, gender identity claims are manifested in action, and actions are subject to moral evaluation, while one's race and sex are not. Existing and proposed gender identity laws are not intended simply to allow people who identify as transgender to engage in certain actions themselves; they are also designed to compel others to endorse and support those actions. They aren't deployed as shields to protect people from unjust discrimination, but as swords to impose a new sexual orthodoxy on private citizens.[82] They penalize people for choosing not to facilitate or participate in actions—such as sex reassignment surgeries—that they reasonably deem to be unhelpful or immoral.[83] It is one thing for the government to allow or even endorse conduct that many citizens consider immoral, but quite another thing for the government to force others to condone and facilitate such conduct in violation of their convictions.

There is also a practical reason why outlawing "discrimination" on the basis of gender identity is not comparable to prohibiting discrimination on the basis of race or sex, and it has to do with the overt, systemic character of the latter forms of discrimination in our national history. When the Civil Rights Act of 1964 was enacted, black Americans were treated as second-class citizens. Individuals, businesses, and associations across the country excluded them in ways that caused grave material and social harm, without justification, and with the tacit or even explicit backing of government. They were refused loans, kept out of decent homes, and denied job opportunities—except as servants, janitors, and manual laborers. These policies built on and exacerbated a prejudicial view of black people as less intelligent, less skilled, and even less fully human than white people.

Making it harder for blacks and whites to mingle on equal terms was not just an incidental consequence of those policies; it was the whole purpose. No claims of benign motives are plausible. Racial discrimination was so pervasive that those who practiced it risked little in terms of economic opportunity or social standing. Market forces and social norms tended to reward instead of punish discrimination, sometimes with assistance from the state. This is why a remedy in law was necessary.[84]

The situation of people who identify as transgender in America today is not comparable. There is nothing akin to Jim Crow laws designed to segregate people who identify as transgender and make them second-class citizens. There is no denial of the right to vote, no lynching of people who identify as transgender, no signs over water fountains saying "Trans" and "Cis." Granted, there has been historic bigotry against those who identify as transgender, and it has not vanished. If people are being turned away from restaurants or denied basic medical care solely on grounds of a transgender identity, that is real discrimination and it should be addressed appropriately so that people are treated with dignity and respect. But any injustice to people on the basis of gender identity today cannot be compared to the systematic mistreatment of people on the basis of race that blemished our nation's past. Thus the legal remedies that were appropriate for combatting the legacy of slavery and segregation are not suited to the problems arising from transgender identities.

But once again, the purpose of the gender identity antidiscrimination laws and policies now being pushed is not to guarantee basic civil rights, but to impose a radical ideology on society. The policies are used as swords, not shields. These laws use the power of the state to send the message that traditional convictions about human nature are false, discriminatory, and rooted in animus. Gender identity policies are designed to penalize Americans who believe that we are created male and female, and to replace that conviction with a new orthodoxy in which one can be male, female, none, or some combination—regardless of biology.[85] They treat any dissent as irrational, bigoted, and unjust.

What Is "Discrimination"?

Just as gender identity is fundamentally subjective, the concept of "discrimination" is also vague, and antidiscrimination policies pertaining to gender identity do not adequately define what counts as discriminatory. Making categorical distinctions between people and treating them differently on that basis does not always amount to invidious discrimination. The law must be nuanced enough to capture the differences among various kinds of "discrimination" in the general sense of drawing a distinction.

Some types of discrimination are clearly invidious and unjustified. Racially segregated water fountains, for example, were an instance of taking race into consideration in a context where it was completely irrelevant, and using that distinction to treat some Americans as second-class citizens merely because they were black. The entire point of making a racial distinction was to treat some Americans as socially inferior. Such policies have correctly been deemed invidious race-based discrimination and have rightly been outlawed.

Similarly, through much of American history, girls and women were not afforded educational opportunities equal to those available to boys and men. These restrictive policies took sex into consideration in a realm where it should have been irrelevant, and then treated girls and women as inferior precisely because of their sex. Such policies were correctly deemed unjust sex-based discrimination, and Title IX of the Education Amendments was enacted to ensure that girls and women receive equal educational opportunities.

In important respects, however, the distinction between men and women is more fundamental than racial differences. This is why our courts have ruled that whereas "separate but equal" is not a legitimate principle when it comes to race-based distinctions in education, "separate but comparable" is a legitimate principle in providing certain kinds of facilities for men and women. When Title IX was enacted in 1972 and its implementing regulations were promulgated in 1975, the law made clear that sex-specific housing, bathrooms, and locker rooms did not constitute unlawful discrimination. Such policies take sex into consideration, but not in order to treat women as inferior to men, or vice versa. They "discriminate" in the nonpejorative sense of "distinguish" in order to protect the dignity and privacy of men and women equally.[86] We would certainly be treating people unequally if access to intimate facilities were based on factors wholly unrelated to privacy concerns, such as race. But forcing men and women, boys and girls to undress in front of each other would render the guarantee of equal protection "superficial," as Justice Kennedy understood. Our laws have long reflected the commonsense view that sex-specific intimate facilities are not discriminatory, while racially segregated facilities have rightly been made unlawful.

The principle of "disparate impact" complicates the question of whether distinctions are always wrongfully discriminatory. Is it always correct to apply the same policies to all if the results are noticeably different between one group and another? For example, people with disabilities often have limited access to various facilities, not out of hostility toward them but only because no provisions have been made for their particular needs. Since those needs were so widely overlooked that people with disabilities were excluded from full participation in society, Congress passed the Americans with Disabilities Act, to provide wheelchair ramps and other accommodations in public places. Recognizing differences was essential to securing more equal opportunities.

Other uses of the "disparate impact" concept are more dubious. For example, many women contend that any limits on abortion are inherently sexist. But the fact that only women can get pregnant has no bearing whatsoever on the judgment of the conscientious pro-life doctor or nurse who refuses to kill the unborn. Pro-life medical practices do not take sex into consideration at all, as this thought experiment will illustrate: LGBT activists now insist that men can become pregnant, and tabloids have trumpeted the story of a transgender "man" bearing a child. Would a pro-life doctor be happy to perform an abortion if such a person requested it?

That hypothetical scenario is comparable to cases that have actually come up in relation to gender identity. One woman sued a Catholic hospital for declining to remove her healthy uterus as part of a sex reassignment process, and she deemed this refusal to be discrimination on the basis of gender identity.[87] A transgender activist explained the reasoning behind this view, referring to the HHS directive on applying the antidiscrimination provisions of Obamacare:

"What the rule says is if you provide a particular service to anybody, you can't refuse to provide it to anyone," said Sarah Warbelow, the legal director for the Human Rights Campaign. That means a transgender person who shows up at an emergency room with something as basic as a twisted ankle cannot be denied care, as sometimes happens, Warbelow said. That also means if a doctor provides breast reconstruction surgery or hormone therapy, those services cannot be denied to transgender patients seeking them for gender dysphoria, she said.[88]

Warbelow's argument conflates real and imaginary discrimination. A hospital that refused to treat a twisted ankle simply because the injured person identifies as transgender would indeed be engaging in invidious discrimination. And there is no evidence—even on the HRC website—for the claim that this kind of thing "sometimes happens." If it did, the negative media attention would quickly cause the hospital to reverse course, without any governmental intervention. But a hospital that declines to remove the perfectly healthy uterus of a woman who identifies as a man is not discriminating on the basis of gender identity, because the doctors who object to removing healthy uteruses do not perform such a procedure on *any* patients, whether they "identify as" women or men. Gender identity plays no part in the decision.[89]

If a school were to say that students who identify with their biological sex may use the water fountains but students who identify as transgender may not, that would be discrimination on the basis of gender identity. It would take a student's gender identity into account where it has no relation to the matter at hand, in order to disadvantage the student. And it would rightly be prohibited.

Nothing of the sort is happening when it comes to school policies on sex-specific bathrooms, locker rooms, showers, and sports teams. These policies make reasonable—and plainly lawful—distinctions based on sex. All biological males, regardless of gender identity, may use the men's room, and all biological females, regardless of gender identity, may use the women's room. Gender identity is not taken into account at all. Rather, entrance to certain intimate facilities is determined on the basis of anatomy, physiology, and biology—an objective standard that Title IX and its implementing regulations expressly permit.

The Obama administration once understood that providing sex-specific facilities does not constitute gender identity discrimination. Recall that its 2012

Equal Access Rule for HUD housing aimed to ban unreasonable discrimination on the basis of gender identity but recognized that basing access to emergency shelters on biological sex was reasonable and not discriminatory. In 2016, the administration revised the policy to reflect a misguided understanding of discrimination.

In fact, the Obama administration's guidance for schools would *require* discrimination on the basis of gender identity in determining access to locker rooms and showers. The following table indicates who does and does not get access to the girls' facilities and to the boys' facilities.

Access to Lockers and Showers Under Obama Administration Guidance

Access to Girls' Lockers and Showers			Access to Boys' Lockers and Showers		
Sex	Gender Identity	Access	Sex	Gender Identity	Access
Female	Female	Allowed	Male	Male	Allowed
Female	Male	Allowed	Male	Female	Allowed
Male	Female	Allowed	Female	Male	Allowed
Male	Male	Denied	Female	Female	Denied

Source: Ryan T. Anderson and Melody Wood: "Gender Identity Policies in Schools: What Congress, the Courts, and the Trump Administration Should Do," Heritage Foundation, March 23, 2017.

In this scheme, it is *only* students who identify with their biological sex—who are not transgender—who must be denied access to one facility or another. That looks like gender identity discrimination under the administration's own logic.

What Needs to Be Done

In February 2017, the Trump administration took steps to reverse the unlawful Obama redefinition of "sex" in antidiscrimination law and return authority to parents and teachers in the states. Civil rights officers in the Department of Justice and the Department of Education issued a joint letter saying the administration was rescinding the Obama policy, which had required schools to allow students who identify as transgender to use the restrooms, locker rooms and similar facilities of their choice—or face a loss of federal funds. The letter said that the Obama mandate did not show "due regard for the primary role of the states and local school districts" in making education policy.[90]

Congress should ratify this action and prevent a future administration from undoing it, by specifying that the word "sex" in our civil rights laws does not mean "gender identity" unless the people, through their elected representatives, explicitly say so. And the people should not say so. Neither Congress nor the states should elevate "gender identity" as a protected class in our civil rights laws. They should specify that access to sex-specific facilities in public institutions is generally to be based on biology, while granting that anyone who is uncomfortable using the bathroom designated for their biological sex should be given a reasonable accommodation. Private institutions should be allowed to make their own policies.

Here are three actions that Congress could take to prevent administrative agencies from making "gender identity" a protected class in Title IX and other civil rights laws:

1. Congress could specify that "sex" does not mean "gender identity" in all civil rights laws. Language included in H.R. 5812, the Civil Rights Uniformity Act, would do exactly that.[91] Introduced by Representative Pete Olson (R-TX) in 2016, the act clarifies that for the purpose of interpreting civil rights statutes, the term "sex" does not mean "gender identity." This would prevent abuses of Title IX and other civil rights laws, ensuring that unelected bureaucrats and judges cannot reshape these policies to the detriment of women and girls. Schools could continue to provide separate bathrooms and locker rooms and sports teams based on biological sex, and religious schools could continue to operate in accordance with their beliefs without fear of punitive agency action. At the same time, such legislation could leave the door open for the reasonable accommodation of people who identify as transgender. Health-care professionals would not have to perform sex reassignment procedures, and health-care plans would not have to cover them.

2. Congress could make the same clarification in a statute targeted at the specific federal laws that have already been abused, such as Title IX of the Education Amendments of 1972, Title VII of the Civil Rights Act of 1964, and Section 1557 of the Affordable Care Act (the section that was reinterpreted to produce a transgender health-care mandate). Such a statute would reiterate that what Congress meant in referring to a person's "sex" when it passed these laws is what the word referred to at the time and still does: biological reality, not gender identity. This would achieve in piecemeal fashion what the Civil Rights Uniformity Act would achieve wholesale.

3. Congress, based on its power of the purse, could specify that the Departments of Education, Justice, and Health and Human Services, as well as the Equal Employment Opportunity Commission, may not use any funds to implement or enforce any new administrative gender identity directives or regulations against persons, institutions, schools, businesses, or governments that allegedly do not comply with those directives. Additionally, Congress could specify that these agencies may not revoke federal funding for any purported noncompliance with administrative regulations on gender identity.

The courts should respect the authority of the legislature to make policy in this area, and should refrain from reinterpreting "sex" to mean "gender identity." Title IX and other laws banning sex discrimination could then function once more according to their original purposes.

States and local governments likewise should not elevate gender identity as a protected class in their own civil rights and antidiscrimination statutes. They should, however, clarify how access to sex-specific facilities is to be governed. For example, while leaving private institutions free to establish their own policies, states and municipalities should clarify that access to sex-specific facilities in public institutions (such as schools) will generally be based on biological sex, and that reasonable accommodations will be provided for anyone who is uncomfortable using the bathroom designated for their biological sex.[92]

Few Americans had ever had a conversation about these or other transgender issues before the primetime interview with the celebrity then known as Bruce Jenner in April 2015. We should be encouraging such a conversation, and allowing parents, teachers, and local school districts the time and flexibility to find solutions that work best for everyone. Future presidential administrations should respect federalism, local decision making, and parental authority in education. We should allow the American people to weigh all relevant concerns and have a voice in devising reasonable policies that serve *all* Americans. Congress should support such efforts, and the courts should uphold them.

Conclusion

When I told people that I was working on a book about the transgender moment, many asked me why. Why spend precious time on something so silly? Why do diligent research and write carefully reasoned arguments about something that runs on emotion? Why open yourself up to charges of transphobia and bigotry?

The simple answer is that I couldn't shake from my mind the stories of people who had detransitioned. They are heartbreaking. I had to do what I could to prevent more people from suffering the same way. Those most vulnerable to the transgender moment needed a book like this, and I had the resources to research and write it. I probably won't persuade committed trans ideologues, but most Americans aren't ideologues of any sort and many Americans are open to arguments on this issue. Many people simply want to know the truth about "gender identity" and whether someone can actually be "trapped in the wrong body." They wish to be compassionate toward those who have such feelings, and they may sense that the "transitioning" approach is unhelpful and that the notion of gender fluidity is deeply mistaken.

Gender ideology has rapidly made inroads into our culture and public policy. Hollywood and various media outlets portray transgender identities and transitioning in a heroic light, or as simply normal. The government has brought lawsuits against "gender identity discrimination." Corporations boast of their transgender-friendly policies. Powerful interests have launched boycotts of states that don't get with the program. Even so, ordinary Americans recognize the transgender moment to be a politically correct fad built on a shaky platform, and many are pushing back. This book is intended to arm them with knowledge.

Is the Transgender Moment Here to Stay?

American consumers across the country made their opinions known through the power of the purse after Target criticized North Carolina's "bathroom bill" and announced its own "inclusive" policy in a blog post in April 2016. Customers, it said, would be free to use the restroom of their choice, regardless of biological sex. In response, over 1.4 million people pledged not to shop at Target unless and until the company changed its policy. Target continues to insist that the controversy has not affected sales, but stock value and retail numbers tell a different story.

Bathroom Break?

Target's same-store sales fell each quarter after its April 19 blog post. The retailer, which faced multiple competitive challenges in the period, says the post's impact wasn't material.

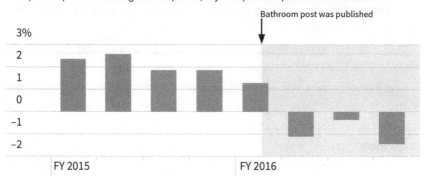

Source: Khadeeja Safdar, "How Target Botched Its Response to the North Carolina Bathroom Law," *Wall Street Journal*, April 5, 2017.

In April 2017, the *Wall Street Journal* reported that "Target's stock has fallen about 25% this year; Wal-Mart's has climbed 4%."[1] *Business Insider* reported that the boycott had cost Target many millions of dollars in lost sales and increased expenses. After Target announced its policy online, "Shopper traffic and same-store sales started sliding for the first time in years." In-store sales had declined every quarter since that blog post appeared. The company meanwhile spent $20 million to install single-occupancy restrooms in all its stores, "to give critics of the policy more privacy."[2] (*Critics of the policy.* Note that people who identify as transgender would not be expected to use the special facilities.)

Clearly it isn't just a fringe of right-wing zealots who object to transgender access policies like the one that Target adopted. In fact, the transgender moment has created some unlikely alliances, such as the group of women who call themselves the "Hands Across the Aisle Coalition." Here's how they describe their organization:

> For the first time, progressive and conservative women have come together to challenge the notion that gender is the same as sex. We are radical feminists, lesbians, Christians and conservatives that are tabling our ideological differences to stand in solidarity against gender identity legislation, which we have come to recognize as the erasure of our own hard-won civil rights. As the Hands Across the Aisle Coalition, we are committed to working together, rising above our differences, and leveraging our collective resources to oppose the transgender agenda.[3]

I was honored to host the coalition's first public event, a panel discussion at the Heritage Foundation titled "Biology Isn't Bigotry: Why Sex Matters in the Age of Gender Identity."[4] (You can watch the whole event by following the link in the endnote.) The discussion highlighted the concerns that women face when sex is redefined as gender identity. As one participant put it, "When gender identity wins, women always lose."[5]

One of the women who spoke at Heritage that afternoon was Miriam Ben-Shalom, a lesbian and gay rights activist. She was discharged from the U.S. Army after her sexuality became public, then reinstated, and finally discharged again after a long legal battle. Ben-Shalom began her remarks by saying: "I am indebted to the Heritage Foundation because they've offered us something that no organization from the left did, which was a safe place to speak." She explained that the women were joining together across the ideological divide because of the many ways that women's safety is threatened by "gender identity" policies:

> It is about bathrooms, locker rooms, women's shelters, women's jails, and women's spaces, and the real issue here is male violence. That's what

it is, and that's what we're talking about here. If trans women were really women, they would understand that the issue is male violence and they would sit down with us and civilly work together to find an acceptable solution to this problem.[6]

Another participant in the discussion, Mary Lou Singleton, opened her remarks much as Ben-Shalom did: "As a long-term leftist, I cannot believe the next sentence I'm about to say: I would like to thank the Heritage Foundation for making this conversation possible." Singleton is an active member of the Women's Liberation Front, the radical feminist organization that filed a lawsuit against the Obama administration to restore Title IX rights to women and girls. She described herself and her concern about gender identity policies this way:

My driving goal in life is making the world a better place for girls and women, the people who are oppressed globally on the basis of female biological sex. These people are aborted in the womb or smothered to death as infants because they have vulvas. They are sold in childhood to men as sex and breeding slaves and the world calls it "child marriage." They perform countless hours of uncompensated labor and are treated as servants by men of all cultures. They are trafficked as commodities in the global prostitution and surrogacy industries. They go to jail for suspicious miscarriages. They are criminalized for having home births and for extended breastfeeding. They suffer court-ordered forced caesareans. The list goes on and on.

Transgender ideology tells us there is no such thing as biological sex and robs us of our ability to name the class of people who suffer sex-based oppression. If we cannot name a phenomenon, we certainly cannot fight it. Gender ideology is harmful to women and girls.[7]

While Heritage offered these women a safe space to express their concerns, Professor Gail Heriot had a different experience with the U.S. House of Representatives. A professor of law and a member of the U.S. Commission on Civil Rights, she testified before the House Judiciary Committee in May 2016 on issues of bureaucratic overreach, after submitting twenty-one pages of carefully reasoned written testimony on the separation of powers and administrative authority.[8] Representative Zoe Lofgren read aloud a brief passage from Heriot's testimony, dealing with gender identity policies: "If I believe I'm a Russian princess, that doesn't make me a Russian princess, even if my friends and acquaintances are willing to indulge my fantasy. Nor am I a Great Horned Owl just because—as I have been told—I happen to share some personality traits with those feathered creatures."[9] Lofgren then attacked Heriot, saying, "I think you're a bigot, lady. I think you are an ignorant bigot." When the chairman of the committee interrupted to stop the breach of decorum, Lofgren shot back:

> LOFGREN: "Mr. Chairman, it is my time, and I would just like to say that we allow witnesses to say offensive things, but I cannot allow that kind of bigotry to go into the record unchallenged."
> HERIOT: "Does that mean you think I am a Russian princess?"
> LOFGREN: "I have no idea."[10]

The video clip of the two-minute exchange went viral on the Internet, and Lofgren was hailed as a champion of tolerance and social justice. What Lofgren deliberately omitted was the context of the sentences about owls and Russian princesses, in which Heriot had carefully balanced the principle of individual freedom with the societal concerns that enter into public policy. Here's how they read:

> There is no reason in the world that any federal, state or local government should be telling anyone that he or she needs to conform to the expectations of others regarding members of his or her sex. That's what freedom is all about. But it's one thing to butt out of an individual's decision to dress and behave like a member of the opposite sex and it is quite another to declare that this makes that individual an actual member of the opposite sex and mandate that every federally-funded school in America act accordingly.
>
> We are teaching young people a terrible lesson. If I believe that I am a Russian princess, that doesn't make me a Russian princess, even if my friends and acquaintances are willing to indulge my fantasy. Nor am I a Great Horned Owl just because—as I have been told—I happen to share some personality traits with those feathered creatures. I should add that very few actual transgender individuals are confused in this way. They understand perfectly that their sex and their gender do not align. Some choose surgery to make their bodies better align with their gender. Most choose not to.[11]

This is an entirely reasonable statement, acknowledging that people are different in various ways, and even people who identify as transgender have differing aims and priorities. But as Stanley Kurtz pointed out, Lofgren didn't want to have a serious discussion of the issues: "Lofgren's most revealing remark during her exchange with Heriot was, 'I don't want to get into a debate about it.' Exactly." She couldn't refute Heriot's case, so she cherry-picked a snippet that might sound inflammatory, and then played the "bigot" card. "This has become the standard-issue leftist response to thoughtful conservative arguments on almost all issues," Kurtz observes.[12] To many viewers of the video, Lofgren's condescension toward the values of average Americans was the take-home point. The congresswoman displayed what has been called "the smug style" of American liberalism.[13] That style is unpersuasive to many people, including some liberals.

Two friends of mine on the political left have given me cause to believe that transgender activists may have overplayed their hand and provoked a pushback. One of these friends is a twenty-something man who, with some bemusement, pointed me to the viral video du jour in which someone who describes herself as an "intersectional feminist," a "queer girl," etc., declared that having "genital preferences" is transphobic, and that "preferences for women with vaginas over women with penises might be partially informed by the influence of a cissexist society."[14] And no, this was not satire.

The video lecture went on: "If you're a woman who only likes women, go ahead, identify as a lesbian! But some women have penises. And if the fact that some lesbians might be attracted to those women offends you, it's because you don't think trans women are real women."[15] My friend objected to being judged transphobic and cissexist merely on the grounds that he dates biological women only. And when lesbians are accused of bigotry because they prefer women who don't have male equipment, you have to wonder how long the "L" and the "T" can be held together in LGBT advocacy.

More significant doubts were expressed by a liberal friend who is the father of several children. He told me that he doesn't care all that much about gay marriage; it doesn't really affect him.[16] But he cares very much about what affects his kids. He doesn't want his daughter coming home from school to say that a boy who thinks he's a girl is sharing a locker room with her. He doesn't want his son to announce that he's "gender-fluid." Average parents of various political stripes are not on board with "gender identity" access policies or school lessons about gender ideology.

The tide may turn eventually, and the culture may return to acknowledging the truth about sex. But as with other controversial social issues, the special interests and deep-pocketed elites are lined up against ordinary Americans. We need a strategy for fighting back politically and culturally, and for offering healthier ways to deal with gender dysphoria.

A Plan of Action

First and foremost, as we advocate for the truth, we must be careful not to stigmatize those who are suffering. Many people who have detransitioned say they felt pressured to transition and are now being attacked from the political left for detransitioning. But many also say that people on the political right made them feel like misfits in society, and that's part of what led to their desire to transition in the first place. We must avoid adding to the pain experienced by people with gender dysphoria, while we present them with alternatives to transitioning.

In order to offer real alternatives, we need to create a network of clinicians who are ready to help those with gender dysphoria in ways that don't endorse transgender ideology or aim to change people's bodies. It isn't enough to highlight the risks and harms of social transition for young children, puberty blocking, cross-sex hormones, and sex reassignment surgery. Medical experts not blinded by a PC ideology must also work together to devise good standards of care for treating people—especially children—with gender dysphoria. Clinicians need to be trained in these methods. Parents need alternatives to the forty-five transgender-affirming pediatric gender clinics in the United States today.

A network of good doctors and therapists across the nation needs to be assembled, with the primary goal of helping people find healthy alternatives to transitioning, so that they feel comfortable in their own skin. This network must also help those who seek to detransition and get their lives back. This will require standards of care for detransitioning, and surgeons and endocrinologists who can undo some of the damage done by sex reassignment procedures and hormone treatment. It will also require mental health professionals and other social workers who can help people deal with the issues underlying their dysphoria and the added suffering brought by transitioning, so they can return to living as the sex that they are.

Meanwhile, we'll also need to engage the broader culture. We need a new generation of scholars and physicians like Paul McHugh to challenge the misdirection of the medical profession today. The media will keep hyping the politically correct experts, so we'll need honest researchers to debunk their bogus studies and conduct rigorous ones.

We'll also need people who are ready and willing to defend the truth in the public square. Among those best equipped to do this are people who can give personal testimony of struggling with gender dysphoria and overcoming it. They may have transitioned and then regretted it, or they may have found a remedy without transitioning in the first place. We are narrative creatures, and first-person stories in particular can move our hearts.

Those personal narratives can help illustrate the truth that sex is not a subjective matter, or whatever one chooses. Being against today's gender ideology is not sufficient; we also need to promote a sound cultural understanding of gender, an understanding of why and how bodily sex matters. We'll need to shape a culture that honors sex differences while also celebrating individuality and the rich variety of ways to be male or female.

Religious leaders can contribute to these efforts in various ways. They'll need to provide pastoral care to people struggling with their gender identity, to people who have transitioned, and to their families and communities. Pastors will need to teach their flocks the truth about the human person, male and female. They can do this by drawing from reason and revelation, philosophy and theology, psychology and biology. In addition to the resources and talents they already possess, they'll need education specifically in gender identity issues.

Finally, we'll need lawyers and politicians with a clear understanding of what's at stake. We'll need lawyers to protect the right of doctors to practice good medicine and the right of parents to seek it out for their children. We'll need legal advocates for privacy and safety in bathrooms and locker rooms and other sex-specific facilities. And we may need lawyers willing to bring malpractice lawsuits against physicians who recklessly transition minors. The work of lawyers will be more successful if political leaders enact good public policy on these issues and refuse to be cowed by the trans lobby.

What's at stake in the transgender moment is the human person. If trans activists succeed in their political agenda, our nation's children will be indoctrinated in a harmful ideology, and some will live by its lies about their own bodies, at great cost to themselves physically, psychologically, and socially.

Lives will be ruined, but pointing out the damage will be forbidden. Dissent from the transgender worldview will be punished in schools, workplaces, and medical clinics. Trying to live in accordance with the truth will be made harder.

This doesn't have to happen. Everyone can play a role in bearing witness to the truth and ministering compassionately to people in pain. For anyone who takes part in this important work, Dr. McHugh offers some advice: "Gird your loins if you would confront this matter. Hell hath no fury like a vested interest masquerading as a moral principle."[17]

Postscript to the
Paperback Edition

The reactions to *When Harry Became Sally* have been revealing. While people on the right typically praised the book, people on the left either ignored it, or grossly mischaracterized it with no sign of having ever read it. *Two* op-eds in the *New York Times* attacked the book, and a *Washington Post* article about the book was so inaccurate that it had to be rewritten.

The second of the two *New York Times* op-eds, by Andrea Long Chu, has been discussed in the preface. The first was written by Jennifer Finney Boylan, a contributing opinion writer for the *Times* and a professor of English at Barnard College of Columbia University.

Boylan claims I wrote "a book that suggests that transgender people are crazy, and that what we [people who identify as transgender] deserve at every turn is scorn, contempt, and belittlement." You've now finished reading the book. Does that sound like an accurate description?

Boylan did not produce even a snippet from my book in support of those claims. Indeed, anyone who had read this book would have known that they are baseless. Boylan's op-ed was simply a hit piece containing no discussion of what I actually wrote, no quotation of my words, not even the briefest summary of a single claim I make.

This wasn't the first time that a mainstream media outlet treated the book in such a manner. Before it was released, the *Washington Post* wrote an embarrassingly bad story about it, chock-full of factual errors.[1] Before the day was done, the *Post* had entirely rewritten the first half of the piece, but never even acknowledged its own errors.[2]

While the mainstream Left either ignored the book or misrepresented it, not everyone on the left responded so dismissively. Some brave individuals realized that the book was presenting the truth—and they wanted to work together to address common concerns. In particular, they had concerns about likely consequences of the so-called "Equality Act," which would add "gender identity" as well as "sexual orientation" to the classes protected under the Civil Rights Act of 1964. First introduced in 2016, the Equality Act was again gaining traction in Congress. And so, in January 2019, I hosted an event at the Heritage Foundation titled "The Inequality of the Equality Act: Concerns from the Left."

Was Heritage changing its political stripes? Not quite. The event came about at Heritage because no left-leaning institution was willing to host such a forum. One of the organizers needed to remain anonymous, because she has a teenage daughter who was four years into the process of transitioning. Throughout that time she's been trying to get left-leaning media and think tanks and professional associations to take seriously the concerns coming from the left about transgender policy, and instead she's found herself and her colleagues essentially deplatformed.

In December she reached out to me to see if the Heritage Foundation would be willing to provide a platform. Gladly.

Heritage's founder, Dr. Ed Feulner, is famous for saying that it's better to add and multiply than to divide and subtract. Undoubtedly, the people who were on the panel, like the people in the audience that day, disagree about many things. We likely disagree about abortion, gay marriage, taxes, trade, foreign policy—just to name a few. And that's OK.

Just because we disagree about some things, even many things, that does not mean we disagree about everything. And where we do agree, we can and should work together. Addition and multiplication. Not division and subtraction.

As I spoke with that anonymous mother about the possibility of a public event, several things became clear about how transgender issues are presented in the media.

First, the transgender cause is portrayed as the next wave of civil rights and as the natural extension of the past decade of LGBT successes. If you support what the media call gay rights, you have to support trans rights. If you support what the media call marriage equality, you have to support trans equality. There's little willingness to recognize that the LGB and the T are radically dissimilar, especially as applied to children.

Second, the media present this issue as one of science versus faith. We're to accept that there's a consensus among doctors that people are born trans, that children as young as two or three can know their "real" gender identity, and that social transitioning and sex reassignment procedures—now referred to as "gender affirmation" or "gender confirmation"—are a safe and effective treatment protocol. And that the only people who could think otherwise must be acting on bigotry and blind dogma.

Third, the media disregard all the costs and risks of mainstreaming transgender ideology. They don't care about the damage being done to young people's bodies and minds—in fact they celebrate it as a civil right. They don't care about the privacy and safety and equality of girls when boys who identify as girls can share female-only spaces—like showers and locker rooms and bathrooms—or when boys who identify as girls can participate in female athletic competitions. They don't care about the ability of doctors to practice good medicine when bad medicine becomes mandated as a civil right, while good medicine becomes outlawed as a civil wrong. And they don't care about the rights of parents to find the best care for their kids.

Sadly, some religious people give support to the media's transgender narrative when they agree to accept "gender identity" laws, provided that they get a religious exemption for themselves or their organization. But bad public policy doesn't become good by exemptions for oneself that do nothing to protect the privacy, safety, equality, or liberty of others.

Whether we support it or not, "gender identity" ideology will affect everyone. Right and Left. Conservative and liberal. Religious and secular. I was more than happy to host that event at Heritage in order to give voice to concerns about the consequences of this ideology from a perspective that has been suppressed.

It is my hope that more bridges will be built, that more hands will reach across the aisle, that this issue will be seen as a human issue—not a political or partisan issue. And that we all will work together to find ways to bring healing and wholeness to people who are suffering.

Acknowledgments

The Heritage Foundation, under the leadership of Senator Jim DeMint and Dr. Ed Feulner, and with the financial support of over 500,000 ordinary Americans, provided me with an encouraging home to do this project. At Heritage, Jennifer Marshall and Emilie Kao, my bosses, protected my time to do the research and the writing, and provided me with helpful and timely feedback. Melody Wood and Monica Burke, outstanding research assistants in my department, along with Andrea Jones, Laura Cermak, and Zack Jones, our wonderful interns over the past year, provided assistance both big and small. I am grateful to them all, but special thanks go to Andrea: without her diligent research in the initial stages, this book would not exist.

Maureen Condic, Sherif Girgis, Dr. Paul Hruz, Dr. Allan Josephson, Margaret McCarthy, Mark Regnerus, Dr. Craig Stump, and Chris Tollefsen all read portions of this book—sometimes large portions—and provided me with critically helpful feedback. The book is much better because of their careful reading. Special thanks are owed to Sherif, who commented on the entire manuscript and helped me think through the whole project. Michael Hanby, Dr. Patrick Lappert, Dr. Quentin Van Meter, and Thomas Joseph White pointed me to helpful sources, and Gary McCaleb and Jeff Shafer of Alliance Defending Freedom put me in touch with several physicians and academics who assisted me in my research. Thank you.

I'm grateful to my agent, Keith Urbahn, cofounder and president of Javelin, and to Roger Kimball, publisher of Encounter Books, for their faith in this endeavor. But most thanks of all go to Carol Staswick, whose excellent editing made this book readable.

There are several other physicians, professors, and lawyers who gave me assistance, but I cannot mention them by name due to their very valid fears of professional repercussions. My hope is that this book helps create a culture where they can speak freely. I am especially grateful to the scholars willing to support this effort publicly by writing endorsements, and to Dr. Paul McHugh in particular for his steadfast devotion to the well-being of his patients, and to the truth.

Notes

.

PREFACE TO THE PAPERBACK EDITION

1. Andrea Long Chu, "My New Vagina Won't Make Me Happy," Opinion, *New York Times*, November 24, 2018, https://www.nytimes.com/2018/11/24/opinion /sunday/vaginoplasty-transgender-medicine.html.

2. For the most recent citations, see Ryan T. Anderson, "Understanding and Responding to Our Transgender Moment," *Fellowship of Catholic Scholars Quarterly*, vol. 41, no. 1 (Spring 2018), available at SSRN: https://ssrn.com /abstract=3172277.

3. Tamara Syrek Jensen et al., "Decision Memo for Gender Dysphoria and Gender Reassignment Surgery," U.S. Centers for Medicare and Medicaid Services, File no. CAG-00446N (August 30, 2016), https://www.cms.gov /medicare-coverage-database/details/nca-decision-memo.aspx?NCAId=282&b c=ACAAAAAAQAAA&.

4. Ibid., discussing Cecilia Dhejne et al., "Long-term follow-up of transsexual persons undergoing sex reassignment surgery: cohort study in Sweden," *PLOS ONE 6* (February 2011): e16885.

5. Ibid.

6. Leon R. Kass, *Leading a Worthy Life: Finding Meaning in Modern Times* (New York: Encounter Books, 2017), p. 204.

7. The first of these op-eds was Jennifer Finney Boylan, "It's Not a Disaster Movie. It's Reality," Opinion, New York Times, February 27, 2018, https:// www.nytimes.com/2018/02/27/opinion/transgender-rights.html.

INTRODUCTION

1. The term "transgender moment" has been used by people on the left and the right, in secular and religious media. See, for example, Brandon Griggs, "America's transgender moment," CNN, June 1, 2015; Sonali Kohli, "Pop Culture's Transgender Moment: Why Online TV Is Leading the Way," *Atlantic*, September 26, 2014; Deborah Sontag, "'A Whole New Being': How Kricket Nimmons Seized the Transgender Moment," *New York Times*, December 12, 2015; Rebecca Juro, "Bruce Jenner and America's transgender moment," MSNBC, April 25, 2015; Justin Peligri, "After marriage, it's a transgender moment," *Washington Blade*, April 30, 2015; John W. Kennedy, "The Transgender Moment," *Christianity Today*, February 12, 2008; Rand Richards Cooper, "The Transgender Moment," *Commonweal*, December 16, 2015.

2. Boston Children's Hospital, "Disorders of Sex Development (DSD) and Gender Management Service (GeMS) Overview," http://www.childrenshospital.org/centers-and-services/disorders-of-sexual-development-dsd-and-gender-management-service-program (accessed May 10, 2017).

3. Human Rights Campaign, "Interactive Map: Clinical Care Programs for Gender-Expansive Children and Adolescents," https://www.hrc.org/resources/interactive-map-clinical-care-programs-for-gender-nonconforming-childr (accessed October 17, 2017).

4. See Paul R. McHugh, Paul Hruz, and Lawrence S. Mayer, Brief of *Amici Curiae* in Support of Petitioner, *Gloucester County School Board v. G.G.*, Supreme Court of the United States, No. 16-273 (January 10, 2017), 12; and Jesse Singal, "What's Missing From the Conversation About Transgender Kids," Science of Us, *New York*, July 25, 2016.

5. Anne P. Haas, Philip L. Rodgers, and Jody Herman, "Suicide Attempts Among Transgender and Gender Non-Conforming Adults: Findings of the National Transgender Discrimination Survey," Williams Institute, UCLA School of Law (January 2014).

6. Cecilia Dhejne et al., "Long-term follow-up of transsexual persons undergoing sex reassignment surgery: cohort study in Sweden," *PLOS ONE* 6 (February 2011): e16885.

7. Joe Shute, "Sex change regret: Gender reversal surgery is on the rise, so why aren't we talking about it?" *Telegraph*, October 1, 2017.

8. Petula Dvorak, "Transgender at Five," *Washington Post*, May 19, 2012.

CHAPTER 1: OUR TRANSGENDER MOMENT

1. Hank Stuever, "TV review: 'Becoming Chaz' on OWN—Chastity Bono's emotional transformation," *Washington Post*, May 9, 2011.

2. Sophie Roberts, "Meet the Male Mums: The first ever pregnant man is now a dad-of-three ... and transgender men are following suit by preparing to give birth on the NHS," *Sun* (UK), July 31, 2016; and Britni de la Cretaz, "What It's Like to Chestfeed," *Atlantic*, August 23, 2016.

3. Katy Steinmetz, "The Transgender Tipping Point," *Time*, May 29, 2014.

4. Aleksandra Gjorgievska and Lily Rothman, "Laverne Cox Is the First Transgender Person Nominated for an Emmy—She Explains Why That Matters," *Time*, July 10, 2014.

5. Alex Morris, "The Advocate: Laverne Cox," *Glamour*, November 4, 2014.

6. Kevin Williamson, "Speaking of Men Who Have Had Their Testicles Removed," *National Review Online*, June 3, 2014; and Dani Heffernan, "Chicago Sun-Times removes grossly inaccurate op-ed and apologizes," GLAAD Blog, June 3, 2014.

7. Taffy Brodesser-Akner, "Can Jill Soloway Do Justice to the Trans Movement?" *New York Times Magazine*, August 29, 2014.

8. Alyssa Shapiro, "Emmy winners Jeffrey Tambor and Jill Soloway celebrate at Amazon's party," *Los Angeles Times*, September 19, 2016.

9. Devon Ivie, "Jill Soloway on Season 3 of *Transparent,* Intersectionality, and Why It's 'Unacceptable' for Cis Men to Play Trans Women," *Vulture*, September 23, 2016.

10. Buzz Bissinger, "Caitlyn Jenner: The Full Story," *Vanity Fair*, June 25, 2015.

11. AP, "Emotional Caitlyn Jenner accepts Arthur Ashe Courage Award at ESPYs," *USA Today*, July 15, 2015.

12. Thomas Page McBee, "Caitlyn Jenner, Trans Champion: 'Maybe This Is Why God Put Me on Earth,'" *Glamour*, October 29, 2015.

13. "I Am Cait," IMDb, http://www.imdb.com/title/tt4733278/ (accessed May 10, 2017); and Elizabeth Wagmeister, "Caitlyn Jenner's 'I Am Cait' Cancelled After 2 Seasons at E!," *Variety*, August 16, 2016.

14. Erin Carlson, "It's not just Caitlyn: Transgender people are having their TV moment," *Fortune*, June 10, 2015.

15. National Geographic Staff, "Our Gender Issue Prompted Many Comments. Here We Respond," *National Geographic*, December 2016.

16. Susan Goldberg, "Why We Put a Transgender Girl on the Cover of National Geographic," *National Geographic*, January 2017.

17. I thank Mary Rice Hasson for pointing this out to me.

18. Ryan T. Anderson and Melody Wood, "Gender Identity Policies in Schools: What Congress, the Courts, and the Trump Administration Should Do," Heritage Foundation Backgrounder no. 3201, March 23, 2017.

19. Ryan T. Anderson, "New Obamacare Transgender Regulations Threaten Freedom of Physicians," *Daily Signal*, May 13, 2016.

20. Centers for Medicare and Medicaid Services, "Proposed Decision Memo for Gender Dysphoria and Gender Reassignment Surgery (CAG-00446N)," CMS. gov, https://www.cms.gov/medicare-coverage-database/details/nca-proposed-decision-memo.aspx?NCAId=282 (accessed May 10, 2017).

21. U.S. Department of Housing and Urban Development, "HUD Issues Final Rule to Ensure Equal Access to Housing and Services Regardless of Gender Identity," Press Release, September 20, 2016, https://portal.hud.gov/hudportal/HUD?src=/press/press_releases_media_advisories/2016/HUDNo_16-137 (accessed May 10, 2017).

22. The law also said that North Carolina would have one set of regulations for the entire state when it comes to civil rights laws for employment and public accommodations, rather than additional piecemeal regulations city by city.

23. North Carolina Department of Health and Human Services, "Myths vs. Facts: What New York Times, Huffington Post and other media outlets aren't saying about common-sense privacy law," Press Release, March 25, 2016, https://

www.ncdhhs.gov/news/press-releases/myths-vs-facts-what-new-york-times-huffington-post-and-other-media-outlets-arent (accessed May 10, 2017).

24. Mark Berman, Sarah Larimer, and Sari Horwitz, "North Carolina, Justice Dept. file dueling lawsuits over transgender rights," *Washington Post*, May 9, 2016.

25. "San Francisco mayor bans city workers from travelling to North Carolina," Fox News Politics, March 26, 2016.

26. "North Carolina governor fires back at New York governor," *Fox & Friends* video, Fox News, March 31, 2016.

27. Bryce Covert, "The Backlash Against North Carolina's Anti-LGBT Law Is Growing," *ThinkProgress*, March 26, 2016.

28. Emery P. Dalesio, "Backlash grows over North Carolina LGBT discrimination law," AP News, April 6, 2016.

29. Peter Hasson, "Malaysia Jails Gays But PayPal Still Opened An Office There," *Daily Caller*, April 6, 2016.

30. John Money, "Hermaphroditism, gender and precocity in hyperadrenocorticism: psychologic findings," *Bulletin of the John Hopkins Hospital* 95, no. 6 (1955): 253–64, http://www.ncbi.nlm.nih.gov/pubmed/14378807. And see Lawrence S. Mayer, M.B., M.S., Ph.D., and Paul R. McHugh, M.D., "Sexuality and Gender Findings from the Biological, Psychological, and Social Sciences," *New Atlantis* 50 (Fall 2016): 91. On academic use of the word "gender," see David Haig, "The Inexorable Rise of Gender and the Decline of Sex: Social Change in Academic Titles, 1945–2001," *Archives of Sexual Behavior* 33, no. 2 (April 2004): 87–96.

31. See John Colapinto, *As Nature Made Him: The Boy Who Was Raised as a Girl* (New York: HarperCollins, 2000).

32. Paul R. McHugh, "Surgical Sex," *First Things*, November 2004.

33. Ibid.

34. Ibid.

35. Ibid.

36. Ibid.

37. Ibid.

38. Ibid.

39. Ibid.

40. Paul McHugh, "Transgender Surgery Isn't the Solution," *Wall Street Journal*, June 12, 2014 (updated May 13, 2016).

41. Paul McHugh, "Transgenderism: A Pathogenic Meme," *Public Discourse*, June 10, 2015.

42. Ibid.

43. Erin Rook, "Johns Hopkins Medicine will resume transgender surgeries after 40 years," *LGBTQ Nation*, October 23, 2016.

44. Zack Ford, "Johns Hopkins to resume gender-affirming surgeries after nearly 40 years," *ThinkProgress*, October 18, 2016.

45. Human Rights Campaign, *Foundation Overview*, December 2015, p. 26, https://www.hrc.org/resources/foundation-overview (accessed May 10, 2017).

46. Ibid., 27.

47. Brian Moulton and Liz Seaton, *Transgender Americans: A Handbook for Understanding*, Human Rights Campaign Foundation (2005), 25, https://www.ithaca.edu/sacl/lgbt/docs/basicresources/understandingtrans.pdf.

48. Human Rights Campaign, *Foundation Overview*, 27.

49. "LGBT Awareness and Support," Johns Hopkins Medicine, July 13, 2016.

50. Dawn Ennis, "Human Rights Campaign Sets Sights on Johns Hopkins After Controversial Trans Report," NBC News, September 1, 2016.

51. Jonathan V. Last, "We Have Ways to Make You Conform," *Weekly Standard*, April 17, 2017.

52. Ibid.

53. Declaration of Quentin L. Van Meter, M.D., U.S. District Court, Middle District of North Carolina, Case 1:16-cv-00425-TDS-JEP, Exhibit I.

54. Jesse Singal, "How the Fight Over Transgender Kids Got a Leading Sex Researcher Fired," Science of Us, *New York*, February 7, 2016.

55. Ibid.

56. Ibid.

57. Ibid.

58. Ibid.

59. Ibid.

CHAPTER 2: WHAT THE ACTIVISTS SAY

1. Brian Moulton and Liz Seaton, *Transgender Americans: A Handbook for Understanding*, Human Rights Campaign Foundation (2005), p. 5, https://www.ithaca.edu/sacl/lgbt/docs/basicresources/understandingtrans.pdf.

2. Human Rights Campaign, "Reporting About Transgender People? Read This," http://www.hrc.org/resources/reporting-about-transgender-people-read-this.

3. American Psychological Association, "Answers to Your Questions About Transgender People, Gender Identity, and Gender Expression," p. 1, http://www.apa.org/topics/lgbt/transgender.pdf.

4. Moulton and Seaton, *Transgender Americans: A Handbook for Understanding*, 5.

5. Declaration of Deanna Adkins, M.D., U.S. District Court, Middle District of North Carolina, Case 1:16-cv-00236-TDS-JEP, p. 5.

6. Ibid.

7. Ibid., 6.

8. Ibid., 7.

9. Ibid., 4.

10. American Psychological Association, "Answers to Your Questions About Transgender People, Gender Identity, and Gender Expression," 1.

11. Declaration of Deanna Adkins, 6.

12. Sam Killermann, "The Genderbread Person v3," *It's Pronounced Metrosexual*, March 16, 2015.

13. Mey Rude, "It's Time For People to Stop Using the Social Construct of 'Biological Sex' to Defend Their Transmisogyny," *Autostraddle*, June 5, 2014.

14. Trans Student Educational Resources, "The Gender Unicorn," http://www. transstudent.org/gender.

15. Ibid.

16. Declaration of George R. Brown, M.D., DFAPA, U.S. District Court, Middle District of North Carolina, Case 1:16-cv-00425, p. 7.

17. Declaration of Deanna Adkins, 4.

18. Declaration of George R. Brown, 8.

19. Declaration of Deanna Adkins, 4.

20. Declaration of George R. Brown, 12.

21. Declaration of Deanna Adkins, 5–6.

22. Declaration of Randi Ettner, Ph.D., U.S. District Court, Middle District of North Carolina, Case 1:16-cv-236-TDS-JEP, p. 5.

23. Declaration of Deanna Adkins, 6.

24. PFLAG, *Our Trans Loved Ones: Questions and Answers for Parents, Families, and Friends of People Who Are Transgender and Gender Expansive* (2008, 2015), p. 9, https://www.pflag.org/ourtranslovedones.

25. Human Rights Campaign, *Schools In Transition: A Guide for Supporting Transgender Students in K–12 Schools*, p. 8, http://assets.hrc.org//files/assets /resources/Schools-In-Transition.pdf.

26. Declaration of Scott F. Leibowitz, M.D., U.S. District Court, Middle District of North Carolina, Case 1:16-cv-00425, p. 6.

27. PFLAG, *Our Trans Loved Ones*, 18.

28. Ibid., 19.

29. Ibid., 27.

30. Ibid., 28.

31. Declaration of Deanna Adkins, 5.

32. Ibid., 7.

33. Ibid., 6.

34. Declaration of George R. Brown, 17.

35. Children's National Medical Center, "If You Are Concerned About Your Child's Gender Behaviors," p. 14, https://childrensnational.org/~/media /cnhs-site/files/departments/gender-and-sexuality-development-program /gvparentbrochure.ashx?la=en/.

36. See Ryan T. Anderson, "How to Think About Sexual Orientation and Gender Identity (SOGI) Policies and Religious Freedom," Heritage Foundation Backgrounder no. 3194, February 13, 2017.

37. Eugene Volokh, "You can be fined for not calling people 'ze' or 'hir,' if that's the pronoun they demand that you use," *Washington Post*, May 17, 2016.

38. The text of California's Senate Bill 219 is here: https://leginfo.legislature. ca.gov/faces/billNavClient.xhtml?bill_id=201720180SB219; *see also* Amy Swearer, "California Lawmakers Want to Force Doctors, Nursing Home Staffs to Deny Their Consciences," *Daily Signal*, August 30, 2017.

39. Human Rights Campaign, *Schools In Transition*, 3.

40. Ibid., 2.
41. Ibid., 20.
42. Ibid., 22.
43. Ibid., 24.
44. Lauren Booker, "What it means to be gender-fluid," CNN, April 13, 2016.
45. Human Rights Campaign, *Schools In Transition*, 15.
46. Ibid., 30.
47. Ibid., 16.
48. Ibid., 27.
49. Ibid., 26.
50. Ibid., 25.
51. Ibid.
52. Ibid., 26.
53. Ibid.
54. Ibid., 28.
55. Declaration of George R. Brown, 15.
56. Ibid., 19.
57. Declaration of Randi Ettner, 8.
58. Ibid., 7.
59. Ibid, 8.
60. Declaration of Scott F. Leibowitz, 9.
61. Expert Rebuttal Declaration of Lawrence S. Mayer, M.D., M.S., Ph.D., U.S. District Court, Middle District of North Carolina, Case 1:16-cv-236-TDS-JEP, pp. 7, 10.
62. Human Rights Campaign, *Schools In Transition*, 2.
63. Ibid., 16.
64. GLSEN, "Model District Policy on Transgender and Gender Nonconforming Students," revised February 2016, p. 4, https://www.glsen.org/article /transgender-model-district-policy.
65. Human Rights Campaign, *Schools In Transition*, 32.
66. GLSEN, "Model District Policy," 9.
67. Human Rights Campaign, *Schools In Transition*, 34.
68. Ibid., 44.
69. Suicidality Symposium, USPATH 2017 (excerpt), https://vimeo. com/205696206, quoted in "'Reportable trauma'? US gender docs 'train' judges & call CPS on balking parents," *4thWaveNow*, February 25, 2017.

CHAPTER 3: DETRANSITIONERS TELL THEIR STORIES

1. Katy Winter, "'I was born a boy, became a girl, and now I want to be a boy again': Britain's youngest sex swap patient to reverse her sex change treatment," *Daily Mail*, October 30, 2012.
2. Ibid.

3. Grace Macaskill, "'I was a boy...then a girl... now I want to be a boy again': Agony of teen who is Britain's youngest sex-swap patient," *Mirror*, October 28, 2012.

4. Anonymous, "Experience: I regret transitioning," *Guardian*, February 3, 2017.

5. Ibid.

6. Cari Stella, "Response to Julia Serano: Detransition, Desistance, and Disinformation," video posted on YouTube, August 9, 2016, https://www.youtube.com/watch?v=9L2jyEDwpEw; and here with a transcript: http://guideonragingstars.tumblr.com/post/148691943070/detransition-desistance-and-disinformation-by.

7. Ibid.

8. Ibid.

9. Ibid.

10. Cari Stella, "Why I detransitioned and what I want medical providers to know (USPATH 2017)," video posted on YouTube, February 6, 2017, https://www.youtube.com/watch?v=Q3-r7ttcw6c.

11. Ibid.

12. Ibid.

13. Cari Stella, "Response to Julia Serano."

14. Ibid.

15. Ibid.

16. Ibid.

17. Bornwrong, "choice," *Born Wrong*, January 4, 2017, https://bornwrong.wordpress.com/2017/01/04/choice/.

18. Ibid.

19. Ibid.

20. Ibid.

21. Ibid.

22. Ibid.

23. Ibid.

24. Ibid.

25. Crash ChaosCats, "Why I Detransitioned (made for USPATH presentation)," video posted on YouTube, February 6, 2017, https://www.youtube.com/watch?v=1-UmP1inIFo.

26. Crashchaoscats, "Lost to Follow-Up/How Far Can You Follow Me?" *Crashchaoscats*, January 30, 2017, https://crashchaoscats.wordpress.com/tag/detransitioned-women/.

27. Crash ChaosCats, "Why I Detransitioned (made for USPATH presentation)."

28. Ibid.

29. Crashchaoscats, "Lost to Follow-Up/How Far Can You Follow Me?"

30. Ibid.

31. Ibid.

32. "TWT – Now on Video! Another detransitioner speaks," *Third Way Trans*, August 24, 2016, https://thirdwaytrans.com/2016/08/24/twt-now-on-video/.

33. Ibid.

34. Ibid.

35. Ibid.

36. Ibid.

37. Ibid.

38. TWT, "To the Young Gender Questioners, I Was You," *Third Way Trans,* September 21, 2014, https://thirdwaytrans.com/2014/09/21/to-the-young-gender-questioners-i-was-you/.

39. "TWT – Now on Video!"

40. Ibid.

41. TWT, "To the Young Gender Questioners, I Was You."

42. "TWT – Now on Video!"

43. Ibid.

44. Ibid.

45. Ibid.

46. TWT, "About the Author," *Third Way Trans,* https://thirdwaytrans.com/about-the-author/.

47. "TWT – Now on Video!"

48. Ibid.

49. TWT, "To the Young Gender Questioners, I Was You."

50. Carey Callahan, "Why I think minors should not medically transition—a detransitioner's perspective," video posted on YouTube, December 20, 2016, https://www.youtube.com/watch?v=QkaQ6_Q6owk.

51. Carey Callahan, "Real Live Detransitioner," video posted on YouTube, July 29, 2016, https://www.youtube.com/watch?v=ohEMLbUxRQA.

52. David French, "The Tragic Transgender Contagion," *National Review,* August 18, 2016.

53. Callahan, "Real Live Detransitioner."

54. Callahan, "Why I think minors should not medically transition."

55. Ibid. One can join the U.S. armed forces at age seventeen with parental consent.

56. Walt Heyer, "I Was a Transgender Woman," *Public Discourse,* April 1, 2015.

57. Ibid.

58. Walt Heyer, "I Used to Be Transgender. Here's My Take on Kids Who Think They Are Transgender," *Daily Signal,* February 16, 2016.

59. Heyer, "I Was a Transgender Woman."

60. Ibid.

61. Walt Heyer, "Transgender Characters May Win Emmys, But Transgender People Hurt Themselves," *Federalist,* February 22, 2015.

62. Heyer, "I Was a Transgender Woman."

63. Heyer, "I Used to Be Transgender."

64. Heyer, "I Was a Transgender Woman."

65. Walt Heyer, "'Sex Change' Surgery: What Bruce Jenner, Diane Sawyer, and You Should Know," *Public Discourse,* April 27, 2015.

66. Walt Heyer, "Regret Isn't Rare: The Dangerous Lie of Sex Change Surgery's Success," *Public Discourse*, June 17, 2016.

67. Ibid.

68. Ibid.

69. Walt Heyer, "Transgender Identities Are Not Always Permanent," *Public Discourse*, September 27, 2016.

70. Heyer, "Transgender Characters May Win Emmys, But Transgender People Hurt Themselves."

71. Heyer, "Regret Isn't Rare."

72. David Batty, "Sex changes are not effective, say researchers," *Guardian*, July 30, 2004.

73. Cecilia Dhejne et al., "Long-term follow-up of transsexual persons undergoing sex reassignment surgery: cohort study in Sweden," *PLOS ONE* 6 (February 2011): e16885.

74. Crashchaoscats, "An Open Letter to Julia Serano from One of the Detransitioned People You Claim to 'Support,'" *Crashchaoscats*, August 8, 2016.

CHAPTER 4: WHAT MAKES US A MAN OR A WOMAN

1. T. W. Sadler, *Langman's Medical Embryology* (Philadelphia: Lippincott Williams & Wilkins, 2004), 40.

2. William J. Larsen, *Human Embryology* (New York: Churchill Livingstone, 2001), 519.

3. Keith L. Moore and T.V.N. Persaud, *The Developing Human: Clinically Oriented Embryology* (Philadelphia: Saunders/Elsevier, 2003), 35.

4. "Sexual Dimorphism," *Encyclopedia Britannica* (2016).

5. Maureen L. Condic and Samuel B. Condic, "Defining Organisms by Organization," *National Catholic Bioethics Quarterly* 5, no. 2 (Summer 2005): 336.

6. Sherif Girgis, "Windsor: Lochnerizing on Marriage?" *Case Western Reserve Law Review* 64 (2014): 988.

7. Lawrence S. Mayer, M.B., M.S., Ph.D., and Paul R. McHugh, M.D., "Sexuality and Gender Findings from the Biological, Psychological, and Social Sciences," Special Report, *New Atlantis* 50 (Fall 2016): 89.

8. Ibid., 90.

9. Expert Rebuttal Declaration of Lawrence S. Mayer, M.D., M.S., Ph.D., U.S. District Court, Middle District of North Carolina, Case 1:16-cv-00425-TDS-JEP.

10. Scott F. Gilbert, *Developmental Biology* (Sunderland, Mass.: Sinauer Associates, 2016), 519–20; and William J. Larsen, *Human Embryology* (New York: Churchill Livingstone, 2001), 307.

11. Larsen, *Human Embryology*, 307.

12. Moore and Persaud, *The Developing Human*, 304.

13. Ibid., 307.

14. Nichole Rigby and Rob J. Kulathinal, "Genetic architecture of sexual dimorphism in humans," *Journal of Cellular Physiology* 230, no. 10 (2015): 2305.

15. The formation of the testes gives rise to the sertoli cells, which produce anti-Mullerian hormone (AMH), also known as Mullerian inhibiting substance (MIS) or factor (MIF), which stops further development of the Mullerian ducts (which otherwise would develop into the uterus and fallopian tubes) and causes their regression.

16. This development is guided by several genes, including RSPO1, WNT4, and FOXL2.

17. Jonathan C. K. Wells, "Sexual dimorphism of body composition," *Best Practice & Research: Clinical Endocrinology & Metabolism* 21 (2007): 415.

18. Ibid., 416.

19. Ibid., 415.

20. Larry Cahill, "His Brain, Her Brain," *Scientific American*, October 1, 2012.

21. In addition to Cahill, see Amber N. V. Ruigrok et al., "A meta-analysis of sex differences in human brain structure," *Neuroscience & Biobehavioral Reviews* 39 (2014): 34–50.

22. Larry Cahill, "A Half-Truth Is a Whole Lie: On the Necessity of Investigating Sex Influences on the Brain," *Endocrinology* 153 (2012): 2542.

23. Cahill, "His Brain, Her Brain."

24. Ibid.

25. Ibid.

26. Madhura Ingalhalikar et al., "Sex differences in the structural connectome of the human brain," *Proceedings of the National Academy of Sciences* 111 (January 2014): 823–28.

27. Institute of Medicine, Committee on Understanding the Biology of Sex and Gender Differences, *Exploring the Biological Contributions to Human Health: Does Sex Matter?* ed. Theresa M. Wizeman and Mary-Lou Pardue (Washington, D.C.: National Academies Press, 2001), Executive Summary, 1, https://www.ncbi.nlm.nih.gov/books/NBK222287/.

28. Ibid., 3.

29. Ibid., 4.

30. Of course our "genetic code" isn't as straightforward as sometimes assumed. Some of our genes can be expressed—turned "on" or "off"—in a process known as epigenetic change. Epigenetic changes, such as DNA methylation and histone acetylation, lead to differential effects in human development as various developmental genes are turned on or off. For a discussion of this, see: Forger N. "Epigenetic mechanisms in sexual differentiation of the brain and behavior," *Philosophical Transactions of the Royal Society B: Biological Sciences* 371 (2016): 1688.

31. Institute of Medicine, *Exploring the Biological Contributions to Human Health*, 5.

32. Ibid., 6.

33. Ruigrok et al., "A meta-analysis of sex differences in human brain structure," 35.

34. Rigby and Kulathinal, "Genetic architecture of sexual dimorphism in humans," 2304.

35. Ibid., 2306.

36. Ibid., 2304.

37. Institute of Medicine, *Exploring the Biological Contributions to Human Health*, 7.

38. Cahill, "His Brain, Her Brain."

39. Ibid.; and Cahill, "A Half-Truth Is a Whole Lie," 2542.

40. Jill M. Goldstein et al., "Fetal hormonal programming of sex differences in depression: linking women's mental health with sex differences in the brain across the lifespan," *Frontiers in Neuroscience* 8 (September 2014), https://www.ncbi.nlm.nih.gov/pmc/articles/PMC4157606/.

41. Peter A. Lee et al., "Global Disorders of Sex Development Update since 2006: Perceptions, Approach and Care," *Hormone Research in Paediatrics* 85 (2016): 159.

42. Declaration of Quentin L. Van Meter, M.D., U.S. District Court, Middle District of North Carolina, Case 1:16-cv-00425-TDS-JEP, Exhibit I.

43. Moore and Persaud, *The Developing Human*, 307.

44. Ibid.

45. Bonnie McCann-Crosby and V. Reid Sutton, "Disorders of Sexual Development," *Clinics in Perinatology* 42 (June 2015): 403.

46. Ibid., 406.

47. Gilbert, *Developmental Biology*, 531.

48. Adriana A. Carrillo, Middey Damian, and Gary Berkovitz, "Disorders of Sexual Differentiation," Chapter 15 in *Pediatric Endocrinology*, 5th ed., ed. Fima Lifshitz (New York: Informa Healthcare, 2009), 2:374.

49. McCann-Crosby and Sutton, "Disorders of Sexual Development," 402.

50. Ibid., 402.

51. See Alexandre Serra et al., "Uniparental Disomy in Somatic Mosaicism 45, X/46, XY/46, XX Associated with Ambiguous Genitalia," *Sexual Development* 9 (June 2015): 136–43; and Marion S. Verp et al., "Chimerism as the etiology of a 46, XX/46, XY fertile true hermaphrodite," *Fertility and Sterility* 57 (February 1992): 346–49.

52. Carrillo et al., "Disorders of Sexual Differentiation," 373–74.

53. Ibid., 377.

54. Lee et al., "Global Disorders of Sex Development Update since 2006," 159.

55. Ibid.

56. Carrillo et al., "Disorders of Sexual Differentiation," 382.

CHAPTER 5: TRANSGENDER IDENTITY AND SEX "REASSIGNMENT"

1. Lawrence S. Mayer, M.B., M.S., Ph.D., and Paul R. McHugh, M.D., "Sexuality and Gender Findings from the Biological, Psychological, and Social Sciences," Special Report, *New Atlantis* 50 (Fall 2016): 8.

2. Anne P. Haas, Philip L. Rodgers, and Jody Herman, "Suicide Attempts Among

Transgender and Gender Non-Conforming Adults: Findings of the National Transgender Discrimination Survey," Williams Institute, UCLA School of Law, January 2014, http://williamsinstitute.law.ucla.edu/wp-content/uploads /AFSP-Williams-Suicide-Report-Final.pdf.

3. Mayer and McHugh, "Sexuality and Gender Findings," 73.

4. Cecilia Dhejne et al., "Long-term follow-up of transsexual persons undergoing sex reassignment surgery: cohort study in Sweden," *PLOS ONE* 6 (February 2011): e16885.

5. Mayer and McHugh, "Sexuality and Gender Findings," 114.

6. Ibid.

7. Ibid., 8.

8. Declaration of Quentin L. Van Meter, M.D., U.S. District Court, Middle District of North Carolina, Case 1:16-cv-00425-TDS-JEP, Exhibit I.

9. Mayer and McHugh, "Sexuality and Gender Findings," 95.

10. American Psychiatric Association, "Gender Dysphoria," *Diagnostic and Statistical Manual of Mental Disorders*, 5th ed. (Arlington, Va.: American Psychiatric Publishing, 2013), 452.

11. Paul McHugh, "Transgender Surgery Isn't the Solution," *Wall Street Journal*, May 13, 2016.

12. Declaration of Allan M. Josephson, M.D., U.S. District Court, Middle District of North Carolina, Case 1:16-cv-00425-TDS-JEP, Exhibit J.

13. Ibid.

14. McHugh, "Transgender Surgery Isn't the Solution."

15. Declaration of Allan M. Josephson.

16. Michelle A. Cretella, "Gender Dysphoria in Children and Suppression of Debate," *Journal of American Physicians and Surgeons* 21 (Summer 2016): 51.

17. McHugh, "Transgender Surgery Isn't the Solution."

18. Cretella, "Gender Dysphoria in Children and Suppression of Debate," 51.

19. Wylie C. Hembree et al., "Endocrine Treatment of Transsexual Persons: An Endocrine Society Clinical Practice Guideline," *Journal of Clinical Endocrinology and Metabolism* 94 (September 2009).

20. Wylie C. Hembree et al., "Endocrine Treatment of Gender-Dysphoric/Gender -Incongruent Persons: An Endocrine Society Clinical Practice Guideline," *Journal of Clinical Endocrinology & Metabolism*, September 13, 2017, https://doi .org/10.1210/jc.2017-01658.

21. World Professional Association for Transgender Health, *Standards of Care for the Health of Transsexual, Transgender, and Gender Nonconforming People*, 7th version (2011), 33, http://www.wpath.org/site_page.cfm?pk_association _webpage_menu=1351.

22. Ibid., 36.

23. Ibid., 47.

24. Ibid., 54.

25. Hembree et al., "Endocrine Treatment of Transsexual Persons," 3149.

26. Robert P. George, "Gnostic Liberalism," *First Things*, December 2016.

27. Mayer and McHugh, "Sexuality and Gender Findings," 93.

28. Christopher O. Tollefsen, "Sex Identity," *Public Discourse*, July 13, 2015.

29. Ibid.

30. Declaration of Lawrence S. Mayer, M.D., M.S., Ph.D., U.S. District Court, Middle District of North Carolina, Case 1:16-cv-00425-TDS-JEP, Exhibit K.

31. Paul McHugh, "Transgenderism: A Pathogenic Meme," *Public Discourse*, June 10, 2015.

32. Mayer and McHugh, M.D., "Sexuality and Gender Findings," Part 2.

33. David Batty, "Mistaken identity," *Guardian*, July 30, 2004.

34. Dr. Paul R. McHugh, M.D., Dr. Paul Hruz, M.D., Ph.D., and Dr. Lawrence S. Mayer, Ph.D., Brief of *Amici Curiae* in Support of Petitioner, *Gloucester County School Board v. G.G.*, Supreme Court of the United States, No. 16-273 (January 10, 2017), 18–19, 20, http://www.scotusblog.com/wp-content/uploads/2017/01/16-273-amicus-petitioner-mchugh.pdf.

35. Hayes, Inc., "Hormone therapy for the treatment of gender dysphoria," *Hayes Medical Technology Directory* (Lansdale, Pa.. Winifred Hayes, May 2014), quoted in Cretella, "Gender Dysphoria in Children and Suppression of Debate," 52. See also "Sex reassignment surgery for the treatment of gender dysphoria," *Hayes Medical Technology Directory* (2014).

36. Annette Kuhn et al., "Quality of life 15 years after sex reassignment surgery for transsexualism," *Fertility and Sterility* 92 (November 2009): 1685–89.

37. Mayer and McHugh, "Sexuality and Gender Findings," 111–12.

38. Dhejne et al., "Long-term follow-up of transsexual persons undergoing sex reassignment surgery," e16885.

39. Mayer and McHugh, "Sexuality and Gender Findings," 111.

40. Ibid.

41. Ibid., 112.

42. Thomas Nagel, "What Is It Like to Be a Bat?" *Philosophical Review* 83 (October 1974): 435–50.

43. American Psychiatric Association, "Gender Dysphoria," 452.

44. Mayer and McHugh, "Sexuality and Gender Findings," 96.

45. Ibid., 115.

46. George, "Gnostic Liberalism."

47. Ibid.

48. For an extended discussion, see Patrick Lee and Robert P. George, *Body-Self Dualism in Contemporary Ethics and Politics* (New York: Cambridge University Press, 2008).

49. Robert Sapolsky, "Caught Between Male and Female," *Wall Street Journal*, December 6, 2013.

50. Mayer and McHugh, "Sexuality and Gender Findings," 98.

51. Ibid., 8.

52. Ibid., 102.

53. Ibid.

54. Ibid., 103.
55. Ibid.
56. Ibid., 104.
57. Declaration of Paul W. Hruz, M.D, Ph.D., U.S. District Court, Middle District of North Carolina, Case 1:16-cv-00425-TDS-JEP, Exhibit H.
58. Milton Diamond, "Transsexuality Among Twins: Identity Concordance, Transition, Rearing, and Orientation," *International Journal of Transgenderism* 14 (May 2013): 24–38.
59. Declaration of Quentin L. Van Meter, M.D., U.S. District Court, Middle District of North Carolina, Case 1:16-cv-00425-TDS-JEP, Exhibit I, 10.
60. Mayer and McHugh, "Sexuality and Gender Findings," 8.
61. Ibid., 105.
62. Paul R. McHugh, "Surgical Sex," *First Things*, November 2004.
63. Ibid.
64. J. Michael Bailey and Kiira Triea, "What Many Transgender Activists Don't Want You to Know: and why you should know it anyway," *Perspectives in Biology and Medicine* 50 (Autumn 2007).
65. Ibid., 521.
66. Ibid., 522.
67. Ibid., 527.
68. Ibid., 524.
69. Ibid., 524–25.
70. Ibid., 523.
71. Ibid., 525.
72. Ibid., 524.
73. Ibid., 523.
74. McHugh, "Transgenderism: A Pathogenic Meme."
75. Bailey and Triea, "What Many Transgender Activists Don't Want You to Know," 527.
76. Ibid., 528.
77. Hembree et al., "Endocrine Treatment of Transsexual Persons," 3135.
78. Declaration of Quentin L. Van Meter.
79. Hembree et al., "Endocrine Treatment of Transsexual Persons," 3132.
80. Declaration of Quentin L. Van Meter.
81. Declaration of Paul W. Hruz.
82. Cretella, "Gender Dysphoria in Children and Suppression of Debate," 51.
83. Leon R. Kass, "Neither for Love nor Money: Why Doctors Must Not Kill," *Public Interest* 94 (Winter 1989): 28.
84. Ibid., 29, 39. For more on this, see my report "Always Care, Never Kill: How Physician-Assisted Suicide Endangers the Weak, Corrupts Medicine, Compromises the Family, and Violates Human Dignity and Equality," Heritage Foundation, March 24, 2015.

85. Paul W. Hruz, Lawrence B. Mayer, and Paul R. McHugh, "Growing Pains: The Problems with Puberty Suppression in Treating Gender Dysphoria," *New Atlantis* 52 (Spring 2017): 21.

86. Cretella, "Gender Dysphoria in Children and Suppression of Debate," 51. I would slightly tweak Dr. Cretella's phrasing here. The Ph.D. philosopher inside of me bristles a little at her definition of normality as applied to the brain. After all, plenty of people have false beliefs about reality, including physical reality: think about our debates over global warming and climate change. Both sides of the debate can't be right, but that doesn't mean one side is delusional. After all, disagreement about contested issues is the norm for human rationality: frequently we don't immediately see the correct answer. We have to discover it discursively, usually in a communal process of give and take, point and counterpoint. I'm sure Cretella agrees and would readily acknowledge all of this.

87. Declaration of Allan M. Josephson.

CHAPTER 6: CHILDHOOD DYSPHORIA AND DESISTANCE

1. Petula Dvorak, "Transgender at Five," *Washington Post*, May 19, 2012.

2. Ibid.

3. Petula Dvorak, "Transgender at 8: Tyler remains certain he's a boy as the world changes around him," *Washington Post*, October 12, 2015.

4. Ibid.

5. Jesse Singal, "You Should Watch the BBC's Controversial Documentary on the Gender-Dysphoria Researcher Kenneth Zucker (Updated)," Science of Us, *New York*, January 13, 2017.

6. See Paul R. McHugh, Paul Hruz, and Lawrence S. Mayer, Brief of *Amici Curiae* in Support of Petitioner, *Gloucester County School Board v. G.G.*, Supreme Court of the United States, No. 16-273 (January 10, 2017), 12, http://www.americanbar.org/content/dam/aba/publications/supreme_court_preview/briefs_2016_2017/16-273_amicus_pet_mchugh.authcheckdam.pdf; and Jesse Singal, "What's Missing From the Conversation About Transgender Kids," Science of Us, *New York*, July 25, 2016.

7. Singal, "What's Missing From the Conversation About Transgender Kids."

8. Paul W. Hruz, Lawrence B. Mayer, and Paul R. McHugh, "Growing Pains: The Problems with Puberty Suppression in Treating Gender Dysphoria," *New Atlantis* 52 (Spring 2017): 17, citing from the *European Journal of Endocrinology*.

9. Ibid.

10. Ibid.

11. Kate Lyons, "UK doctor prescribing cross-sex hormones to children as young as 12," *Guardian*, July 11, 2016.

12. Jesse Singal, "How the Fight Over Transgender Kids Got a Leading Sex Researcher Fired," Science of Us, *New York*, February 7, 2016.

13. Wylie C. Hembree et al., "Endocrine Treatment of Transsexual Persons: An Endocrine Society Clinical Practice Guideline," *Journal of Clinical Endocrinology and Metabolism* 94 (September 2009): 3140.

14. World Professional Association for Transgender Health, *Standards of Care for*

the Health of Transsexual, Transgender, and Gender Nonconforming People, 7th version, (2011), 20.

15. Ibid., 19.
16. Hembree et al., "Endocrine Treatment of Transsexual Persons," 3140.
17. Peggy T. Cohen-Kettenis, Henriette A. Delemarre-van de Waal, and Louis J.G. Gooren, "The Treatment of Adolescent Transsexuals: Changing Insights," *Journal of Sexual Medicine* 5 (August 2008): 1894.
18. Hruz, Mayer, and McHugh, "Growing Pains."
19. Ibid.
20. McHugh, Hruz, and Mayer, Brief of *Amici Curiae*, 12.
21. Singal, "What's Missing From the Conversation About Transgender Kids."
22. Hruz, Mayer, and McHugh, "Growing Pains."
23. Singal, "What's Missing From the Conversation About Transgender Kids."
24. Singal, "How the Fight Over Transgender Kids Got a Leading Sex Researcher Fired."
25. Ibid.
26. Ibid.
27. Michelle A. Cretella, "Gender Dysphoria in Children and Suppression of Debate," *Journal of American Physicians and Surgeons* 21 (Summer 2016): 53.
28. Declaration of Paul W. Hruz, M.D, Ph.D., U.S. District Court, Middle District of North Carolina, Case 1:16-cv-00425-TDS-JEP, Exhibit H.
29. Singal, "You Should Watch the BBC's Controversial Documentary on the Gender-Dysphoria Researcher Kenneth Zucker (Updated)."
30. Singal, "How the Fight Over Transgender Kids Got a Leading Sex Researcher Fired."
31. Hruz, Mayer, and McHugh, "Growing Pains."
32. Ibid.
33. Ibid.
34. See a listing of prominent examples in ibid.
35. Ibid.
36. Ibid.
37. Ibid.
38. See discussion in ibid.
39. Declaration of Paul W. Hruz.
40. Hruz, Mayer, and McHugh, "Growing Pains."
41. Hembree et al., "Endocrine Treatment of Transsexual Persons," 3142.
42. Ibid., 3132.
43. Hruz, Mayer, and McHugh, "Growing Pains."
44. McHugh, Hruz, and Mayer, Brief of *Amici Curiae*, 18.
45. Cretella, "Gender Dysphoria in Children and Suppression of Debate," 52.
46. Hruz, Mayer, and McHugh, "Growing Pains."
47. Ibid.
48. Singal, "How the Fight Over Transgender Kids Got a Leading Sex Researcher Fired."

49. Human Rights Campaign, "Interactive Map: Clinical Care Programs for Gender-Expansive Children and Adolescents," https://www.hrc.org/resources/interactive-map-clinical-care-programs-for-gender-nonconforming-childr (accessed October 17, 2017).

50. Lawrence S. Mayer and Paul R. McHugh, "Sexuality and Gender Findings from the Biological, Psychological, and Social Sciences," Special Report, *New Atlantis* 50 (Fall 2016): 107.

51. Paul McHugh, "Transgenderism: A Pathogenic Meme," *Public Discourse*, June 10, 2015.

52. Paul McHugh, "Transgender Surgery Isn't the Solution," *Wall Street Journal*, May 13, 2016.

53. McHugh, "Transgenderism: A Pathogenic Meme."

54. McHugh, Hruz, and Mayer, Brief of *Amici Curiae*, 13.

55. Kenneth J. Zucker, "Children with gender identity disorder: Is there a best practice?" *Neuropsychiatrie de l'Enfance et de l'Adolescence* 56 (September 2008): 358.

56. Kenneth Zucker, Hayley Wood, Devita Singh, and Susan J. Bradley, "A Developmental, Biopsychosocial Model for the Treatment of Children with Gender Identity Disorder," *Journal of Homosexuality* 59 (March 2012): 375.

57. Zucker, "Children with gender identity disorder: Is there a best practice?" 363.

58. Zucker et al., "A Developmental, Biopsychosocial Model for the Treatment of Children with Gender Identity Disorder," 375.

59. Ibid.

60. Ibid., 376.

61. Ibid.

62. Ibid., 377.

63. Ibid., 378.

64. Ibid.

65. Derek Glidden et al., "Gender Dysphoria and Autism Spectrum Disorder: A Systematic Review of the Literature," *Sexual Medicine Review* 4 (January 2016): 9.

66. Zucker et al., "A Developmental, Biopsychosocial Model for the Treatment of Children with Gender Identity Disorder," 379.

67. Ibid.

68. Ibid., 380.

69. Ibid., 380–81.

70. Zucker, "Children with gender identity disorder: Is there a best practice?" 360.

71. Zucker et al., "A Developmental, Biopsychosocial Model for the Treatment of Children with Gender Identity Disorder," 381.

72. Ibid., 382.

73. Ibid., 383.

74. Zucker, "Children with gender identity disorder: Is there a best practice?" 363.

75. Zucker et al., "A Developmental, Biopsychosocial Model for the Treatment of Children with Gender Identity Disorder," 383.

76. Ibid.

77. Ibid., 388.

78. Zucker, "Children with gender identity disorder: Is there a best practice?" 361.

79. Zucker et al., "A Developmental, Biopsychosocial Model for the Treatment of Children with Gender Identity Disorder," 389.

80. Ibid.; Zucker, "Children with gender identity disorder: Is there a best practice?" 360–61.

81. New Mexico Senate Bill 121, 53rd Legislature, 1st sess. (2017), https://www.nmlegis.gov/Sessions/17%20Regular/bills/senate/SB0121.html; Stephen Peters, "New Mexico Governor Signs Into Law Bill Protecting LGBTQ Youth From 'Conversion' Therapy," Human Rights Campaign, April 7, 2017.

82. Dominic Holden, "New Mexico May Become Seventh State To Ban LGBT Conversion Therapy," *BuzzFeed*, March 9, 2017; Mike Savino, "State outlaws conversion therapy aimed at changing minors' sexual orientation, gender identity," *Record-Journal* (Connecticut), May 16, 2017.

83. American Psychoanalytic Association, "2012 – Position Statement on Attempts to Change Sexual Orientation, Gender Identity, or Gender Expression," June 2012, http://www.apsa.org/content/2012-position-statement-attempts-change-sexual-orientation-gender-identity-or-gender.

84. Human Rights Campaign, "Policy and Position Statements on Conversion Therapy," http://www.hrc.org/resources/policy-and-position-statements-on-conversion-therapy.

85. Human Rights Campaign, "The Lies and Dangers of Efforts to Change Sexual Orientation or Gender Identity," http://www.hrc.org/resources/the-lies-and-dangers-of-reparative-therapy.

86. World Professional Association for Transgender Health, *Standards of Care for the Health of Transsexual, Transgender, and Gender Nonconforming People*, 7th version (2011), 16.

87. Quoted in Zucker, "Children with gender identity disorder: Is there a best practice?" 359.

88. Ibid.

CHAPTER 7: GENDER AND CULTURE

1. Ashley Parker, "Karen Pence is the vice president's 'prayer warrior,' gut check and shield," *Washington Post*, March 28, 2017.

2. Joanna L. Grossman, "Vice President Pence's 'never dine alone with a woman' rule isn't honorable. It's probably illegal," *Vox*, March 31, 2017.

3. Mary Vought, "I worked for Mike Pence. Being a woman never held me back," *Washington Post*, April 1, 2017. For the record, Mary Vought is a friend of mine.

4. Ibid.

5. Sarrah Le Marquand, "It should be illegal to be a stay-at-home mum," *Daily Telegraph*, March 20, 2017.

6. Quoted by Christina Hoff Sommers, "Feminism and Freedom," *American Spectator*, July 2, 2008.

7. Le Marquand, "It should be illegal to be a stay-at-home mum."

8. Ibid.

9. American Psychological Association, "Answers to Your Questions About Transgender People, Gender Identity and Gender Expression," http://www .apa.org/topics/lgbt/transgender.pdf.

10. John Stuart Mill, "The Subjection of Women," 1869, http://www.constitution. org/jsm/women.htm.

11. Scott Yenor, "Sex, Gender, and the Origin of the Culture Wars: An Intellectual History," Heritage Foundation, June 30, 2017.

12. For a good discussion of this alternative early strand of feminism, see Hoff Sommers, "Feminism and Freedom."

13. Simone de Beauvoir, *The Second Sex*, trans. H. M. Parshley (London: Jonathan Cape, 1953, 2009), 294.

14. Margaret H. McCarthy, "Gender Ideology and the Humanum," *Communio* 43 (Summer 2016): 278.

15. Ibid., citing Kate Millett, *Sexual Politics* (1970). Sr. Allen points out that Millett (following John Money and Robert Stoller) pioneered the use of the term "gender" as something "so arbitrary... that it may even be contrary to physiology." Sr. Mary Prudence Allen, "Gender Reality," *Solidarity: The Journal of Catholic Social Thought and Secular Ethics* 4 (2014): 15, citing Millett, *Sexual Politics*.

16. Betty Friedan, *The Feminine Mystique* (New York: W. W. Norton, 1963, 2010), 495.

17. Ibid., 462.

18. Beauvoir, *The Second Sex*, 44.

19. McCarthy, "Gender Ideology and the Humanum," 280.

20. Shulamith Firestone, *The Dialectic of Sex: The Case for Feminist Revolution* (1970; New York: Farrar, Straus & Giroux, 2003), 11.

21. Alice Schwarzer, *After the Second Sex: Conversations with Simone de Beauvoir* (New York: Pantheon, 1984), 39.

22. Ibid., 40.

23. Cleta Mitchell, "No Room for Dissent in Women's Movement Today," *New York Times*, March 31, 2017.

24. See Kate Millett, *Sexual Politics* (Garden City, N.Y.: Doubleday, 1970), 30–31; and Beauvoir, *The Second Sex*, 10–11, 404.

25. Robert J. Stoller, *Sex and Gender: On the Development of Masculinity and Femininity* (New York: Science House, 1968), 48.

26. John Money and Patricia Tucker, *Sexual Signatures: On Being a Man or a Woman* (Boston: Little, Brown & Co., 1975), 90–91, 98.

27. Yenor, "Sex, Gender, and the Origin of the Culture Wars: An Intellectual History."

28. McCarthy summarizes Butler's thinking about the body in "Gender Ideology and the Humanum," 283.

29. Judith Butler, *Undoing Gender* (New York: Routledge, 2004), 64–65.

30. McCarthy, "Gender Ideology and the Humanum," 289.

31. See, for example, Judith Butler, *Gender Trouble: Feminism and the Subversion of Identity* (New York: Routledge, 2006), 171–80.

32. Butler, *Undoing Gender*, 28.

33. Ibid.

34. Ibid., 29.

35. McCarthy, "Gender Ideology and the Humanum," 283–84, 288.

36. "Kindergarten Teacher Bans Legos For Boys Citing 'Gender Equity,'" CBS Seattle, November 15, 2015.

37. Christina Hoff Sommers, "You Can Give a Boy a Doll, but You Can't Make Him Play With It," *Atlantic*, December 6, 2012.

38. Ibid.

39. Kate Stanton, "Lego gets sales boost from girl-friendly toy series," UPI, February 28, 2013.

40. Jonathan V. Last, "The Lego Disney Castle: Finally a Death Star for Girls," *Weekly Standard*, July 12, 2016.

41. Christina Hoff Sommers, "What 'Lean In' Misunderstands About Gender Differences," *Atlantic*, March 19, 2013.

42. Ibid.

43. Ibid.

44. Ibid.

45. W. Bradford Wilcox, "Surprisingly, Most Married Families Today Tilt Neo-Traditional," Institute for Family Studies, February 26, 2014.

46. W. Bradford Wilcox and Samuel Sturgeon, "Why would millennial men prefer stay-at-home wives? Race and feminism," *Washington Post*, April 5, 2017.

47. Ibid.

48. Christina Hoff Sommers, "Ambitious Women Should Be Prepared to Work 60 Hour Weeks," *New York Times*, November 8, 2015.

49. On "natural goodness" see Philippa Foot, *Natural Goodness* (Oxford: Clarendon Press, 2001); and Rosalind Hursthouse, *On Virtue Ethics* (Oxford: Oxford University Press, 2002). See also Elizabeth Anscombe and Alasdair MacIntyre generally.

50. For more on natural law ethics, see: John Finnis, *Natural Law and Natural Rights* (Oxford: Oxford University Press, 2011); Finnis, *Fundamentals of Ethics* (Washington, D.C.: Georgetown University Press, 1983); Finnis, *Aquinas: Moral, Legal, Political Thinker* (Oxford: Oxford University Press, 1998); Robert P. George, *In Defense of Natural Law* (Oxford: Oxford University Press, 2001); and Patrick Lee and Robert P. George, *Body-Self Dualism in Contemporary Ethics and Politics* (New York: Cambridge University Press, 2008).

51. J. Richard Udry, "Biological Limits of Gender Construction," *American Sociological Review* 65, no. 3 (June 2000): 443–57, http://dx.doi.org/10.2307/2657466.

52. Sr. Mary Prudence Allen, "Gender Reality," *Solidarity: The Journal of Catholic Social Thought and Secular Ethics* 4 (2014): 25.

53. Ibid., 26–27.

54. Margaret Harper McCarthy, "The Emperor's (New) Clothes: A Look at the logic of the (not so) new 'gender ideology,'" Catholic Women's Forum, confidential working paper (on file with author), 18.

55. Ibid., 23.

56. See Sherif Girgis, Ryan T. Anderson, and Robert P. George, *What Is Marriage? Man and Woman: A Defense* (New York: Encounter Books, 2012), 25.

57. McCarthy, "Gender Ideology and the Humanum," 291–92.

58. Ibid., 290.

59. Christopher O. Tollefsen, "Gender Identity," *Public Discourse*, July 14, 2015.

60. Amy A. Kass, "A Case for Courtship," Institute for American Values, Working Paper no. 73 (September 22, 1999), 3, http://americanvalues.org/catalog/pdfs/wp-73.pdf.

61. Anthony Esolen, *Out of the Ashes: Rebuilding American Culture* (Washington, D.C.: Regnery, 2017), 96.

62. Ibid., 97, 99.

63. Ibid., 97–98.

64. Pete Williams, "Boy Scouts Will Admit Girls, Allow Them to Earn Eagle Scout Rank," NBC News, October 11, 2017.

65. Esolen, *Out of the Ashes*, 99–100.

66. Ibid., 100.

67. C. S. Lewis, *The Four Loves* (New York: Harcourt, 1960), 67.

68. Ibid., 73.

69. Adrian F. Ward, "Men and Women Can't Be 'Just Friends,'" *Scientific American*, October 23, 2012.

70. See Ta-Nehisi Coates, "The Case for Reparations," *Atlantic*, June 2014; and *Between the World and Me* (New York: Spiegel & Grau, 2015).

71. Ta-Nehisi Coates, "Violence and the Social Compact," *Atlantic*, December 20, 2012.

72. See Ryan T. Anderson, *Truth Overruled: The Future of Marriage and Religious Freedom* (Washington, D.C.: Regnery, 2015).

73. W. Bradford Wilcox, "Reconcilable Differences: What Social Sciences Show about the Complementarity of the Sexes and Parenting," *Touchstone* 18, no. 9 (November 2005), 32, 36.

74. David Popenoe, *Life without Father: Compelling New Evidence That Fatherhood and Marriage Are Indispensable for the Good of Children and Society* (New York: The Free Press, 1996), 146.

75. Ibid., 197.

76. Wilcox, "Reconcilable Differences," 33.

77. Popenoe, *Life without Father*, 145–46.

78. Wilcox, "Reconcilable Differences," 35.

79. "One study found that about 35 percent of girls in the United States whose fathers left before age 6 became pregnant as teenagers, that 10 percent of

girls in the United States whose fathers left them between the ages of 6 and 18 became pregnant as teenagers, and that only 5 percent of girls whose fathers stayed with them throughout childhood became pregnant." Wilcox, "Reconcilable Differences," 35.

80. For the relevant studies, see Chapters 1 and 7 of my book *Truth Overruled*. See also The Witherspoon Institute, *Marriage and the Public Good: Ten Principles* (Princeton, N.J., 2008), 9–19, http://winst.org/wp-content/uploads/WI _Marriage_and_the_Public_Good.pdf. Signed by some seventy scholars, this document presents extensive evidence from the social sciences about the welfare of children and adults. See also Kristin Anderson Moore, Susan M. Jekielek, and Carol Emig, "Marriage from a Child's Perspective: How Does Family Structure Affect Children, and What Can We Do About It?" Child Trends Research Brief (June 2002), 1, 6, http://www.childtrends.org /wp-content/uploads/2013/03/MarriageRB602.pdf; Wendy D. Manning and Kathleen A. Lamb, "Adolescent Well-Being in Cohabiting, Married, and Single-Parent Families," *Journal of Marriage and Family* 65, no. 4 (November 2003): 876, 890; Sara McLanahan, Elisabeth Donahue, and Ron Haskins, "Introducing the Issue," *Marriage and Child Wellbeing* 15, no. 2 (Fall 2005), http://www.princeton.edu/futureofchildren/publications/docs/15_02_01.pdf; Mary Parke, "Are Married Parents Really Better for Children?" Center for Law and Social Policy, May 2003, http://www.clasp.org/admin/site/publications _states/files/0086.pdf; and W. Bradford Wilcox et al., *Why Marriage Matters: Twenty-Six Conclusions from the Social Sciences*, 2nd ed. (New York: Institute for American Values, 2005), 6, online at http://americanvalues.org/catalog /pdfs/why_marriage_matters2.pdf.

81. Esolen, *Out of the Ashes*, 124.

82. Christopher Lasch, *Women and the Common Life* (1997), cited in Margaret Harper McCarthy, "A Mother's Work Is Never Done!" *Humanum*, Spring 2013 (*A Mother's Work*), 10.

83. Leon R. Kass, "The End of Courtship," *National Affairs* 31 (Winter 1997): 50–51.

84. McCarthy, "A Mother's Work Is Never Done!" 13.

85. G. K. Chesterton, *What's Wrong with the World*, quoted in McCarthy, "A Mother's Work Is Never Done!" 14.

86. Esolen, *Out of the Ashes*, 127.

87. Ibid., 130.

88. Dorothy L. Sayers, "Are Women Human? Address Given to a Women's Society, 1938," *Logos: A Journal of Catholic Thought and Culture* 8, no. 4 (Fall 2005): 169–70.

89. McCarthy, "A Mother's Work Is Never Done!" 15.

90. Ibid., 11

91. Esolen, *Out of the Ashes*, 128.

92. Ibid.

93. Steven E. Rhoads, "Lean In's Biggest Hurdle: What Most Moms Want," Institute for Family Studies, March 16, 2017, https://ifstudies.org/blog /lean-ins-biggest-hurdle-what-most-moms-want.

94. Ibid.

95. Ibid.

96. David Cloutier and Luke Timothy Johnson, "The Church and Transgender Identity," *Commonweal*, February 27, 2017.

97. Ibid.

98. Ibid.

99. Ibid.

CHAPTER 8: POLICY IN THE COMMON INTEREST

1. The regulation from the Department of Health and Human Services reinterpreted Section 1557 of the Affordable Care Act, which prohibits discrimination on the basis of "race, color, national origin, sex, age, or disability," so that "sex" would include "gender identity," thus requiring coverage and performance of sex reassignment surgeries and access to facilities based on patients' chosen gender identity. See Ryan T. Anderson, "New Obamacare Transgender Regulations Threaten Freedom of Physicians," *Daily Signal*, May 13, 2016.

2. Ryan T. Anderson, "Obama Unilaterally Rewrites Law, Imposes Transgender Policy on Nation's Schools," *Daily Signal*, May 13, 2016; U.S. Department of Justice, Office of Public Affairs, "U.S. Departments of Justice and Education Release Joint Guidance to Help Schools Ensure the Civil Rights of Transgender Students," May 13, 2016, https://www.justice.gov/opa/pr/us-departments-justice-and-education-release-joint-guidance-help-schools-ensure-civil-rights (links to the "Dear Colleague" letter).

3. U.S. Department of Housing and Urban Development, "HUD Issues Final Rule to Ensure Equal Access to Housing and Services Regardless of Gender Identity," Press Release, September 20, 2016, https://portal.hud.gov/hudportal/HUD?src=/press/press_releases_media_advisories/2016/HUDNo_16-137.

4. Eugene Volokh, "Claims by transgender schoolteacher (who wants to be called 'they') yield $60,000 settlement, agreement to create disciplinary rules regulating 'pronoun usage,'" *Washington Post*, May 25, 2016. Emphasis added by Volokh.

5. Katharine Kersten, "Transgender Conformity," *First Things*, December 2016.

6. Kelsey Harkness, "Nationally Ranked School Counters Complaint of Transgender Discrimination," *Daily Signal*, May 2, 2016.

7. Kersten, "Transgender Conformity."

8. Emily Zinos, "Time for Parents to Resist Transgender Activism," *First Things*, January 20, 2017.

9. Emily Zinos, "Biology Isn't Bigotry: Christians, Lesbians, and Radical Feminists Unite to Fight Gender Ideology," *Public Discourse*, March 6, 2017.

10. Paul R. McHugh, Paul Hruz, and Lawrence S. Mayer, Brief of *Amici Curiae* in Support of Petitioner, *Gloucester County School Board v. G.G.*, Supreme Court of the United States, No. 16-273 (January 10, 2017), 16, http://www.scotusblog.com/wp-content/uploads/2017/01/16-273-amicus-petitioner-mchugh.pdf.

11. Ibid., 20.

12. Expert Rebuttal Declaration of Paul W. Hruz, M.D, Ph.D., U.S. District Court, Middle District of North Carolina, Case 1:16-cv-00425-TDS-JEP.

13. Declaration of Paul W. Hruz, M.D, Ph.D., U.S. District Court, Middle District of North Carolina, Case 1:16-cv-00425-TDS-JEP, Exhibit H.

14. Zinos, "Biology Isn't Bigotry."

15. The next three sections draw on a report I co-authored with Melody Wood: "Gender Identity Policies in Schools: What Congress, the Courts, and the Trump Administration Should Do," Heritage Foundation, March 23, 2017.

16. *United States v. Virginia et al.*, 518 U.S. 151, 550 n.19 (1996), https://supreme. justia.com/cases/federal/us/518/515/case.html.

17. Eugene Volokh, "Prominent feminist: bans on sex discrimination 'emphatically' do not 'require unisex bathrooms,'" *Washington Post*, May 9, 2016; and Ruth Bader Ginsburg, "The Fear of the Equal Rights Amendment," *Washington Post*, April 7, 1975, https://www.washingtonpost.com/news /volokh-conspiracy/wp-content/uploads/sites/14/2016/05/ginsburg.jpg.

18. *Faulkner v. Jones*, 10 F.3d 226, 232 (4th Cir. 1993).

19. 28 CFR § 115.15(d), quoted in Defendant's and Intervenor-Defendants' Brief in Opposition to the United States' Motion for Preliminary Injunction, *United States of America v. State of North Carolina et al.*, U.S. District Court, Middle District of North Carolina, Case 1:16-CV-00425-TDS-JEP (August 17, 2016), 68, http://files.eqcf.org/cases/116-cv-00425-149/. Cited hereafter as Defendants' and Intervenor-Defendants' Brief.

20. Women's Liberation Front and Family Policy Alliance, Brief of *Amici Curiae* in Support of Petitioner, *Gloucester County School Board v. G.G.*, Supreme Court of the United States, No. 16-273 (January 10, 2017), 6, www.scotusblog.com/ wp-content/uploads/2017/01/16-273_amicus_pet_womens_liberation _front_and_family_policy_alliance.pdf. Emphasis in original.

21. *Students and Parents for Privacy v. United States Department of Education; John B. King, Jr.; United States Department of Justice; Loretta E. Lynch; and School Directors of Township High School District 211, County of Cook and State of Illinois*, U.S. District Court, Northern District of Illinois, Case 1:16-cv-04945, Verified Complaint for Injunctive and Declaratory Relief (May 4, 2016), 55, http://www.adfmedia.org/files/SPPcomplaint.pdf.

22. Ibid., 56.

23. Declaration of Y.K., Defendants' and Intervenor-Defendants' Brief, Exhibit O, 2–3.

24. Declaration of S.H., Defendants' and Intervenor-Defendants' Brief, Exhibit Q, 1–3.

25. Safe Spaces for Women, Brief of *Amicus Curiae* Supporting Neither Party, *Gloucester County School Board v. G.G.*, Supreme Court of the United States, No. 16-273 (January 2017), 2, http://www.scotusblog.com/wp-content /uploads/2017/01/16-273-amicus-np-SSW.pdf.

26. Ibid., 3.

27. Ibid., 14.

28. Jessica Chasmar, "Ga. ACLU Leader Resigns over Obama's Transgender Bathroom Directive," *Washington Times*, June 2, 2016.

29. Jeannie Suk Gersen, "The Transgender Bathroom Debate and the Looming Title IX Crisis," *New Yorker*, May 24, 2016.

30. Expert Opinion of Sheriff Tim Hutchison (Retired), Defendants' and Intervenor-Defendants' Brief, Exhibit N, 6–7.

31. Kenneth V. Lanning, *Child Molesters: A Behavioral Analysis for Professionals Investigating the Sexual Exploitation of Children*, 5th ed. (Alexandria, Va.: National Center for Missing and Exploited Children, 2010), http://www .missingkids.com/en_US/publications/NC70.pdf.

32. Expert Declaration and Report of Kenneth V. Lanning, Defendants' and Intervenor-Defendants' Brief, Exhibit M, 12. Sheriff Tim Hutchison agrees: "The risks of GIBAPs do not come from transgender use of public facilities that do not line up with birth certificates. Rather, non-transgender male sex offenders who prefer female victims will use GIBAPs to obtain better access to their victims for different types of sex crimes." Expert Opinion of Sheriff Tim Hutchison (Retired), 8.

33. Expert Declaration and Report of Kenneth V. Lanning, 13.

34. Ibid.

35. Expert Opinion of Sheriff Tim Hutchison (Retired), 12.

36. Ibid., 15.

37. Ibid., 7.

38. Expert Declaration and Report of Kenneth V. Lanning, 18.

39. Expert Opinion of Sheriff Tim Hutchison (Retired), 10

40. Expert Declaration and Report of Kenneth V. Lanning, 14.

41. Expert Opinion of Sheriff Tim Hutchison (Retired), 10.

42. Ibid.; Expert Declaration and Report of Kenneth V. Lanning, 14.

43. Sam Pazzano, "Predator Who Claimed to Be Transgender Declared Dangerous Offender," *Toronto Sun*, February 26, 2014.

44. "Man Dressed as Woman Spies into Mall Bathroom Stall in Virginia, Police Say," NBC Washington, October 14, 2015.

45. Mariana Barillas, "Man Allowed to Use Women's Locker Room at Swimming Pool Without Citing Gender Identity," *Daily Signal*, February 23, 2016.

46. Jessica Chin, "University of Toronto Gender-Neutral Bathrooms Reduced After Voyeurism Reports," *Huffington Post*, October 6, 2015.

47. Kelsey Harkness, "Minnesota Students and Parents File Lawsuit Against Obama's Bathroom Mandate," *Daily Signal*, September 8, 2016.

48. Rick Bella, "Cross-Dressing Sex Offender Released to Community Supervision," *Oregonian*, May 3, 2012.

49. "Police: Man in bra and wig found in women's bathroom," KOMO News, March 16, 2012.

50. Niraj Chokshi, "Transgender Woman Is Charged with Voyeurism at Target in Idaho," *New York Times*, July 14, 2016.

51. *State of Idaho v. Sean Patrick Smith*, District Court of the Seventh Judicial District, State of Idaho, County of Bonneville, Magaistrate [*sic*] Division, No. CR-16-8468, Affidavit of Probable Cause for Warrantless Arrest Under I.C.R. 5

(July 12, 2016), 2, http://assets.eastidahonews.com/wp-content /uploads/2016/07/13132732/state-of-idaho-vs-smith-affadavit.pdf.

52. "Man Seen Reaching Under Stall with Phone in Target Dressing Room in New Jersey," ABC7 Eyewitness News, September 12, 2016.

53. Anderson and Wood, "Gender Identity Policies in Schools: What Congress, the Courts, and the Trump Administration Should Do."

54. Expert Declaration and Report of Kenneth V. Lanning, 17.

55. Ibid., 18.

56. Expert Opinion of Sheriff Tim Hutchison (Retired), 11.

57. Women's Liberation Front, Brief of *Amicus Curiae* in Support of Petitioner, *Gloucester County School Board v. G.G.*, Supreme Court of the United States, No. 16-273 (September 2016), 16, www.scotusblog.com/wp-content /uploads/2016/09/16-273-cert-amicus-WLF.pdf.

58. Ibid., 2.

59. Women's Liberation Front and Family Policy Alliance, Brief of *Amici Curiae*, 1.

60. Ibid., 18. Emphasis in original.

61. Ibid., 1.

62. Ibid., 28. Emphasis in original.

63. Family Policy Alliance, "Ask Me First About Fairness: Tanner," video posted on YouTube, August 2, 2016, https://www.youtube.com/watch?v=Jk_ CKFkm8sI; and Melody Wood, "The NBA's Transgender Bathroom Advocacy Could Point to End of Women's Sports," *Daily Signal*, August 1, 2016.

64. Associated Press, "Transgender Boy Wins Texas Girls' Wrestling Title," *New York Times*, February 25, 2017.

65. Expert Declaration and Report of Kenneth V. Lanning, 17.

66. Ibid., 17–18.

67. *Tuan Anh Nguyen and Joseph Boulias, Petitioners v. Immigration and Naturalization Service*, 533 U.S. 53, 18 (2001), https://www.law.cornell.edu /supct/pdf/99-2071P.ZO.

68. Neither the agency memo issued by an acting assistant deputy director in the *G.G.* case nor the 2016 Obama administration DOE/DOJ "Dear Colleague" letter went through the appropriate rulemaking process under the Administrative Procedure Act (APA), which requires that regulations and binding agency guidance must be subject to public notice and comment before finalization. Because the Title IX memo and letter did not follow the APA rules, they should not be given any deference. They also should be rejected because they do not offer a plausible alternative interpretation of the unambiguous word "sex."

69. *State of Texas et al. v. United States of America et al.*, No. 7:16-cv-0054-0, Preliminary Injunction Order, August 21, 2016, p. 31. Section 106.33 of Title 34 (Education) in the Code of Federal Regulations reads as follows: "Comparable facilities. A recipient may provide separate toilet, locker room, and shower facilities on the basis of sex, but such facilities provided for students of one sex shall be comparable to such facilities provided for students of the other sex." 34 CFR § 106.33, https://www.law.cornell.edu/cfr/text/34/106.33.

70. *Seamus Johnston v. University of Pittsburgh of the Commonwealth System of Higher Education et al.*, U.S. District Court, Western District of Pennsylvania, Civil Action No. 3:13-213, Memorandum Opinion and Order (March 31, 2015), 26, http://cases.justia.com/federal/district-courts/pennsylvania/pawdce/3:2013 cv00213/212325/43/0.pdf?ts=1427935122.

71. Ibid., 23.

72. Ibid., 29–30.

73. *G.G. v. Gloucester County School Board*, U.S. Court of Appeals for the Fourth Circuit, No. 15-2056 (April 19, 2016), 47, http://www.ca4.uscourts.gov /Opinions/Published/152056.P.pdfm.

74. Ibid., 48.

75. Declaration of Paul W. Hruz, M.D, Ph.D., U.S. District Court, Middle District of North Carolina, Case 1:16-cv-00425-TDS-JEP, Exhibit H.

76. For more on this, see Anderson and Wood, "Gender Identity Policies in Schools."

77. S. 47, Violence Against Women Reauthorization Act of 2013, 113th Cong., 1st sess., https://www.gpo.gov/fdsys/pkg/BILLS-113s47enr/pdf/BILLS-113s47enr. pdf; Matthew Shepard and James Byrd, Jr., Hate Crimes Prevention Act, 18 U.S. Code § 249, https://www.law.cornell.edu/uscode/text/18/249.

78. Executive Order 13672, "Further Amendments to Executive Order 11478, Equal Employment Opportunity in the Federal Government, and Executive Order 11246, Equal Employment Opportunity," July 21, 2014, *Federal Register*, vol. 79, no. 141 (July 23, 2014), pp. 42971–42972, https://www.gpo.gov/fdsys/pkg /FR-2014-07-23/pdf/2014-17522.pdf (accessed March 3, 2017).

79. Jerome Hunt, "A History of the Employment Non-Discrimination Act," Center for American Progress, July 19, 2011.

80. Ryan T. Anderson, "How the So-Called 'Equality Act' Threatens Religious Freedom," *Daily Signal*, July 23, 2015.

81. Human Rights Campaign, "Student Non-Discrimination Act," last updated January 4, 2017, http://www.hrc.org/resources/student-non-discrimination-act.

82. See Ryan T. Anderson, forthcoming in *National Affairs*.

83. People opposed to interracial marriage or racially integrated lunch counters could claim they were opposed to certain actions when blacks and whites did them together, but that stops the inquiry too soon. Why were they opposed? The reason they were against blacks and whites doing things together was an attitude of white supremacy that viewed and treated blacks as less intelligent, less skilled, and in some respects less human. They thus opposed blacks interacting with whites on an equal plane. One can and should hold that we are created male and female, with male and female created for each other, without holding any hostility toward people who identify as LGBT. For more on this, see John Corvino, Ryan T. Anderson, and Sherif Girgis, *Debating Religious Liberty and Discrimination* (New York: Oxford University Press, 2017).

84. Portions of this paragraph are adapted from ibid.

85. For more on this, see Ryan T. Anderson, *Truth Overruled: The Future of Marriage and Religious Freedom* (Washington, D.C.: Regnery, 2015).

86. During the debate on Title IX, there was concern that its enactment would mean the end of sex-specific educational programs and sex-specific intimate facilities like bathrooms, locker rooms, and showers. Because of this concern, Congress explicitly constructed Title IX to ensure that access to living facilities could take biology into account: Section 1686 states that "nothing contained herein shall be construed to prohibit any educational institution receiving funds under this Act, from maintaining separate living facilities for the different sexes." Three years later, the Department of Health, Education, and Welfare's implementing regulations made clear that Title IX "permits separate but comparable toilet, locker room, and shower facilities on the basis of sex," thereby preserving sex-specific facilities while ensuring that women's facilities would not be inferior to men's, and vice versa. "Implementing Title IX: The HEW Regulations," *University of Pennsylvania Law Review* 124 (1976): 826. Title IX provided equal opportunities for women in education without violating their privacy. Its implementation over subsequent years shows that it is possible to acknowledge genuine differences between the sexes while granting women equivalent opportunities to participate in school and extracurricular activities, including sports.

87. Sandhya Somashekhar, "Transgender man sues Catholic hospital for refusing surgery," *Washington Post*, January 6, 2017.

88. Sandhya Somashekhar, "Catholic groups sue over Obama administration transgender requirement," *Washington Post*, December 29, 2016.

89. See Ryan T. Anderson, "How to Think About Sexual Orientation and Gender Identity (SOGI) Policies and Religious Freedom," Heritage Foundation Backgrounder no. 3194, February 13, 2017, especially "Definition of Key Terms: 'Discrimination.'"

90. Ryan T. Anderson, "Trump Right to Fix Obama's Unlawful Transgender School Policy," *Daily Signal*, February 22, 2017.

91. See H.R. 5812, Civil Rights Uniformity Act of 2016, 114th Cong., 2nd sess., https://www.congress.gov/bill/114th-congress/house-bill/5812/text?format=txt.

92. Adults who have undergone sex reassignment therapies and changed the sex on their legal IDs could be allowed access to sex-specific facilities in accordance with their new legal sex.

CONCLUSION

1. Khadeeja Safdar, "How Target Botched Its Response to the North Carolina Bathroom Law," *Wall Street Journal*, April 5, 2017.

2. Hayley Peterson, "The Target boycott cost more than anyone expected—and the CEO was blindsided," *Business Insider*, April 6, 2017.

3. Hands Across the Aisle, "Who We Are," February 6, 2017, https://handsacrosstheaislewomen.com/2017/02/06/who-we-are/ (accessed May 10, 2017).

4. Ryan T. Anderson, "Biology Isn't Bigotry: Why Sex Matters in the Age of Gender Identity," Heritage Foundation Commentary, February 16, 2017, http://www.heritage.org/gender/commentary/biology-isnt-bigotry-why-sex-matters-the-age-gender-identity.

5. Andrea Jones and Melody Wood, "Feminists and Conservatives Link Arms to Confront Transgender Ideology," *Daily Signal*, March 3, 2017.

6. Ibid.

7. Hands Across the Aisle, "Voices from Hands Across the Aisle," https://handsacrosstheaislewomen.com/about/ (accessed May 10, 2017).

8. Testimony of Gail Heriot, Professor of Law, University of San Diego, to the House Judiciary Committee, United States Congress, hearing on "The Federal Government on Autopilot: Delegation of Regulatory Authority to an Unaccountable Bureaucracy," May 24, 2016, https://judiciary.house.gov/wp-content/uploads/2016/05/HHRG-114-JU00-Wstate-HeriotG-20160524.pdf.

9. Ibid., 16.

10. Paige Lavendar, "Congresswoman Shuts Down Transphobic Woman: 'You're a Bigot, Lady,'" *Huffington Post*, May 26, 2016.

11. Testimony of Gail Heriot, 16.

12. Stanley Kurtz, "Zoe Lofgren's Epic Cheap-Shot at Gail Heriot," *National Review*, May 27, 2016.

13. Emmett Rensin, "The smug style in American liberalism," *Vox*, April 21, 2016.

14. Riley J. Dennis, "Can Having Genital Preferences for Dating Mean You're Anti-Trans?" *Everyday Feminism*, April 21, 2017.

15. Ibid.

16. I happen to think he's wrong about this, but leave that to the side for now. See my book *Truth Overruled: The Future of Marriage and Religious Freedom* (Washington, D.C.: Regnery, 2015).

17. Paul McHugh, "Transgenderism: A Pathogenic Meme," *Public Discourse*, June 10, 2015.

POSTSCRIPT TO THE PAPERBACK EDITION

1. See Professor Matthew J. Franck's tweet-thread on the many errors of the piece and the subsequent changes at https://twitter.com/MatthewJFranck/status/959852549548503041.

2. Ariana Eunjung Cha, "Ryan Anderson's book on transgender people is creating an uproar," Washington Post, February 2, 2018, https://www.washingtonpost.com/news/to-your-health/wp/2018/02/02/ryan-andersons-book-calling-transgender-people-mentally-ill-is-creating-an-uproar/?utm_term=.207f55085b5d. See also Matthew Franck, https://twitter.com/MatthewJFranck/status/959855125216088065.

Index

abortion, 152, 199
Academy Awards, 11
ACLU, 36, 38, 178, 186
Adkins, Deanna, 30, 32–34, 36–37, 81
Affordable Care Act (Obamacare), 175, 192, 200, 202
Allen, Sr. Mary Prudence, 159
Alliance Defending Freedom, 183
American Academy of Pediatrics, 96
American College of Pediatrics, 96
American Psychiatric Association, 14, 110
American Psychoanalytic Association, 143
American Psychological Association, 29, 30, 148–49
Americans with Disabilities Act, 199
anorexia nervosa, 5, 87, 96, 116, 132–33
Anthony, Susan B., 150
Apple, Inc., 15
Arcadia School District (Calif.), 12
athletics, 41, 190, 191–92
autism spectrum disorder, 137–38
autogynephilia, 109–11

Bailey, J. Michael, 109–11
Beauvoir, Simone de, 147–48, 150–52
Becoming Chaz (film), 10
Becoming Us (TV show), 11
Being Jazz (Jennings), 11
Benioff Children's Hospital, 35
Ben-Shalom, Miriam, 207–8
Benson, Thomas Lee, 189
Blanchard, Ray, 109, 111

body dysmorphic disorder, 96, 116, 132
Bono, Chastity/Chaz, 10, 117
Boston Children's Hospital, 2
Boys' Clubs of America, 162
Boy Scouts of America, 162
brain structure, 5, 33, 106–8; and neuroplasticity, 33, 107, 125, 180; sex differences in, 84–85, 87, 154, 162
Brown, George R., 32–33, 37, 41
Buehler, Taylor, 189
Butler, Judith, 153–54

Cahill, Larry, 84–85
California, 38, 142
Callahan, Carey, 67–68
Catholic hospitals, 175, 199–200
Centers for Medicare and Medicaid Services, 13
Centre for Addiction and Mental Health (CAMH, Toronto), 21–24
Charlotte-Mecklenburg schools (Va.), 183
Chesterton, G. K., 168–69
Chicago Gender Center, 34
Chicago Sun-Times, 10
Child Molesters: A Behavioral Analysis (Lanning), 186–87
Children's Hospital Los Angeles, 124
Children's National Medical Center, 37
Civil Rights Act of 1964, 14, 195, 197, 202
Civil Rights Uniformity Act, 202–3
Clarke Institute of Psychiatry, 109
Clinton, Bill, 146

Clinton, Hillary, 168
Cloutier, David, 173
Coates, Ta-Nehisi, 163
Condic, Maureen, 79
Condic, Samuel, 79
Connecticut, 142
"conversion" therapy, 22–24, 37, 142–43
Cooper, Ria, 49–50
Cox, Laverne, 10, 31
Cretella, Michelle: on dysphorias, 96–97;
    on evidentiary weakness, 131; on self-
    fulfilling protocol, 125; on well-being, 114,
    115–16
Cuomo, Andrew, 15

Daily Mail (UK), 49
Dancing with the Stars (TV show), 10, 117
Danish Girl, The (film), 1, 11
depression, 36, 48, 92; and family rejection,
    50, 69, 70–81; female susceptibility to, 87
desistance, 23, 123–26; denial of, 55–56, 123;
    discouragement of, 123–24, 181; rates of, 2,
    36–37, 119, 123, 125
Developing Human, The, 78, 82, 89
developmental biology, 77–88; disorders in,
    88–92
Dheyne, Cecilia, 103
Diagnostic and Statistical Manual of Mental
    Disorders (DSM), 22, 28, 95, 104
Dialectic of Sex, The (Firestone), 151–52
Diamond, Milton, 108
disease susceptibility, 85–87
disorders of sexual development (DSD),
    88–92
Duke Center for Child and Adolescent
    Gender Care, 30

Ehrensaft, Diane, 35–36
Emmy Awards, 10–11
Emperor's New Clothes, The (Andersen), 18
Employment Non-Discrimination Act
    (ENDA), 37, 195
Endocrine Society: on adolescent choices,
    130; on limits of knowledge, 111–12; on
    puberty blockers, 121–22; on reassignment
    therapy, 96–99
Equal Employment Opportunity
    Commission, 203
Equality Act, 37, 195
Equality Texas, 27
Equal Rights Amendment, 182
Esolen, Anthony, 161–63, 168, 169, 171
Ettner, Randi, 33, 41–42
Exploring the Biological Contributions to

Human Health: Does Sex Matter? (Institute
    of Medicine), 85–86

Facebook, 15, 145
family dynamics: activist concerns about, 43–
    45; as causal factor, 138–40; and rejection,
    50; sex differences in, 146, 151–52, 157
Family Policy Alliance, 182–83, 191
Feminine Mystique, The (Friedan), 150
feminism, 147–55
Firestone, Shulamith, 151–52
Fortune magazine, 11
Friedan, Betty, 151, 170

Genderbread Person, 31–32
gender clinics, 64, 132, 133, 136–37; pediatric,
    2, 211
Gender Spectrum, 38
Gender Unicorn, 31–33
George, Robert P., 100, 105–6
Gersen, Jeannie Suk, 186
Gibson, Kim R., 193–94
Gingrich, Newt, 146
Ginsburg, Ruth Bader, 181–82
Girgis, Sherif, 79–80
Girl Scouts of America, 162
Glamour magazine, 11
Gloucester County Public Schools (Va.), 12
GLSEN, 43
GnRH analogues, 126–27
Goldstein, Jill, 87
Google, 15
Graham, Billy, 146, 165
Guardian (UK), 51–51, 102, 121

Hands Across the Aisle Coalition, 206–8
Hasbro, 155
Hayes, Inc., 102–3
Heriot, Gail, 208–10
Heritage Foundation, 207–8
Heyer, Walt, 69–72
Hobby Lobby, 175
Hoff Sommers, Christina, 155–57
"homosexual transsexuals," 108–9
hormone treatment, 35, 44, 68, 97–98;
    for children, 119–22, 125, 128, 130; and
    competitive sports, 191–92; results of,
    50–53, 64, 66, 71–72, 101–3; see also puberty
    blockers
Hruz, Paul: on adolescent choices, 130;
    on consensus statements, 112–13;
    on desistance, 123, 125; on false
    assumptions, 133; on medical duty, 115;
    on neuroplasticity, 180–81; on puberty

blockers, 122, 127–29; on redefining "sex," 194; on twin studies, 108
Human Embryology (Larsen), 78
Human Rights Campaign (HRC): on "conversion" therapy, 143; Corporate Equality Index, 19–20; Healthcare Equality Index, 20–21; on medical discrimination, 200; school guide, 35, 38–41; Student Non-Discrimination Act, 195–96; terminology change, 28, 29
Hutchison, Tim, 186–88, 190
Hyde, Chris, 102

I Am Cait (TV show), 11
I Am Jazz (Jennings/Herthel), 11, 179
I Am Jazz (TV show), 11
IBM, 15
Illinois, 142
Industrial Revolution, 169–70
Institute of Medicine (National Academy of Sciences), 85–86
International Journal of Transgenderism, 108
International Olympic Committee, 192

Jackson, Avery, 11–12
Jenner, Bruce/Caitlyn, 116; ABC interview of, 9, 11, 119, 203; and autogynephilia theory, 111; as "success" story, 52
Jennings, Jazz, 11, 179
Jim Crow laws, 197
Johns Hopkins Hospital, 2, 15–21, 153; and HRC, 20–21
Josephson, Allen, 95, 96
Journal of Cellular Biology, 82
Journal of Personality and Social Psychology, 156

Karolinska Institute, 103
Kass, Amy, 161
Kass, Leon, 114–15, 168
Kennedy, Anthony, 192
Kennedy, Ted, 146
Kurtz, Stanley, 209

Langman's Medical Embryology, 78
Lanning, Kenneth V., 186–88, 190
Larsen, William J., 78
Lasch, Christopher, 168
Last, Jonathan, 21
Lawrence, Anne, 96
Lego Group, 155, 156
Leibowitz, Scott, 35, 42
Le Marquand, Sarrah, 147–48
Lewis, C. S., 164

LGBTQ Nation, 19
Little Sisters of the Poor, 175
Lofgren, Zoe, 208–10
Luce, Clare Boothe, 150
Lynch, Loretta, 14

Manning, Bradley/Chelsea, 13–14
Matthew Shepard and James Byrd, Jr., Hate Crimes Prevention Act, 195
Mayer, Lawrence, 116; on classifying sex, 80–81, 101; on desistance, 123; on DSM criteria, 104–5; on false assumptions, 133; and HRC, 20, 21; on medical duty, 115; on mental health risks, 93, 103; on neurobiological theory, 106–7, 108; on neuroplasticity, 180–81; on puberty blockers, 122, 127–29
McCarthy, Margaret: on Beauvoir, 151; on Butler, 153–54; on "gender," 160; on women's work, 168, 170–71
McCrory, Pat, 15
McHugh, Paul, 2, 6, 16–21, 116, 213; on autogynephilia, 109, 111; on classifying sex, 80–81, 101–2; on desistance, 123; on DSM criteria, 104–5; on false assumptions, 95–96, 97, 132–33; on ideological fads, 17–19; on medical duty, 115; on mental health risks, 93, 103; on neurobiological theory, 106–7, 108; on neuroplasticity, 180–81; on puberty blockers, 122, 127–29
Meyer, Jon, 17, 109
military policy, 13–14, 207
Mill, John Stuart, 149–50
Millett, Kate, 150
Mirror (UK), 50
Mitchell, Cleta, 152
Money, John, 15–16, 153
More, Hannah, 150
My Princess Boy (Kilodavis), 179

Nagel, Thomas, 104
National Basketball Association (NBA), 15
National Center for Lesbian Rights, 38
National Center for Transgender Equality, 43
National Collegiate Athletic Association, 192
National Education Association, 38, 178
National Geographic, 11–12
natural law ethics, 158
neuroplasticity, 33, 107, 125, 180–81
New Jersey, 142
New Mexico, 142
New York (state), 15, 142
New York City, 38
New York magazine, 22–24, 119

Niemeyer, Paul, 194
North Carolina: HB2 (bathroom bill), 14–15, 30, 182; and Target policy, 206
Nova Classical Academy, 178–80

Obama, Barack, and administration: "gender identity" policy, 12–14, 175–77, 182, 190, 192–96, 201; and Manning, 13–14; North Carolina suit, 14, 182
Obamacare (Affordable Care Act), 175, 192, 200, 202
O'Connor, Reed, 193
Olson, Pete, 202
Olson-Kennedy, Johanna, 124
Orange Is the New Black (TV show), 10
Oregon, 142
Oxford Dictionary of English Etymology, 159

Palatine School District (Ill.), 12
PayPal, 15
Pediatric Endocrine Society, 112–13
Pence, Karen, 146–47
Pence, Mike, 146–47, 165
PFLAG, 34, 35
Popenoe, David, 166
puberty blockers, 118–22; effects of, 126–29; for precocious puberty, 126–27; reversibility claim, 122, 127–28

racial discrimination, 197–99
"reparative" therapy, 22–23, 37
Rhoads, Steven, 173–74
Rude, Mey, 31

Safe Spaces for Women, 184–85
Salesforce, 15
San Francisco, 14–15
Sapolsky, Robert, 206
Sawyer, Diane, 9
Sayers, Dorothy, 169–70
schools, 12, 175–77; activist agenda for, 38–44; and equality, 190–92; ideology in, 178–81; and parental authority, 42–45; privacy & safety in, 40–42, 181–90
Schools in Transition (HRC/ACLU), 38–41
Scientific American, 164
Second Sex, The (Beauvoir), 150–51
sexual predators, 180–90
Singal, Jesse, 22–24, 119–20; on desistance, 123–26; on political agendas, 131–32
Singh, Devita, 133, 134
Singleton, Mary Lou, 208
Smith, Maya Dillard, 185–86
Smith, Sean Patrick, 189
Soell, Leo, 178
Soloway, Jill, 11

Sommers, Christina Hoff, 153–54
sports, 41, 190, 191–92
Stanton, Elizabeth Cady, 150
Stella, Cari, 52–56
Stoller, Robert, 153
Student Non-Discrimination Act, 195–96
Sturgeon, Samuel, 157
"Subjection of Women, The" (Mill), 149–50
suicide, 45, 49, 56–57, 132; rates of, 2, 36, 78, 93, 103
surgery (reassignment), 34–35, 68, 121; insurance coverage for, 13, 20; at Johns Hopkins, 15–17, 19–20; procedures, 98–99, 121; results of, 17, 50–52, 54, 56–58, 69–73, 99–103

Target, 189, 206–7
ThinkProgress, 19
Third Way Trans (blog), 64
Time magazine, 10, 31
Title IX of Education Amendments (1972): purpose of, 176, 192–96, 198–99, 201, 202–3; reinterpretation of, 12, 173, 175–76, 192–96; and sports, 191–92
Tollefsen, Christopher, 100–1, 161
TransActive Gender Center, 53
Transgender Americans: A Handbook for Understanding (HRC), 19–20, 28
Transparent (TV show), 10–11
Trans Students Educational Resources, 32
Triea, Kiira, 109–11
Trump, Donald, and administration, 13–14, 178, 201–2

Udry, J. Richard, 158–59
University Hospital & University of Bern, 93
University of Birmingham, 73, 102
University of California, Los Angeles, 153
University of California, San Francisco: Benioff Children's Hospital, 35–36
University of Pittsburgh, 193
University of Texas at Austin School of Law, 27
U.S. Army, 207
U.S. Congress, 195–96, 208–10
U.S. Court of Appeals for the Fourth Circuit, 182, 194
U.S. Department of Education: "gender identity" policy, 12, 175–76, 182; Trump policy reversal, 201–2
U.S. Department of Health and Human Services (HHS), 12–13, 175–76, 192, 200
U.S. Department of Housing and Urban Development, 13, 177, 201
U.S. Department of Justice: "gender identity" policy, 12, 175–76, 182; and North

Carolina, 14, 182; Trump policy reversal, 201–2
U.S. Department of State, 190
U.S. Supreme Court: on contraception mandate, 175; and "gender identity" policies, 123, 183–85, 191; on same-sex marriage, 9, 80; on VMI coeducation, 181–82
USPATH, 44–45, 54

Vanity Fair magazine, 11
Van Meter, Quentin L., 88, 108, 112
Vermont, 142
Vindication of the Rights of Woman, A (Wollstonecraft), 149
Violence Against Women Reauthorization Act (2013), 195
Virginia Military Institute, 182
Vought, Mary, 147

Walker, Paul, 69, 71
Warbelow, Sarah, 200
Washington Post, 5, 117–19, 131; Pence story in, 146–47
Washington State Human Rights Commission, 185
Wegener, Einar ("Lili Elbe"), 1, 11

When Harry Met Sally (film), 1, 163–64
Wilcox, W. Bradford, 157, 166–67
Willard, Frances, 150
Williamson, Kevin, 10
Wollstonecraft, Mary, 149
Women's Liberation Front, 182–83, 190–91, 208
Women's March on Washington (2017), 152
Wood, Melody, 189
World Professional Association for Transgender Health (WPATH), 32; on "conversion" therapy, 153; on puberty blockers, 122; standard of care, 35, 57, 69, 97–98; U.S. branch, 44–45, 54; and Zucker firing, 22

Yenor, Scott, 153
Young Men's Christian Association, 162

Zinos, Emily, 179–80, 181
Zucker, Kenneth, 21–24, 123; on causes of GID, 132–40; on "conversion," 143–44; on desistance, 133–34; treatment protocol of, 140–42